AGAINST

THE

ODDS

Against the Odds

A Single Mother's Battle for Love, Family, and Respect

TRICIA OBEN

Foreword by Regina Mundi

SPEARS BOOKS
Denver, Colorado

SPEARS BOOKS
AN IMPRINT OF SPEARS MEDIA PRESS LLC
21699 E. Quincy Ave, Unit F #167
Aurora, CO 80015
United States of America

First Published in the United States of America in 2025 by Spears Books
www.spearsbooks.org
info@spearsmedia.com
Information on this title: https://spearsbooks.org/product/against-the-odds/

© 2025 Tricia Oben née Efange
All rights reserved.

No part of this publication may be reproduced, distributed, or transmitted in any form or by any means, including photocopying, recording, or other electronic or mechanical methods, without the prior written permission of the publisher, except in the case of brief quotations embodied in critical reviews and certain other noncommercial uses permitted by copyright law. For permission requests, write to the publisher, addressed "Attention: Permissions Coordinator," at the above address.

ISBN: 9781957296593 (Paperback)
Also available in Kindle, Google Books & Apple Books

Spears Media Press has no responsibility for the persistence or accuracy of urls for external or third-party internet websites referred to in this publication, and does not guarantee that any content on such websites is, or will remain, accurate or appropriate.

Designed and typeset by Spears Media Press LLC
Cover design: D. Kambem

The characters and events portrayed in this book are real.

In Loving Memory of My Mother, Susan Mbi Enoh
(February 1940–November 2015)
The woman whose love and guidance illuminated our lives, whose strength and kindness shaped our characters, and whose memory continues to inspire us each day.
In remembrance of the countless moments of joy, wisdom, sorrow, great challenges, and unwavering support you shared with us—your children, both biological and non-biological, and the community you cherished.
Your legacy lives on in the love we continue to share, the kindness we extend to strangers, and the lessons you imparted, forever etched in our hearts.
With boundless gratitude and everlasting love,

Tricia Oben (née Patricia Agbor Enange Efange)
(Your first child)

Contents
***

Foreword *ix*
Introduction *1*
1. Early Years *6*
2. Life in Mamfe's Polygamous Households *11*
3. Sunday at Main Street *26*
4. The Morning of the Python *34*
5. My Grandfather's Clock *39*
6. From Mamfe to Onitsha via Enugu by Road *42*
7. The British Godfather *50*
8. Reme and Big Papa Enotanya *55*
9. The Tiger *63*
10. Mami Susanna, the Matriarch *67*
11. Weathering the Storm *71*
12. The Dance with Devils *75*
13. Secondary School at QRC Okoyong *80*
14. The School Grounds *86*
15. Bamenda to Mamfe *92*
16. Settling Down *96*
17. The Wedding Feast *99*
18. The Bond is Broken *109*
19. Clerks' Quarters Set the Foundation *114*
20. Happenings at Clerks' Quarters *121*
21. Mami Waka Waka *132*
22. Our Neighbors *138*
23. Entrepreneurial spirit *144*
24. The Journey of the Ibeagha Family *148*

25. My mother and Josephine, and the
Bonds of Friendship   *153*
26. A Mother's Triumph   *157*
27. Our House at Kalla Street   *170*
28. Her Workplace and the Coming of Francophones   *175*
29. The Abdication   *187*
30. Her Tenants   *191*
31. Sibling Fights and Squabbles   *194*
32. Health is Wealth   *197*
33. Merrily Around the World   *200*
34. A New Beginning in Mile 4   *204*
35. Aversion to Politics   *207*
36. My Mother Buys a Car   *213*
37. Parenting Style   *218*
38. The Strength of Solitude   *223*
39. The Spirit as Partner   *229*
40. The Rhythms of our Home   *231*
41. The Absence of a Father   *239*
42. Maintaining a Closed Book   *247*
43. Was there Ever a Love Life?   *255*
44. QRC Okoyong … Again!   *258*
45. Following in Her Footsteps   *266*
46. A Mother's Faith, a Daughter's Flight   *273*
47. Retirement and Old Age   *277*
48. CANCER, The big C!   *282*
49. Legacy   *292*
Postscript   *296*

About the author   *299*

Foreword

***

It is with great pleasure that I introduce you to the extraordinary life of a woman whose indomitable spirit has inspired countless individuals over the years. In the following pages, you will embark on a captivating journey through the biography of Susan Mbi Enoh, a true embodiment of focus, courage, resilience, and determination—a woman of character and real substance.

This biography, penned by a highly respected journalist, her daughter Tricia, skillfully delves into the remarkable life of Susan. I had the privilege of being Susan's classmate for six years in the 1950s in the first girls' secondary school in Cameroon, Queen of the Rosary College, Okoyong, Mamfe. When we arrived in Okoyong, everything was new to us. At the time, we had no role models. With bright eyes and open hearts, we took in all the novelty unfolding around us: language, clothing, Western-style education, library, refectory... even our religion was new. It was an exciting time, but we only realized this long after we had left QRC and become individuals in our own right.

In those days, mostly during holidays, we would visit our various homes and tell all kinds of stories to the excited village crowds. They looked at us like beings from outer space.

As teenage girls, we all had our dreams, real or imaginary. We were encouraged to dream through many forms, not least through the teachers who traveled long distances to come to Mamfe. The Reverend Sisters had traveled sometimes over ten thousand miles to come and teach us.

I witnessed the seeds of Susan's dreams taking root in QRC. We faced challenges in grasping unfamiliar subjects and comprehending novel concepts (Physics, Chemistry). Adapting to new styles of attire, acquiring a different language, and embracing a new religion required significant effort. Although it was a considerable amount to undertake simultaneously, we quickly demonstrated our ability and versatility to rise to the occasion.

Susan was remarkably both smart and hardworking, and her dreams grew into a reality that overcame all challenges. Starting from humble beginnings with parents who had no clue what their children were studying, she quickly rose to success.

It wasn't until much later that I discovered she had secured a good job almost immediately after we left QRC. I also learned that she chose to raise her children on her own, without ever marrying—a very brave thing to do at the time. Reflecting on everything I manage today, I realize that her achievements as a single mother were extraordinary, both then and now.

Susan's unwavering commitment to her aspirations left an indelible mark on the lives she touched.

As you turn the pages of this biography, you will journey alongside Susan, experiencing the triumphs and tribulations that shaped her into the trailblazer she became. Her story serves as a testament to the power of perseverance, reminding us that no obstacle is insurmountable when confronted with unwavering determination.

Prepare to be inspired by this moonbeam of a woman. A woman who could not be held down and who fearlessly carved her path in a world that often sought to confine women.

As we grew older, in our fifties and sixties, Susan and I did not talk much, but we kept in touch. Our classmates kept the bond from our school days strong. When the silver jubilee of QRC Okoyong was celebrated in 1981, our classmates who were still alive convened excitedly at QRC Okoyong, Mamfe, for the memorable event.

May Susan's story ignite a fire within all who read this biography, propelling us to embrace our unique journeys with courage and conviction.

Let us come together to celebrate the life and legacy of an astounding woman who continues to inspire young mothers, especially single mothers, with her remarkable life.

In her story, we find not only inspiration but also a lasting call to action—to boldly pursue our dreams, no matter how formidable the challenges may seem.

Susan Mbi Enoh's life is a testament to the boundless potential that resides within each of us, waiting to be unleashed. It calls on all single mothers not to be afraid and to forge ahead with focus and conviction.

Senator Regina Mundi
September 2023

My mother, Susan Mbi Enoh, did not have an easy life, but she had the life she chose. Here is her story …

Introduction

* * *

Mamfe in 1940, the year my mother was born, was a place where the echoes of tradition vied with the whispers of change. This captivating juxtaposition, unknown to the town's residents, could be overwhelming. But it was mostly a harmonious clash.

It was in this state of transition between tradition and modernity that a remarkable woman emerged, known to all as Susan Mbi Enoh. Her life, like the melodies of an ageless rhyme, carried contradictions through time: the mystery of her early history and beauty, side by side clarity and rarity; the portrayal of love and betrayal of love; life and death.

From the onset, the uncertainty of whether she would live after her birth lent an aura of enigma to her existence. My grandmother, Ma Elizabeth Ekumanka, had had multiple live births before my mother arrived, and none survived. She went on to have a total of twelve births, with only five surviving childhood. My mother's siblings from her mother were Mary Ndip, Peter Enohanyor, Florence Ebai Nyor, and Gloria Tembi. My mother was the first child of their father, Pa Thomas Agbor Enohtanya, who was a prominent businessman and a beacon of prosperity. He was also a polygamist. As a man of means, he firmly navigated the complexities of a polygamous household, keeping his four wives in line. So, my mother had other half-siblings. I got to know only a handful of them: Etarock, Pamela, Becky, Anasthasia, Agbornikoh, and Stephen.

Susan grew up to be a woman of unwavering strength (mental and physical) and steadfast convictions, venturing where few dared. As one of the first girls to grace the halls of higher learning, she shattered stereotypes that sought to relegate women to the kitchen and childbirth.

Earlier, she honed her independence by intuitively managing her relationship with her father, becoming adept at seizing opportunities and making requests that he readily yielded to. As his eldest child, she was independent in an era where her father's peers were already parents to grown-up, adolescent children. Being independent was not beneficial to a young woman in the 1950s. Parents and children, and especially fathers and children, were not friends. As housemates, each understood their role. But Susan's father was not like that. He tolerated his daughter.

Standing tall, Susan was a staunch Catholic thanks to her father and her Catholic secondary education. Her genre of Catholicism and devotion transcended the confines of a church building. As with many things in her life, she succeeded in finding a different way of looking at religion and Christianity. She believed that in her trials, Jesus walked beside her, performing miracles of healing, providing the means, and guiding her through life's tempestuous waters. She also believed she had to put in a lot of effort for Jesus to walk beside her—almost meeting him halfway.

Her passion was deeply rooted in playing music, where the melodies of her heart, whether joy or sorrow, found eloquent expression through the tender touch of piano keys. As a young mother, the piano became her sole luxurious possession for a very long time, and it was only much later that we, her children, understood what the instrument meant to her. Its muffled sounds, sometimes in the dead of night, served as a poignant reflection of her emotional state. She generously imparted her musical gift to her children, kindling within them the flames of their musical journeys, and thus perpetuating the timeless legacy of her artistry. Despite working as a government clerk, her heart belonged to petty trading—a testament to her determination to make ends meet. A testament to what she learned from her father. She was not content with the salary a clerk earned.

As a single mother, she brought six children into the world: Patricia (Tricia), Elizabeth, Jubilant, Vivian, Judith, and Eric. The last two, Judith and Eric, left this world prematurely, leaving an indelible mark on Susan's heart. The pain from the loss of Eric at the age of twenty-four cut very deep, and she mourned for years. Judith died a week after birth from jaundice. After her death, my mother bought a book that became almost as regular a read as her Catholic missal.

The title of the book was "Is Death the End?" The book explored questions about what happens after we die. It discussed various beliefs and perspectives on life after death, including religious teachings, near-death experiences, reincarnation, and some scientific theories. My mother was engrossed in it because she was grappling with the loss of her child. She was seeking comfort or understanding about what happens after death and if she would ever see her child again. I believe the book offered her hope, solace, or a sense of connection to her departed loved one, Judith, at the time. At the death of Eric, she was a more mature woman and had already faced some of the harshest challenges a single mother could face. She came to his death with more understanding of what death is, even if the hurt and grief were no different.

Growing up with Susan as our mother and father rolled

into one, from when we were all born, it became clear what her primary challenge was: to raise her children, provide them with quality education, and ensure that each surpassed her in every way. Her strict yet compassionate approach earned her the respect of many, even in an era where parenthood was often synonymous with tyranny. Our household was full of shared laughter and many tears compared to the families around us, where children hid and were out of sight when their fathers were home. We saw only their tears when facing their parents.

My mother's unwavering belief in education as the key to upward social mobility and a ladder to a brighter future fueled her determination. She strived to ensure her children achieved what she could not. Even with her limited educational journey, she vowed her children would reach greater heights. Through her non-stop dedication and sacrifices, she instilled in them the importance of perseverance and seizing every opportunity that came their way. And so, she raised them with a fierce conviction that everything was possible, preparing them for a world she could not even imagine existed but believed they could conquer.

There is a statement often quoted that "there can be no success without legacy," suggesting that success is intrinsically linked to leaving a lasting impact or legacy behind. While achieving success can certainly contribute to one's legacy, the two concepts are not necessarily inseparable.

Chinua Achebe put it succinctly in one of his interviews: "The truest test of success is whether what you are doing is going to benefit future generations." The famous writer was discussing themes related to leadership, culture, and societal progress. Achebe frequently emphasized the importance of thinking about future generations.

Success, no doubt, can be defined in various ways, including personal achievements, professional accomplishments, or reaching specific goals. Legacy, on the other hand, refers to the lasting impact or influence that an individual leaves behind, whether through their actions, contributions, or values.

While many people strive to achieve success with the hope of leaving a meaningful legacy, it's possible to achieve success without necessarily leaving a lasting legacy. Conversely, one can leave a powerful legacy without necessarily achieving traditional markers of success.

For in Susan's life can be found both. In her life, there was a beacon of hope, an inspiration for single mothers, a testament to the indomitable spirit of a woman who defied the odds. That is the definition of success and also of one who has left a lasting legacy.

As I, Tricia, her first child and a journalist, take up the pen to tell her story, I do so with love, immense gratitude, and the awareness that her enormous contributions to society should not remain hidden. To deliberately take up single parenthood and to succeed in it is an achievement worthy of praise.

As the author of her biography, the task is both a privilege and a solemn duty—one that seeks not only to immortalize her memory but to inspire generations yet unborn. I hope that her life, with its trials and triumphs, will serve as an inspiration to single mothers facing their individual battles. Through Susan's life in this book, her descendants shall discover the roots from which they spring, the blood that courses through their veins, and the responsibility to surpass the legacy of the generations that came before.

This book is the tale of Susan Mbi Enoh, a woman of strength and grace, whose story deserves to be told, remembered, and celebrated.

1

Early Years

* * *

When we talk about true-life stories, the spectacle of a bride leaving her groom stranded at the altar, poised on the brink of matrimony, remains a rare occurrence. Such a dramatic twist is typically confined to the pages of novels or the screens of Nigerian Nollywood films or even Hollywood movies, where tales of love and heartbreak, of promises made and broken, of destinies altered and fulfilled exist. However, "Pseudo-Nollywood" was a reality etched into the annals of my family's history, forever immortalized in the legend of my mother, Susan Mbi Enoh.

Affectionately known as Mami, Mami Pee, Ma'a, Suzy, Suzie, Susa, or simply Reme, her captivating journey embarked from the unassuming township of Mamfe, located within the borders of the Republic of Cameroon. It was in the year 1940 that she made her grand entrance into a world destined to bear witness to her extraordinary life. Her entrance into this book with the story of love and heartbreak challenges the very notion of conventional matrimony. In her unique journey, she dared to defy expectations, leaving an indelible mark on the pages of her biography.

The tale told of my mother's birth is a remarkable testament to the unpredictability of life. Her mother, a teenager at the time, was diligently working on her farmland as she always did, blissfully unaware that her precious bundle of joy was about to make an unexpected entrance. It was amidst lush greenery that it all started. There were yam seedlings neatly stacked in various corners of the farm. There were mounds of soil getting ready for yam planting and sprouting, and by a gentle brook at the edge of the farm, the labor pains intensified. She knew exactly what to do, but she wished there was someone nearby to assist her. She lost her voice momentarily and could only mumble to herself in between the pangs of pain. It was a "déjà vu," she thought.

There, under the open sky, and alone, this teenager brought my mother into the world. This was not her first delivery, but she was nonetheless exhausted, worried, and afraid. The fear was more from thinking that this one, too, might die, and she could end up childless.

In a moment of sheer resourcefulness, she resorted to the sound of clanging her stainless-steel food plate against nearby stones persistently while at the same time screaming the best she could—a desperate call for help. A compassionate woman from the neighboring farm heard the noises and rushed to her side. With some fresh grass, she cleaned a dirty machete that had previously been used for digging and cutting grass. With that instrument, the umbilical cord was severed. With the help of a few other people who had also heard the cry for help and gathered around, my grandmother was hastily transported to the local dispensary. Most other women gave birth at home and never went to the hospital. This was Enotanya's wife, and she got special treatment. The dispensary discharged her a few days later, marking the beginning of a new chapter in the lives of the mother and her daughter. This extraordinary birth tale is a powerful reminder that sometimes, life's most profound moments unfold in the most unexpected of places.

My mother's life was defined by an unwavering focus and fierce independence, qualities that became more apparent as she grew older. From a young age, her aspirations for a brighter future were clear to everyone she encountered. Her actions, words, and attitude set her apart from other girls her age. She was naturally quiet, but when asked a question, she always had a thoughtful response. She also had an innate desire to help, often completing tasks without being asked.

As a child, her notably reserved trait persisted into her adolescent years. Despite her quiet nature, she possessed a strong and assertive personality. Beneath her stoic exterior, however, was a kind and cheerful spirit that could brighten even the gloomiest of days with her infectious laughter.

In her forties, while working as a civil servant, Mami kept a bottle of Martini hidden in a special spot in the house, a bottle she fiercely guarded. A single sip of the cherished drink on a Sunday evening would often send her into fits of giggles. Though we rarely saw her indulge in this secret pleasure, the occasional empty bottles sparked curious speculation among us.

It gave rise to playful inquiries like:
"Na who drink da mimbo?" or
"Whosai empty bottle mimbo commot?"

Astonishingly, a single bottle of Martini could last for three months or more, a testament to her disciplined enjoyment.

Mami's physical appearance as a teenager was equally captivating. With bright, lively eyes that sparkled with vitality, a warm and inviting smile, and a distinctive African nose, she had a unique charm that set her apart. As a child, I was told she bore a striking resemblance to a porcelain doll. Soft and flawless, she had high cheekbones and perfect teeth. Her complexion, a fair and polished hue, was the source of envy among her sisters.

Her skin was akin to polished iroko wood, radiating a natural elegance that made her stand out in the eyes of all who had the privilege of knowing her.

Childhood and early adolescence were enjoyable yet predictable. They unfolded in a rhythm that was both delightful and structured. She began primary school at the age of 7. Her routine was consistent: school from Monday to Friday, and Saturdays were reserved for the family's agricultural activities. She would walk for miles to the farms, either with one of her parents or with her siblings. Cultivating the soil and nurturing the land were pleasurable activities for them. Walking wasn't just limited to the farms; it was their way of getting anywhere.

Back then, school wasn't as accessible as it is today, and mostly boys had the opportunity to attend. Every morning, as the sun began to rise, the streets of Mamfe echoed with the sound of eager young footsteps. The mornings were cooler, and cars were a rare sight—not yet a common means of ferrying children to school as they are today. Instead, everyone made the journey on foot, trudging along dusty paths with bare feet. The roads were rough, not yet blessed with the smoothness of tar we know today. But fate smiled upon Mamfe, and tar eventually made its way to the town. The main street, stretching to Lala Quarters, was adorned with this newfound black luxury. It wasn't the rich, glossy tar of modern roads, but it offered a welcome respite from the relentless dust of the dry season and the ever-present pebbles.

However, this blessing came with its own set of challenges. The scorching sun of Mamfe didn't discriminate, and by the time the children made their way back home from school, the tar had transformed into a treacherous path. It wasn't just the heat from the melting tar that tormented them; it was the tiny pebbles from the nearby river, mixed with the tar to construct the roads, that made each step a painful ordeal. Families could not afford shoes, so some children tied plastic bags, grass, trash, or anything they could find around their feet to ease the pain, running home quickly. But even with these makeshift solutions, they still suffered. Many couldn't run at all, as some schools were located far from home.

For families with many children (families with eleven kids were not uncommon), affording shoes for each child was an unimaginable luxury. Mothers juggled the responsibilities of raising large families, knowing that buying shoes for all their children was simply out of the question. Instead, they relied on the resilience of their children's feet, toughened by years of walking the unforgiving paths of Mamfe. They treated blisters, swellings, and wounds, but the children mostly suffered in silence.

Yet, despite the hardships, progress was made. From a time when shoes were a distant dream for many, to today, where the streets are filled with children wearing footwear, Mamfe has come a long way. Each step, whether taken on dusty paths or newly tarred streets, is a demonstration of the resilience and determination of a community striving for a better future.

2

Life in Mamfe's Polygamous Households

* * *

My mother, the firstborn of my six-foot-four grandfather, entered this world amidst the complexities of an unplanned polygamous family. Her father was a towering figure—known as Papa to his children and as Big Papa to my siblings and cousins. To my mother, as a child, he was flawless.

He was not just a father but a guiding light, a source of warmth and security amid life's uncertainties. She would eagerly trail after him, following his every step whenever she wasn't occupied with schoolwork or homework. Their bond was more than just familial; it was a deep-rooted companionship built on mutual admiration and trust. Yet, as time passed, the family dynamic shifted.

With the arrival of other siblings, particularly those from his relationships with other women, the once-pristine pedestal on which Big Papa stood in my mother's eyes began to erode. Though her devotion to him remained steadfast, the special place she once held in his heart seemed to waver as he was surrounded by the complexities of their expanding family. Still, their bond endured—a manifestation of the strength of their love and the lasting imprint he left on her life.

Papa turned to polygamy because his first wife, Mami Susanna, was unable to bear children. That was how my grandmother, also called Big Mami, came into the picture. He embraced Catholicism fervently when priests arrived in his village of Ntenako, 11 kilometers from Mamfe, and he continued practicing his faith when he later settled in Mamfe town as an adult. Among all the teachings of Christianity, one lesson stood out to him the most: *"Ask, and you will receive."* (Or *Bhep meh* in the Kenyang language).

At the height of his business success, he sometimes carried himself with an air of invincibility, almost as if he were the Almighty himself. His temper could flare unexpectedly, especially when someone needed something but failed to ask in time. If you remained silent about a need and he later discovered it, you could forget about ever receiving it. He stood firm on this principle, treating it as an important life lesson: you must ask to receive—he would not anticipate or arrange it for you.

He admired many aspects of being Catholic, especially as he was seen as an enlightened person. Open to change, he readily adopted new beliefs and ideas. However, as the years passed, he found himself compromising his faith. First, he became only a part-time Catholic, refraining from taking communion in church because he had more than one wife. Societal and familial pressures also significantly influenced his thoughts and decisions.

According to tradition, children were not just farmhands for his vast fields but also blessings from his ancestors. They symbolized wealth, prosperity, and the continuation of the family lineage. Having many children was—and still is—considered a source of pride. So, when one wife couldn't provide the much-needed offspring, he had little choice but to seek an alternative.

My grandmother arrived in this tumultuous setting as a mere teenager. Destiny often weaves lives together in unexpected ways, and so it was with her. At the time, her dream was to escape her small village and live in a big town. She and her cousins would trek long distances from Eyang, searching for buyers for their small agricultural goods.

Coming from the hinterlands, they were often met with disdain by the townspeople, who saw them as primitive. Accustomed to the narrow paths of their villages, they maintained the habit of walking in single file, even on the broader, tarred streets of Mamfe town. They were labeled as *"people from overside,"* a term used to mark their difference. Yet, despite the prejudice they faced, the *overside* women were renowned for their beauty. Their grace and charm stood out against the backdrop of scorn.

For my grandmother and her entourage, their journey often led them down dusty paths as they sought to sell the fruits of their labor to the more affluent inhabitants of Mamfe.

It was during one such venture that fate intervened, leading them to my grandfather's workshop. As the group paused at the entrance, my grandfather, sweating from his labor, was inside setting up a bike. He had no desire to be disturbed. But the group was desperate for a sale that day, so they persisted, calling out their wares over and over. Irritated, he stopped what he was doing and stepped outside, intent on shooing them away.

From among her cousins, my grandmother caught his attention. Who would have thought that a man of means and influence in Mamfe would take notice of a young village girl? With a generosity that hinted at deeper sentiments, he purchased everything they had to offer, paying them handsomely and immediately. It was a gesture not lost on my grandmother—nor on those around her.

As whispers of a wealthy suitor's interest in the young village girl spread like wildfire, the wheels of tradition began to turn. In a world where consent was often an afterthought, the elders of the village seized the opportunity without consulting the one most affected: my grandmother. Such was the custom, ingrained in the fabric of their society, where elders made decisions and fate danced to their tune.

And so, against the backdrop of Mamfe's bustling streets and the murmurs of eager relatives, the stage was set for a union that would shape generations to come. In this dance between tradition and fate, my grandmother's journey into matrimony began—a story of love, resistance, challenges, and the silent sacrifices made in the name of custom.

She was married off at the tender age of thirteen. Her journey to Big Papa's house was no small feat. Her birthplace, Eyang (*Overside water*—literally meaning *across the river*), lay a distant 45 miles from Mamfe. The trek involved navigating dirt tracks and forests teeming with wild animals, as well as crossing rivers on makeshift canoes or on foot during low tide. It was an adventure in its own right.

Big Mami, who had lost her mother at birth and was raised by her grandmother, was now thrust into a new life. Accompanied by family, she crossed the river one last time into matrimony. It would be a very long time before she would return to visit her people.

Big Papa's decision to seek a bride beyond the confines of his own village has always held a certain mystique and mystery for me. In a community where such ventures were rare, his boldness stood out like headlights in the night. As time passed and he took on additional wives, my grandmother's origins became a subject of ridicule among the people around her, and her husband did not shield her from being taunted.

Hailing from a distant village rarely visited by outsiders, she became the target of scorn and derision. Her unfamiliar roots were whispered about in hushed tones, painted with the brush of ignorance and prejudice. Stories of her homeland were distorted into tales of primitive savagery, leaving her vulnerable to the jabs of those who deemed themselves more civilized.

Yet, amidst the taunts and jeers, my grandmother remained strong mentally and physically. Her dignity was unshaken by the shallow judgments of those who failed to see beyond the surface.

With my grandmother safely in the house, three more wives joined the ranks in successive years. The family grew with the addition of children, and eventually, twenty-odd children were born—though, tragically, many didn't make it past their first year. In the grand scheme of things, twenty children might not sound like an astonishing number, especially when you consider some of his contemporaries who boasted families of thirty or more!

In those days, these polygamous families in Mamfe adhered to a distinct and structured way of life. Almost every household was polygamous, and it was the way to go. The setup of such households followed a well-defined pattern that maintained order and harmony within the family.

Each wife occupied her own designated living space, which consisted of a separate bedroom and kitchen. Within these quarters, the wives not only resided but also raised their children. This arrangement allowed each wife a degree of independence and autonomy, enabling her to manage her household affairs as she saw fit.

Living together in a polygamous family came with its own set of pros and cons, shaping the daily routines and interactions of the household members in a distinct manner. The allocation of individual living spaces was a practice that provided both independence and division among the wives.

Polygamy was a common practice in Pa Enotanya's community during the 1950s, shaping the family structure in a way that created harmony and stability. In the compound where my mother grew up, the wives lived in separate quarters but shared communal spaces, fostering a sense of togetherness. Despite the presence of multiple families within one household, there was little animosity or division. Instead, the wives and children interacted like a single, extended family, united by mutual respect and shared responsibilities.

This system of polygamy worked well for Pa Enotanya's family and continues to work in many parts of Cameroon. One of its strengths lies in its ability to bring stability, especially in situations where there are more women than men. In these households, certain facilities were communal, encouraging cooperation and collective responsibility. The wives took pride in their individual roles, yet contributed equally to the household, both in terms of domestic work and farming. Big Papa gave a farm to each of his wives. He would make sure the farms were cleared in time every year for the women to work. Most often, he also provided seeds. The women had to tend the crops and weed the farms until harvest time. However, the food produced was never pooled together. Each wife was able to manage and control her portion.

Polygamy also provided a strong support system during times of hardship. With a large family, there was always someone to lean on. When resources were scarce—whether it was money or food—everyone had an open-door system. Together they shared what little they had, ensuring that no child went hungry. This pooling of resources helped elevate the family's overall economic status, even in difficult times.

Moreover, polygamous marriages, like that of my grandparents, often crossed village lines, fostering alliances between different communities. These unions promoted social cohesion, reducing conflicts, and building stronger bonds across regions. The interconnectedness of the family was not only a source of strength for the individuals involved but also a means of contributing to wider communal harmony.

For Pa Enotanya and his wives, the system worked because it was rooted in shared values of cooperation, respect, and communal living. They managed their household efficiently, ensuring that every member of the family, from the children to the wives, played a vital role in the family's prosperity and happiness. Polygamy, in this context, was not just a family structure; it was a way of life that ensured stability, productivity, and unity.

Located prominently along the bustling Main Street, my grandfather's one-level ranch-style house exuded an air of affluence and distinction. A testament to his prosperity, this prime piece of real estate stood and still stands as a symbol of his success as a businessman. With its sprawling layout, the house boasted five bedrooms, including my grandfather's spacious quarters (bedroom, living room, and veranda), which commanded a presence of its own.

As one ventured to the rear of the house, a series of additional single rooms could be seen, offering a glimpse into the depth of space within. At the back, descending a flight of thirteen steep steps, the courtyard revealed itself within the confines of the property.

Here, in the tranquility of the open space, life had its own rhythm. Across from the stairs, the kitchens were lined up with one for each wife. On a normal evening, this space hummed with activity, with aromatic delights wafting through the air. A small corridor, tucked between two kitchens, led to the rear, where the bathrooms stood, a practical yet discreet addition to the household's amenities.

In this carefully curated space on the main street of Mamfe town, where functionality was the driving force and vision, my grandfather's house stood as a testament to his foresight and position within the community.

However, in the backyard of this household, there were just two bathrooms and two toilets. Now, imagine a family of at least 25 people in this space. This number didn't even include the ever-growing horde of extended relatives and the occasional visitor from the village who, needing a place to stay in town, inevitably joined the fray.

As Chinua Achebe once wrote, "The family is like the forest: when you are outside, it is dense; when you are inside, you see that each tree has its own position." Here, each "tree" struggled for space, privacy, and time. With everyone jockeying for a turn in the shared facilities, it was a recipe for disaster, my friends! Imagine trying to fit a pride of lions into a clown cart—it was bound to turn into a circus, and it was a show almost every day!

This enclosed courtyard served as a central gathering point where family members would interact, bond, and partake in the day-to-day activities of life. It was a bustling hive of domestic commotion, with more relatives, neighbors, cousins, and kids crisscrossing than you would see at a busy city intersection in Douala. It was the epicenter of all their shenanigans—of those who had excellent social etiquette and those without.

But amidst the cacophony of daily life, it was the bathrooms and toilets that took center stage in our comedy of errors. The tale of communal lavatory struggles, where soap suds met showdowns, and bathroom brawls became morning entertainment! It was the common bathrooms and toilets that were the constant sources of comedic chaos. I loved it when my grandmother told such stories.

Even what was not funny, she would turn into funny. Listening to my grandmother's tales was always a joyous affair. Even the most mundane anecdotes would transform into uproarious tales under her magical storytelling prowess. She would start a story by laughing so heartily that we all joined in the laughter before the story was told.

With her unique blend of questionable English, Pidgin English, Bayangi Kenyang language, Keyaka language, and Menkia language, she had a knack for infusing humor into every narrative. Sometimes, we found ourselves laughing, not entirely sure of what she was saying, but utterly captivated by the infectious mirth in her voice. Her stories were a delightful concoction of wit and charm, painting vivid scenes that left us in stitches and longing for more. I miss her so much! In this particular story about the bathroom, she said something in her language akin to "as you can imagine, conflicts in Big Papa's house were as inevitable as roosters crowing in the mornings."

She narrated the following story one morning on one of her visits to us in Victoria. She said that one day, at twilight, as the sleepy-eyed relatives shuffled towards the facilities, squeezing through the narrow passageway to the bathrooms, little did they know that a battleground of drama awaited them.

Cousin Ayuk or Uncle Ayuk was all set for his morning scrub, only to find that his bucket of water had vanished. There was no running water. Water had to be fetched from across the street, down the flight of thirteen steep stairs, and then to the bathrooms. To avoid congestion in the mornings with everyone trying to fetch water, some people carried their water during the day in buckets.

But wait, someone had taken Uncle Ayuk's bucket of water just as he came down and prepared to use the bathroom. Who could it be? The nerve! Accusations flew like a flock of birds startled by a mischievous kid, and soon, the courtyard echoed with furious cries! With accusations, tempers flared faster than a pot of boiling "tatchot" soup.

"Who used my water?" Cousin Ayuk demanded, brandishing

a towel like an obasanjom's shield. The shouting match was about to begin.

Cousin Beteck, on the defensive, retorted, "Not me! I barely had enough water myself!"

Mami Susanna clapped her hands three times.

Peter, in his calm voice, asked Ayuk if he was sure he had the bucket of water because it was rare for a bucket and water to just disappear. Usually, someone would pour out half of their water into their own bucket.

And so it went, a verbal joust had broken out, a shouting match that had erupted like an impromptu choir performance, except this choir was belting out a discordant tune of bathroom blues.

That morning, life in this domestic utopia was anything but dull or tranquil. So, if you ever think that your bathroom woes are a soap opera, remember the legendary back courtyard of our family's past, where every day was a bathroom battle.

"Who took my water?" Mamfe's Bayangi people, known for their language's unique blend of English and pidgin English, were in for a linguistic treat. The familiar sounds of the distinctive three languages melded seamlessly with Ayuk's frustration.

Over and over, the increasingly irate Uncle Ayuk bellowed, causing every door along the courtyard to creak open. Puzzled faces emerged, bleary-eyed and tousled, demanding, "Why are you shouting like the world's about to end?"

His response, still echoing with exasperation in Kenyang, "If na you take ma wata, bring am back before I transform into a morning tiger now now!"

Names were hurled into the slightly foggy air like fishing nets cast into the River Badi. "Ebai Nyor!" he shouted, then "Lucy!" and "Agboanya!" followed suit. After each name, he paused dramatically, as if expecting an admission of guilt from the unseen culprits. A small crowd had now gathered, some urging him to forget the water. "Let sleeping dogs lie," someone showing off their English shouted. Others offered him some of their own water.

As the negotiations were going on, the imposing presence of Big Papa emerged from the bathroom. A hush fell over the courtyard, like a sudden cease-fire during a noisy battle. It was he who had taken the precious bucket of water.

His towering frame was draped in nothing but a small towel cinched around his waist. It was a rare sight for most, as his nakedness had seldom been exposed to prying eyes. His ritual of bathing upon returning from the farm often occurred during the quiet hours of the evening when the household was typically preoccupied with other tasks for those who were home, and most others had not yet returned.

As he made his way through the courtyard towards the stairs leading to his room at the back, the uneasy silence that had settled over the gathering was broken. A smattering of greetings echoed through the air, to which he responded in kind. Big Papa remained oblivious to the tension in the air. Perplexed by the unusual gathering, yet without awaiting an answer, he swiftly commanded them to disperse and engage in productive activities befitting the morning hour. He admonished that idleness was the seat of the indolent. Oblivious to the undercurrents, he remained focused, unaware of the events that had just unfolded in his absence.

Everyone present knew the unspoken rule: the patriarch held dominion over any available water source, and nobody dared question it. One by one, they retreated to their quarters, cleaning their "two-rope slippers" on the door mats and chuckling to themselves.

"Poor Ayuk." Another day in Mamfe, with the quirky rhythm

of a polygamous household and its hilarious communal struggles. In the grand scheme of this home, these conflicts were the spice that flavored collective life. Here's to the bathrooms and toilets that united families in chaos, reminding everyone that even in the wildest of shared spaces, there was always room for a good laugh—along with a splash of mayhem!

But the daily routines in these polygamous households weren't just about bathroom battles. Each day began with a 5 a.m. wake-up call, followed by personal hygiene rituals that involved using chewing sticks, charcoal, salt, and other toiletries stored in individual living spaces to maintain cleanliness.

Bathing was a customary practice, often performed twice daily—morning and evening—due to Mamfe's humid climate. Neglecting to bathe before bed was an invitation to discomfort, ensuring a sticky, sweat-soaked night.

In the Main Street house, responsibilities were clearly defined. Each wife had a designated week to prepare meals for her husband and sleep in his bed. However, for their children, the mothers cooked every day. This rotational system ensured that everyone contributed to the household's sustenance.

While some wives were skilled cooks, others—like Big Papa's fourth wife, Mami Agbor-Tambeng—were not as proficient in the kitchen. Even when she could cook, she often refused, relying on leftovers from her husband's table to feed her family.

Big Papa favored her more than his other wives—except Mami Susannah, of course. He would often call Mami Agbor-Tambeng to take some of his food even before he started eating. When it was her turn to cook for him, Big Papa typically relied on another wife, usually the one with the best culinary skills—my grandmother—to prepare his meals. If no food was forthcoming, he never complained. Instead, he resorted to dry-roasted food, patiently waiting for the week to pass.

Life in Mamfe's Polygamous Households

Another distinctive aspect of this family structure was the rotation of sleeping arrangements. Each wife took turns sleeping in Big Papa's room, and this system usually functioned without incident. However, as in any family, occasional challenges arose. Some of Big Papa's wives had a reputation for stirring trouble. Mami Manso, for instance, sometimes refused to fulfill her duties—either by declining to cook or by refusing her turn in Big Papa's quarters. Meanwhile, Big Mami, my grandmother, the youngest of them all, refused to follow any structure at all, systematically causing considerable confusion.

Despite these challenges, Big Papa, known for his gentle and non-confrontational nature, preferred quiet reprimands and often chose not to escalate conflicts. Instead, he sought to maintain peace within the household, opting to move forward rather than dwell on sticky situations.

Pa Enotanya was born in the village of Ntenako (Manyu Division), the second of four children in a stable yet impoverished polygamous home. His parents were food crop farmers, and he quickly learned to follow in their footsteps. Without access to formal Western-style education, he was a restless young man, yearning for more than what his parents could offer. Even if his future lay in farming, he wanted more land, more crops—more opportunity. He possessed the energy of a lion and the strength of an ox.

When my grandfather embarked on the journey from his humble village of Ntenako to the bustling town of Mamfe, his heart brimmed with dreams and aspirations, each more ambitious than the last. The mere act of relocating—a grueling five-hour trek on foot—marked the first step in his pursuit of a better life. His footsteps traced a path through rugged terrain and deep valleys, through forests teeming with wild animals. Each step was a testament to his unwavering resolve, a silent vow to unravel the enigma of his existence.

As day stretched into night and twilight beckoned with promises yet unfulfilled, he pressed on—until at last, he stood at the threshold of the modest town of Mamfe, ready to carve out his future. The town welcomed him gently, with a warmth that melted away his apprehensions. Finding a household of fellow Ntenako natives was easy, and though his mind was clouded with doubt and uncertainty, he settled there for a few months.

Among his many dreams was the desire to explore neighboring villages like Nchang, seeking opportunities to acquire vast expanses of farmland—land that would surpass anything his village had ever known. With relentless determination, he turned this dream into reality, securing hectares of fertile land in Nchang, an enduring legacy now cherished by his descendants.

Yet, Big Papa's ambitions stretched far beyond agriculture. He ventured into commerce, starting as a modest vendor of agricultural produce before transforming into a prominent retailer. From food crops to any marketable goods he could acquire, he thrived in the world of trade.

His entrepreneurial spirit knew no bounds. He diversified his ventures, becoming not only a skilled tailor but also the owner and operator of a bicycle plant, mastering the art of bicycle repair and production. As time passed, his stature in the business world grew, yet his hunger for success only intensified.

In tribute to his enterprising nature, Big Papa expanded into importation, cementing his reputation as a prominent figure in Mamfe. His imported goods, sourced from the distant shores of Enugu, Nigeria, arrived in shiploads—a testament to his remarkable journey from a humble village farmer to a multifaceted business tycoon.

History remembers him as a man who turned dreams into reality through sheer restlessness and unrelenting hard work.

Fueled by a flicker of hope that refused to be extinguished, he embarked on a pilgrimage to Nigeria—one that would define his legacy.

3

Sunday at Main Street

***

Sunday was the first day of the week. Like all other Sundays, they were reserved for church, a sacred tradition my mom, Susan, shared with her father, Big Papa, but not with Big Mami, her mother. Big Mami did not believe in the church. She said she was scared of white people whose practices she said she did not like. Later in her life, she befriended a Catholic priest, Father Arnold, who eventually baptized her. She was already in her 70s when this happened.

On Sundays, she would prepare rice and stew for her family. If they were lucky, the stew would come with chicken. Most families raised chickens for special occasions and holidays. Big Mami knew that her husband, Big Papa, and her children, especially my mum, Susan, loved rice and chicken.

Big Papa adored her daughter, my mother, "Susan", whose name he pronounced "Susa". She was his "handbag" when she was not in school. He was determined to provide her with nothing but the very best, a demonstration of the boundless love he held for his cherished daughter.

My mother's distinctive way of walking never failed to make an impression on those who met her for the first time. Her height, notably tall for her age, bestowed upon her an aura of confidence, evident in her long, energetic strides that deviated from the ordinary. With each step, she covered ground swiftly, a trait that eventually led her to venture into the world of competitive athletics. Her journey as an athlete began during her primary school years at Government Primary School, Mamfe and continued through her secondary education at Queen of the Rosary College, Okoyong.

Throughout her primary school years, Mami stood out as a bright and quick learner. She had an aversion to trouble, instinctively avoiding quarrels and conflicts. Whenever a fight seemed imminent, she would quickly flee after school, choosing instead to seek refuge in the comforting embrace of her parents within the familiar confines of the family house on Main Street.

My grandfather, an enlightened young man in his late thirties, defied the norms of his time. While some families were different, many girls were still confined to domestic roles, early marriages, or, at best, a limited primary education. Determined to break this cycle, he made it his mission to send his first daughter to a "higher" educational institution after she completed primary school.

Despite being showered with love and affection, Susa was not exempt from discipline, both at home and at school. Her upbringing and education were rooted in strict discipline, where reverence for elders was constantly instilled. Every morning, she was expected to greet everyone, either in the local dialect or in English.

Ne Yii (Good morning).

This greeting was repeated about twenty times each morning, depending on how many people you encountered. The combination of domestic tutelage, formal education, and the guidance of kin—including aunts, uncles, and the vast network of extended family—ensured that she absorbed the virtues and ethical principles needed to navigate life with wisdom and grace. Any aunty or uncle could discipline a child at any time for wrongdoing, and it was universally accepted. A parent, even if inclined to spare the rod, had little choice—someone else would enforce it.

Evenings presented a different scene. As the sun dipped below the horizon, casting long, dusky shadows over the house on Main Street, a cherished nightly ritual unfolded. It was a time when the world settled into the gentle embrace of twilight, and my mother's father, affectionately called Pa Enotanya or Big Papa, claimed his usual perch—a high-backed stool, reminiscent of a barstool, on the veranda.

Big Papa's house stood close to the road, barely seven meters away. However, a small gully separated it from passing vehicles and bicycles. Any speeding driver who lost control would find himself in the gully—not on our veranda—unless he somehow took flight.

As always, Big Papa positioned himself to face the road, which stretched in both directions in front of the house. The veranda transformed into a gathering place, where not only family but also neighbors and passersby assembled. My mother, her siblings, and their friends would rush through their evening chores, eager to listen to the elders' rich tales and lose themselves in the melodies of familiar voices.

Yet, on moonlit nights, the gathering on the veranda became more than just storytelling. It evolved into an enchanting dance beneath the celestial glow, a symphony of voices raised in harmonious song. They all came to lose themselves in the joy of moonlit reverie.

The choice of the veranda was entirely arbitrary. It held no particular significance—there were no promised snacks to lure them in, nor the expectation of a grand feast. As Chinua Achebe described in *Things Fall Apart*:

> A man who calls his kinsmen to a feast does not do so to save them from starving. They all have food in their own homes. When we gather together in the moonlit village ground it is not because of the moon. Every man can see it in his own compound.

No, what drew them together was the magnetic pull of shared narratives, the collective wisdom of generations past, and the intoxicating allure of community. The stories became sweeter, carried on the laughter of children, their playful distractions adding to the rhythm of voices weaving tales of the old.

These were evenings when hearts felt unburdened, and spirits soared on the wings of ancestral wisdom. The closest comparison I can make to those moonlit storytelling nights is movie nights at home with grandchildren—though even that does not truly come close.

Under the stars, the adults turned the veranda into a theater of nostalgia, weaving together tales of their journeys and the traditions of their ancestral villages. They often wondered why and how things had changed, always claiming that the past was better. On dim, dusky evenings, the feeble glow of lanterns served as a quiet reminder that bedtime approached swiftly.

Without the guiding hand of the moonlight, the veranda would gradually empty as families retreated to their quarters, their hearts brimming with stories, their dreams alight with the echoes of shared laughter, and their souls warmed by the embrace of kinship.

It was on this veranda that Big Papa wove his stories—tales passed down through generations, rich in African folklore and steeped in tradition. He would always begin in the Kenyang language, using the same familiar phrases:

"*You see, back then, many young girls were stuck doing chores and getting married as babies... I married your mother when she was a child,*" he would say, pointing at my mother and her siblings.

"I will not let anyone here marry as a child".

The stories that followed often revolved around the intricate workings of the animal kingdom. The fox, the tortoise, the cat, the bush rat, the elephant, the hippopotamus, the crocodile, the chicken, the tiger, the hyena, the dog, and countless other creatures each played their roles in these age-old narratives.

Yet, these tales were more than mere entertainment; they carried profound wisdom, imparting valuable life lessons and ethical principles. They embodied the knowledge passed down through generations by their ancestors, ensuring that their timeless messages endured.

Each tale had three distinct components. First, there was the narrative itself, rich with characters, conflicts, and unexpected twists. Then came the accompanying songs, where everyone present had a role to play. The call-and-response pattern echoed through the evening air, drawing listeners deeper into the heart of the story.

"Mbolo mbolo Ma Lucy."
Response: "Yah yah a eh."
"Mbolo mbolo Ma Lucy."
Response: "Yah yah a eh."
"Maya mbenge me mbe poo twoh."
Response: "Yah yah eh."
"Eta ya mbenge me mbe poo twoh
Response: "Yah yah eh."

Or perhaps, other songs like

"Dodo ki do..."

Or

"Ney moh o o"
A nyeh mbeng kwa en'go

Finally, at the end of each story came the lessons learned—the moral of the tale.

These stories served as a conduit for instilling morality, fostering harmony within the community, and guiding individuals toward virtuous living. The messages were clear: how to be good neighbors, how to live in peace, how to be caring siblings, and how to contribute positively to the collective well-being. A sprinkle of African folklore, a dash of wisdom from our crafty grandfathers, and a pinch of education—that was the recipe that shaped our mothers into the remarkable women they became.

Big Papa, my grandfather, often shared stories with my mother and her siblings about his own father, my great-grandfather. Though I never met him, his presence was deeply felt through the lessons and beliefs he passed down to Big Papa.

One of the most striking differences between them was their perspective on life. While Big Papa had a more pragmatic outlook, my great-grandfather held an unwavering belief in the power of ancestral reverence. He believed that the ancestors—those who had passed on—were not truly gone but continued to play an active role in the lives of the living. He taught Big Papa that the spirits of the ancestors could grant blessings, ensure fertility, and even bring justice when wrongs had been committed. Their influence was all-encompassing, shaping decisions and guiding the family's actions. They were seen as the true custodians of balance, mediating between the world of the living and the spiritual realm.

Whenever my mother and her siblings gathered around Big Papa, he would share the wisdom he had inherited from his father. He spoke of the offerings his father made to honor the spirits—small tokens of gratitude meant to ensure peace and prosperity in their household. These stories were not just about rituals; they were about respecting the past and understanding that life was interconnected, spanning generations.

However, Big Papa did not follow these traditions with the same intensity as his father. While he acknowledged the significance of ancestors, his outlook on life had evolved. He often spoke to my mother and her siblings about how much the world had changed—how the connection to the ancestors, though still meaningful, needed to adapt to modern life. It wasn't that Big Papa rejected his father's teachings; instead, he found a way to balance tradition with a more practical approach.

In many ways, these stories shaped my mother's understanding of her place within the family and the broader lineage. Like her siblings, she absorbed these tales, learning to respect the traditions of the past, even as the practice of ancestral reverence shifted over time.

For Big Papa, the stories of his father were not just about rituals; they were about instilling values of respect, continuity, and understanding one's roots.

He often told his children that his father's deep faith in the ancestors had given him strength and guidance, but it was up to each generation to decide how best to honor that legacy. Though my mother grew up in a household where the focus had shifted from ancestral reverence to more contemporary ways of thinking, the echoes of my great-grandfather's beliefs remained, woven into the fabric of their family life.

Of course, my grandfather had his own stories. Some carried the imprint of Christianity, speaking of a man named Jesus, born in a distant land, and the astonishing belief that he had sacrificed himself to redeem humanity.

Big Papa did not fully grasp the rituals of the Catholic Church, but he understood the power of sacrifice. Alongside these tales, he wove narratives of animals in the forest, illustrating God's divine order, where humans were elevated above the beasts.

Though the spiritual undertones of these stories varied, their essence remained the same: they served as a guiding light, a source of wisdom, and a testament to the enduring power of storytelling in shaping lives, cultures, and generations.

4

The Morning of the Python
Courage on the Farm Path

* * *

One Saturday, my mother, the wide-eyed pre-teen, accompanied her mother to the Nchang Bush, as this particular farm was called. It was an ordinary day in August, with dead leaves and grass painted in shades of green, red, and gold all over. Surprisingly, it had not rained for a couple of days, and everywhere was dry. The path they walked on was a narrow trail with my mum in front and her mother behind. They were both barefoot and flanked on both sides by tall, slender grasses that rustled gently in the breeze. The specific name of the grass was unknown to my mum, but she could still recall how the surroundings were quiet, and the grass whispered secrets to the wind, making the landscape feel like a world of enchantment. A few leaves would occasionally take on a new life, flying in the air before settling back in another location. My mother was fascinated by the surroundings and was tempted now and then to stop and listen if her mom would let her.

The sky above was a brilliant, very light blue canvas, stained with the brushstrokes of chirping birds. Their melodious or disturbing songs, depending on the mood of the listener, filled the

The Morning of the Python

air, creating a symphony of nature's sounds. Bees and flies darted busily about, each absorbed in its vital mission. All around, the world buzzed with life, with every nook and cranny of the grassy forest teeming with insects and creatures going about their daily business.

Once in a while, my grandmother would explain a distinct sound, but for the most part, they walked in silence.

My mother was carrying a machete. She had an innocent curiosity; her eyes were always full of wonder at the world that surrounded her. She would turn around from time to time to look at her mother, as if for assurance that all was well. As they walked, a subtle unease crept over her, an inexplicable sense that something was amiss.

Ahead of them, something unsettling began to take shape. The air thickened, and the grasses lining the narrow path shifted—not with the breeze, but as though stirred by something unseen, something or someone watching. The blades swayed with a deliberate rhythm, their motion eerily synchronized, as if guided by an invisible hand. Her pulse quickened, and she found herself fixated on the unnatural movement, unable to look away.

She had been plucking grass absentmindedly, but now her fingers froze, the once-innocent action feeling out of place in this strange atmosphere. Without knowing why, her pace faltered. Her feet felt heavy, dragging against the ground as an inexplicable dread crept up her spine. She slowed down, her heart thudding louder with each step.

Something was wrong.

She glanced back at her mother, but the questions swirling in her mind wouldn't form into words. Her mother's face, calm but distant, offered no comfort. The silence between them seemed to hum with an unseen presence, something lurking just beyond her senses. She turned her gaze forward again, fear tightening in her chest, as the grasses swayed—alive with secrets, as if beckoning something... or someone.

At first, she couldn't quite make out the shape slithering through the tangled undergrowth. It was long and flat, weaving almost imperceptibly beneath the shifting grasses. Her youthful eyes struggled to focus on it. To her innocent mind, it was another oddity of the forest, a "snick," as she called it—a name for the strange and unknown. She felt a sense of fear and foreboding. Was it merely something curious, blending into the shadows?

But something was different. The air held its breath. The ground beneath her feet felt unsteady, as though even the earth itself recoiled. She could hear it now—the faint, unsettling rustle that followed the thing's movements.

Still, she remained oblivious to the danger. Her mind, too young and innocent, couldn't comprehend the silent threat hiding just ahead. The world had yet to teach her that sometimes the unknown could be dangerous.

Unbeknownst to my mother, her keen instincts had not let her down. Her mother, Big Mami, my grandmother, vigilant and experienced, had already recognized the serpent for what it was. Her breath hitched—just slightly, but enough for the tension in the air to deepen. Every muscle in her body tensed.

She didn't have time to warn her daughter not to make a sound, as the creature was no longer hidden, at least not fully. It lay poised, taut, perfectly still, yet its presence pressed against the air like a warning. In a quick and decisive movement, Big Mami reached out, grasped her daughter's hand, and, in the process, yanked her dress as she pulled her back just as she was about to take her next step. Girls did not wear trousers then. The suddenness of the vice-like grip, the harsh yank on her dress, made her heart leap into her throat. Confusion turned into fear as her mother pulled her back with such force that her feet almost momentarily left the ground. Time seemed to slow down. She heard a low hiss, barely audible over the pounding in her ears. My mother realized that the enigmatic "snick" was not a stationary object, but a creature that was very much alive.

They stood frozen, the world narrowing to just the two of them and the snake, waiting—waiting for something terrible to happen. Then a flash of scales glinted in the sunlight.

Without saying a word, her mother continued to hold her back, gently but firmly, communicating the seriousness of the situation through her touch and stern expression. They stood there, a mother and her daughter, frozen in place. The serpent, still concealed by the tall grasses, continued its slow and deliberate journey across the path.

Time seemed to stretch out as they watched its graceful progress, inch by inch. They waited patiently, knowing that any hasty movement could provoke an unwanted reaction from the creature. My mother's heart raced with a mix of fear and fascination as she observed the sinuous beauty of the serpent, its scales glinting in the dappled dew and sunlight.

Finally, as the snake disappeared into the grass on the opposite side of the path, they breathed a collective sigh of relief. Their path was clear once more, and the enchanting journey to the farm could continue.

But my mom burst into tears of emotion, and it took a few minutes of scolding to get back on track. Her mother's strong grip had saved her from stepping right on a python, a potentially perilous encounter that might have left a lasting scar on her young heart.

That day, my mother learned a lesson that would stay with her for a lifetime – the world is filled with hidden wonders and dangers, and the importance of a mother's protective embrace is a treasure beyond measure. The encounter with the snake left an indelible mark on her, a memory of the day she danced on the edge of the unknown, guided safely back by her mother's watchful hand.

5

My Grandfather's Clock

* * *

The story about the clock in the Main Street house was recounted to me by my aunt, Mary Ndip, years ago, as she recounted that of "Hausa dem for Mamfe na so so Bamum" (that is for another chapter). The living room in my grandfather's house was a carefully designed space that captured the essence of family. The walls bore witness to the passage of time, adorned with a gallery of well-framed black-and-white family photographs that spanned across generations.

These precious photo moments were frozen in time, capturing the smiles, laughter, and shared experiences of my ancestors. Each photograph had a story, holding within it a narrative waiting to be told, and collectively, they softly murmured tales of a past era. The attire and postures were different, but the enduring smiles and the stories they evoked were universal and unchanging.

In my aunt's stories about their house, there was something quite special about the pictures on the walls. Children used to come from their own homes just to look at them. Back then, not many people could afford enlarged framed pictures and even those who could did not often think about decorating their walls with pictures. Homes were always left open, and some people would drift from one house to another. No invitation or prior notice was needed!

The same pictures stayed on the walls for a very long time, until I started secondary school in Okoyong Mamfe. It was as if, with old age, my grandfather got tired of them and just let them be. He was on the wall as a young man, but he was not there as an aged man.

But here's what made it even more interesting: there were no photos on the wall of my grandfather's current family—his wives and children. There were pictures of him, yes, and even pictures of him with his car and on his bike, but none of his family. Interesting, now that I think of it.

My mom told us about some people who would come by every day just to stare at those pictures as if they expected something magical to happen by looking at them. What's more, some folks would go to the extent of calling out the names of the people in the photos and making commentaries, even though many of those folks had passed away long ago. It's fascinating how pictures can make you feel as though you're in the presence of those you miss.

In the heart of this family living room stood an imposing and regal clock, adorned with a pendulum that swayed rhythmically, a time watchman in their home. It occupied a prominent place on the wall, its presence commanding attention. Yet, this was no ordinary timekeeping device; it was an esteemed member of their family, an ever-constant presence in their lives.

Whenever the siblings gathered in that cozy living room, their eyes couldn't resist the allure of that magnificent clock. It wasn't just a clock; it was a wise teacher, a sentinel of moments. It was here, beneath its watchful gaze, that the children learned to count. Suzie, my clever mum, seemed to grasp the concept of numbers with swiftness. She would eagerly count out loud, setting the pace for the rest of them. Her patient guidance helped them all learn the ropes of counting. Her enthusiasm was infectious as she led the counting sessions, her voice marking the steady tick-tock of the clock. Soon, everyone was singing the Westminster Chime and counting. This grand clock was therefore not just a silent observer of their lives; it was an active participant in their education.

Every hour, as it struck, the enchanting chime would echo through the room, announcing the time with musical grace. Like clockwork, my mother and her siblings would rush to the living room from all corners of the house to witness this hourly spectacle. One o'clock was a particularly amusing challenge, as everyone had to dash to the living room just to count the number one, but it was a tradition they held dear.

The Westminster Chime melody, with its timeless charm, left a lasting impression on their memories as my aunts continued to tell the story of how their sister taught them to count with the ding dong, ding dong of Big Papa's clock. And as they stood together, huddled around this cherished timepiece, the family bonds grew stronger, and the foundations of knowledge were laid, all to the reassuring cadence of the clock's pendulum. It became a symphony of togetherness, a reminder that, no matter where life took them, they would always share precious moments like those they shared in their father's living room. These were treasurable lessons in the value of family, the importance of tradition, and the magic that resides in the simplest of moments.

6

From Mamfe to Onitsha via Enugu by Road

* * *

Big Papa embarked on his first journey to Enugu and then to Onitsha, the economic powerhouse of former Eastern Nigeria, by following a lorry driver. He was still a young man, brimming with restless ambition. Life in Mamfe, though stable, could no longer contain his growing desire for more. He had built a life for himself, working his farms with his wives and managing small yet steady businesses in the bustling local markets. His crops were reliable, his ventures modestly successful, but a part of him yearned for a greater challenge.

Leaving Mamfe for Enugu, Nigeria, was not an easy decision, but Big Papa never shied away from a difficult path. He had heard stories of opportunities in Nigeria—thriving towns and cities where commerce flourished and fortunes awaited the daring. The journey, however, was no simple feat. The road from Mamfe to Enugu stretched across treacherous terrain—muddy, broken paths winding through dense forests. It was a test of endurance, requiring both mental fortitude and an iron will. But Big Papa was determined; he believed this journey could unlock doors that Mamfe never could.

Before leaving, he gathered his wives in the compound and

From Mamfe to Onitsha via Enugu by Road

explained why he had to go. Although his businesses were growing, Mamfe's market was small, with limited opportunities. In Onitsha, he had heard of new trade routes and the possibility of sourcing goods at lower prices to resell back home. If successful, it would mean not just greater wealth for the family but a stronger foothold in a broader market.

His wives, though anxious, understood his restless spirit. They had seen it in him before—the same drive that had made him an enterprising young man, willing to take risks to secure his family's future. They knew he would return. With quiet resolve, Big Papa packed his few belongings, leaving clear instructions to ensure the farms and businesses ran smoothly in his absence.

He needed to be in Onitsha himself. In the 1960s, the road trip from Mamfe in Cameroon to Enugu, the capital of Eastern Nigeria, was a challenging and time-consuming journey, passing through the border town of Ekok and Abakaliki. Abakaliki, the capital of Ebonyi State in southeastern Nigeria, is located 64 kilometers (40 miles) southeast of Enugu. The distance between Mamfe and Enugu is approximately 130 kilometers. The road, particularly on the Cameroonian side, was largely unpaved and rough, making travel difficult and slow. It sometimes took up to three hours to travel from Cameroon to Nigeria.

Travelers made the journey in overcrowded buses, crossing the border at Ekok. The trip was often prolonged due to frequent checkpoints by local authorities and military personnel, who monitored for smugglers, illegal immigrants, and political dissidents. However, in those days, officials often just waved drivers through.

When I was in Form One in Queen of the Rosary College, Okoyong, Mamfe, my Big Papa told me a hilarious story about one such journey he took to Onitsha during the rainy season. That night, the driver and passengers had to stay at a border town after a cargo truck got stuck in the mud.

"And let me tell you, the rain wasn't helping either," he said, steadying me as I perched on a lopsided kitchen bench. The more the driver and his conductor tried to rev the engine, the deeper the truck sank into the mud. It was like a bad game of *Wheels on the Bus in the Mud*, I concluded with a smile years later as I reminisced.

Eventually, the truck tipped sideways into a ditch, blocking the entire road. With no other option, they spent the night in their uncomfortable vehicle. But the villagers outside were welcoming, offering them boiled cocoyam with red palm oil, seasoned with salt and *njangsa* pepper—an unexpected gourmet meal in the middle of nowhere.

The village had no running water or electricity, and when night fell, the darkness was absolute. Other travelers, also stranded, joined in, sharing stories of hardship and hope. Some passersby stopped to listen, offered assistance, and then continued on their way.

The eerie sounds of the forest grew louder as the night deepened. My Big Papa shuddered, recalling his father's stories about a bird whose ominous call foretold death. For a moment, he imagined something sinister lurking in the shadows. But he forced himself to shake off the unsettling thoughts, focusing instead on his excitement for the journey ahead. Fortunately, the delicious boiled cocoyam had done its magic—banishing his unease entirely.

It also sparked lively conversation, as everyone eagerly commented on the food.

As the sun set over the Cameroon rainforest, the landscape underwent a mesmerizing transformation. Beneath the dense canopy, the forest came alive, revealing a world teeming with nocturnal wonders. This lush and mysterious kingdom, renowned for its extraordinary biodiversity, became a stage for creatures that thrive under the veil of darkness.

With the ascent of the moon, the nocturnal denizens took center stage, and the forest awakened with a symphony of sounds. The night air reverberated with an eclectic chorus—each species eager to make its presence known. Crickets serenaded the night with their rhythmic chirps, their tiny voices blending seamlessly into the growing nocturnal orchestra.

Bats, flitting silently through the night, contributed their distinctive squeaks and squawks, punctuating the darkness. Birds, too, joined the composition, their sharp calls and screeches echoing through the dense foliage.

Amid this symphony, monkeys added their plaintive cries, an eerie counterpoint that deepened the forest's nocturnal opera. Croaking frogs, masters of camouflage, lent their voices to the chorus, their distinct tones providing the bass and harmonizing with the night's melody.

Yet, the enchantment did not end there. As darkness deepened, with the moon on and off, the forest occasionally resounded with spine-tingling calls from elusive nocturnal creatures. Bushbabies, the enigmatic primates of the night, unleashed their ghostly vocalizations, while owls, the silent hunters of the dark, sent forth haunting hoots that rippled through the trees.

Under the cloak of night, the Cameroon rainforest became an auditory wonderland—a showcase of the vibrant and diverse life that thrives in the heart of darkness.

That night, as Big Papa struggled to find a comfortable position on the overcrowded bus, the mosquitoes had a field day, turning the journey into a real-life battle. Their incessant buzzing drove him nearly mad, and he muttered that when a mosquito finally landed before he could swat it away, sinking its proboscis into his skin, it felt like a ninja attack—swift, stealthy, and painfully precise.

"They're like tiny, winged vampires," he grumbled, "thirsty for blood and determined to ruin an already miserable night." The air was hot and stifling, and their relentless presence, coupled with their irritating hum, ensured no one got a wink of sleep. Despite the chaos, my grandfather, a soft-spoken young man by nature, rarely complained. After his meal of boiled cocoyam, he found a way to settle in, responding occasionally to remarks and sharing a joke or two with his fellow passengers. However, he began to notice a shift in mood—what had started as excitement, especially for those traveling to Nigeria for the first time, was now giving way to frustration.

He observed his fellow travelers more closely. The bus, packed to capacity with thirty passengers—mostly men—became a microcosm of human endurance. Some idly indulged in snuff, while others stared out the window, undoubtedly recalculating their now-disrupted plans. What was meant to be a brief journey had turned into an unplanned overnight stay at the border.

Among the sea of weary faces, a quiet scene of domesticity caught my grandfather's attention. At the back of the bus, a woman nursed her baby while her husband sat dutifully by her side. Together, they exuded a rare serenity amidst the surrounding discomfort—a beacon of calm in an otherwise restless night.

Further down the aisle, a man repeatedly stood up, sticking his head out the window to spit, his movements a reflection of the shared discomfort. The heavy air was thick with the mingling scents of sweat and unwashed bodies—a pungent reminder of the tropical heat, tight quarters, and the absence of any natural antiperspirants.

Adding to the discomfort, the unmistakable stench of soiled baby napkins lingered in the air. A bowl of half-eaten food sat abandoned since the journey's inception, while the floor of the bus bore witness to an assortment of discarded plastic bags, crumpled paper, and other refuse—creating an atmosphere of neglect and squalor.

The scene was anything but picturesque. A cacophony of odors assaulted the senses, painting a vivid picture of disarray. Some passengers had resigned themselves to the situation, their heads bowed in contemplation or surrendered to sleep.

Yet, amidst the chaos, my grandfather remained a picture of composure. His unassuming nature rarely betrayed his inner thoughts. After his modest meal of boiled cocoyam, he found a way to settle into the discomfort, exchanging occasional remarks and jests with his fellow travelers.

For the first time, he allowed himself to truly observe the people sharing this journey with him. In his eagerness to reach his destination, he had overlooked the richness of human stories unfolding around him. But as the night stretched on and the truck remained lodged in place, he found solace in the unexpected camaraderie forged through adversity—a reminder of the resilience of the human spirit, even in the face of uncertainty.

Neither the mosquitoes nor the truck blocking the road could dampen his enthusiasm. The excitement of reaching Nigeria for the first time kept him going. The difficulties of the journey paled in comparison to the adventure that lay ahead. He had heard countless stories about Nigeria but had never set foot across the border. Now, the prospect of exploring a new country and discovering fresh opportunities for his business filled him with anticipation.

As the journey neared its end, he felt a deep sense of accomplishment for having made it through the rainforest. His determination and entrepreneurial spirit had carried him forward, and his positive attitude would prove essential in achieving success. This was just one of the first of many trips he would make to Onitsha via Enugu.

When he finally arrived in Nigeria, a wave of wonder and excitement washed over him. Everything was larger, louder, taller and teeming with life. The bustling markets, filled with traders from all over, were unlike anything he had ever seen. He knew that here, he would not only find the goods he had come for but also gain valuable knowledge and insights into new ways of doing business.

The road from Mamfe to Onitsha was more than just a trade route—it was a vital link between two nations, fostering connections between people and commerce. He understood that Nigeria, with its larger population and more developed markets, held countless opportunities. Determined to learn and succeed, he embraced the challenge ahead.

Onitsha was a world of its own—a place where quick thinking and sharp negotiation skills were essential. For Big Papa, this was both exhilarating and demanding. He spent weeks navigating the crowded markets, bargaining with seasoned traders, and immersing himself in the pulse of this dynamic new world.

On that first trip, he brought back simple goods with the bit of money he had—items that were rare and difficult to find in Cameroon at the time, like matches, which he sold at over 200% profit. The success fueled his ambition, and his journeys across the border became more frequent.

When he finally made the long journey back to Mamfe, his return was triumphant. His bags were fuller—not just with goods, but with knowledge and connections that would serve him for years to come. His wives and children welcomed him with relief, their initial anxieties replaced by a sense of pride. He had not only survived the journey but had returned with more than they had ever expected.

In the years that followed, the trip to Onitsha via Enugu

became a defining moment in Big Papa's life. It marked the turning point where his small, steady business began to grow into something greater. His success in Onitsha opened doors, allowing him to expand and dream bigger. Though the road had been difficult, that journey reshaped his future—and, in turn, the future of our family.

7

The British Godfather

* * *

During subsequent trips, Big Papa sought out one man he had heard of, Mr. Oru Samson, a very well-respected engineer who had distinguished himself in Nigeria and was based in Enugu. He was one of Big Papa's kinsmen, and he stayed with him for a few days in Enugu before continuing to Onitsha on each trip.

Their connection blossomed into a lifelong friendship. Over the years, they made many exchange visits, and on one occasion, Big Papa brought his daughter along to Enugu, where they spent the entire trip as Pa Oru's guests.

It was also during one of such trips that Big Papa had the good fortune of crossing paths with a British entrepreneur named David Wilson. Struck by the remarkable qualities of this affable Manyu man—his simplicity, impeccable character, genial disposition, intelligence, and striking handsomeness—Wilson found himself drawn to my grandfather, embracing him as a son and unlocking a world of opportunities for him.

The Briton was a distinguished British manager and businessman. He extended his generosity by negotiating arrangements that transcended mere financial transactions. He ensured a steady supply of goods beyond the funds Big Papa had brought along. This symbiotic relationship took shape as Big Papa would trade, reimburse the principal sum, and then embark on a fresh cycle with increased merchandise and capital. This invaluable support from his "godfather" proved instrumental in rapidly expanding his financial foundation, ultimately propelling him into the realm of a prominent entrepreneur.

His early dealings, which initially involved small bags and cartons, quickly escalated into the procurement of entire truckloads and even shiploads of diverse commodities. His inventory encompassed a broad spectrum of products, including sewing machines and components, fabrics, snuff, matches, towels, cutlasses, soap (in multiple colors), bicycles and their components, thread, sewing accessories, and salt. These were items in high demand, ensuring the steady growth of his burgeoning enterprise.

Thanks to his godfather, Mr. Wilson, Big Papa got a scholarship for a few months to learn to assemble and repair bicycles in Nigeria. Upon his return, he established a bicycle-repair workshop, which became a significant part of his business and a major attraction in Mamfe.

He also learned to sew clothes in Nigeria and set up a dress-making business with several apprentices. He sewed clothes for his family and friends, but more importantly, he sewed them on a commercial scale, and his business grew exponentially. He became very popular and was nicknamed "Tiranoh" (Tailor Enoh in the Kenyang language).

In 1960, as Nigeria celebrated its hard-won independence, a significant shift unfolded in the corporate landscape. British companies, having completed their missions, began packing their bags and making their way back to the United Kingdom. Among those preparing to depart was David, the benevolent figure who had played a crucial role in shaping the path of my grandfather's life.

In a heartfelt journey to Nigeria to bid his mentor farewell, Big Papa took bundles of fabric as parting gifts. With gratitude in his heart and an eagerness to learn more about navigating the intricate world of business without necessarily holding the reins, Big Papa engaged David in a profound conversation about shareholding and a move away from sole proprietorship.

Their conversations eventually culminated in an unexpected yet transformative gesture—a gift that would change the course of my grandfather's life. David, recognizing both the potential and the unquenchable thirst for knowledge in Big Papa, made a decision that was not only generous but visionary. He purchased shares in Nigerian Breweries on my grandfather's behalf, marking the start of a profound and eye-opening education in the world of business.

This gift of shares was far more than a financial investment; it was a doorway into new realms of understanding. For a man like Big Papa, whose instincts for enterprise had always been sharp, this was a pivotal moment. The intricacies of shareholding, the ebb and flow of business partnerships, and the broader implications of corporate investment were concepts that had previously been distant. But David's gesture was the spark that ignited Big Papa's journey into this new world, where business was not just about hard work but also about ownership, strategy, and foresight.

The shares in Nigerian Breweries served as a learning tool, one that introduced him to the broader landscape of financial growth and long-term wealth management. It was a gesture that would resonate through generations, laying the groundwork for a deeper understanding of business for both Big Papa and those who would follow in his footsteps. This pivotal moment not only expanded his vision but also deepened his sense of what was possible in the world of commerce and beyond.

From that moment forward, he became a dedicated attendee of annual shareholders' meetings of Nigerian Breweries, his presence signifying his commitment and thirst for knowledge. He diligently collected dividends annually, a tangible reminder of his journey into the intricate world of business, a journey that would continue to shape his life until his final days.

As he grew older and tired, he gradually sold off his businesses. Even the sewing that he was so passionate about could not escape this fate, and he sold off his machines. By this time, his hands were those of a much older man, jabbed and poked by needles and pins in the tailoring workshop where he would often sew through the night with the help of his tilly lamp until the early morning risers carrying their vegetables to the market would greet him on the way: "Ne yee eh," to which he would respond with his chewing stick in his mouth, "eh ne yee nkuo." His eyes were tired with age, and threading the needle became a problem if one of his children or apprentices were not present.

Before he wrapped up his business ventures, he made an intriguing choice—he decided to acquire a car. But not just any car. His Opel Olympia was a unique acquisition, arriving in Mamfe not via the usual road transport but by boat. It became the first of its kind in Mamfe, quickly becoming the talk of the town. However, a few years later, he found himself in a financial bind. With insufficient funds to complete his fifth block building in the heart of Mamfe, after having already finished two in the village that same year, he reluctantly decided to part with his cherished car.

In his later years, he settled for a humbler mode of transportation—a bicycle. Picture this: a towering figure of a man, slightly hunched over, casually pedaling his way down Main

Street. It was nothing short of a remarkable sight, one that turned heads and captured the imagination of bystanders and neighbors throughout the 1960s.

8

Reme and Big Papa Enotanya

* * *

My mother was awed by her father. She saw him as a calm, fascinating character—slow to speak and even slower to anger. She was special to him in many ways. First, she was his first child after many years of childlessness. As a toddler, she followed him everywhere he went when he was at home and spent time in his workshop.

Then he met with and chatted with so many people daily. She was fascinated by deals he made that she had no clue about. He was always talking to himself and would gaze with penetrating eyes, trying to decipher what he was talking about. He was a very wealthy man, no doubt—one of the wealthiest at the time in Mamfe. But he never flaunted his riches and was always low-key. As a young adult, from photos that I saw, he was very well-built and good-looking, with distinct, almost striking features that added character to his appearance. He could not read or write, but he could count money and understood the role of money in his life and that of his family members.

Starting with his complexion, he possessed a warm and sun-kissed skin tone, indicative of spending significant time outdoors on farms and other businesses. After years of exposure to the

African sun, he had left a subtle, healthy glow on his face, suggesting a life lived close to nature.

His face had a strong, well-defined bone structure, with prominent cheekbones that hinted at his African heritage. As an older man, the lines on his face were etched by years of laughter and wisdom, creating a captivating medley of experiences. Wrinkles uncharacteristically traced the corners of his eyes, revealing the genuine joy and kindness that radiated from within him. By the time I knew him, he already had wrinkles, which also added a whimsical charm to his countenance.

His eyes were deep and expressive, reminiscent of the vast African skies. They were a rich shade of dark brown, with a twinkle that reflected his curiosity about the world around him. The pupils were full of life, always observant, and exuded a sense of calmness and understanding. These eyes had seen both the joys and struggles of life, adding depth to his persona.

His lips were full and wore a perpetual gentle smile. They held the tales of countless conversations and echoed the laughter shared with friends and relatives who stopped by, nonstop. When he was deep in thought, his lips would purse together, emphasizing his contemplative nature. His nose was neither too large nor too small, blending harmoniously with the rest of his facial features. It had an elegant curve, representing the balance between strength and grace. The bridge of his nose showcased small, faint—almost invisible—freckles, perhaps earned through countless hours spent under the sun repairing bikes.

Any hair around his face was always shaved, showing his dedication to a personal grooming routine and hinting at his meticulous nature and love of style.

As he sat outside on his terrace under the burning sun, his face would often reflect a sense of tranquility, contentment, and genuine interest in the world passing by. Lines of concentration would occasionally furrow his brow as he focused on a passing detail, indicating his keen attention to craftsmanship and his surroundings. Every few minutes, he would lift his head to respond to a greeting.

Overall, this middle-aged tailor from the 1950s in Mamfe, Cameroon, possessed a face that carried the wisdom, kindness, and warmth earned through a life well-lived. His facial features, shaped by his experiences and profession, painted a portrait of a man who observed the world with curiosity, care, and a deep appreciation for the beauty found in everyday moments. But Big Papa, towering at an impressive lanky six foot four inches, had a distinctive presence that extended beyond his remarkable height. When you saw him, you revered him.

The man had to bend double to enter his own living room. When he would return home after a long, grueling day, drenched in sweat, he would bend, enter the living room, and go straight to his quarters, where he was met by a cadre of feline companions who adored him. These cats would eagerly gather around him, anticipating the nourishment and affection he brought with him.

Big Papa had a deep affection for certain culinary delights, particularly cassava fufu, yam fufu, or cocoyam fufu paired with an array of savory soups. Whether it was Ogbono (mango) soup, Tatchot soup (Habanero pepper leaves), okro soup, or egusi soup, he relished these dishes. It was on the back veranda, a makeshift dining area, that I witnessed a rather unique spectacle for the first time.

In a household where formal dining areas were not specified, meals were often enjoyed in the kitchen, living room, or on open verandas. It was on this veranda that Big Papa's dining rituals unfolded. The fufu balls he rounded with both palms and consumed were slightly larger than a table tennis ball, and I would gaze in wonder as they descended into his throat, creating a captivating, convoluted journey down his esophagus. The accompanying soup acted as a lubricant, ensuring a smooth passage without the discomfort of gagging or choking. Occasionally, his head would bow slightly, and his eyes would widen if the fufu ball proved particularly sizable—a natural, instinctive response to aid its passage down his throat. Nature's own way of helping it glide down.

Cooking duties were rotated among the wives on a weekly basis, and fufu served as a staple, paired with a variety of delectable sauces and soups. Big Papa, in his culinary preferences, rarely indulged in chewing cassava, plantain, or cocoyam.

As the years wore on, Big Papa underwent a transformation. His elegant gait, characteristic of tall individuals, remained, but physically, he showed signs of weariness. High blood pressure became a relentless adversary, ultimately claiming him at the venerable age of 87. His once brisk steps had slowed, and a wandering eye lent him a perpetually distracted look as if his physical presence were merely a vessel. It was as though his spirit had embarked on a journey that only he could glimpse peripherally, a destination the rest of us could not see but would eventually reach.

Big Mami or Biggie (my mother's mother) was a sharp contrast to her husband. Physically, she was barely five feet two to Big Papa's six feet four. My Biggie was a classic beauty in the true sense of the word. She was very attractive with symmetrical facial features. Her face was strong and defined, with high cheekbones and lips that curved into a happy smile always. Her eyes, a light shade of brown, were her most striking feature. They were like deep, soulful pools and seemed to hold many secrets she could never share. When she laughed, her eyes sparkled, but the same eyes could cut through like a knife when she was mad. Her gaze was intense and unwavering (when she was upset), a proof of the strength and resilience that carried her through life.

Her skin was a rich shade of iroko, smooth and flawless despite the passing of time. It glistened in the sun, especially as she used kernel oil (manyanga) every morning. She was well-proportioned with a deceptive, petite, delicate appearance. Her body was full and curvy. Her legs were slightly curved inwards, and she moved with grace and fluidity, her hips swaying to a rhythm that only she could hear.

She had muscular arms, developed through years of manual labor on farms. When she stood upright, her well-built frame and confident posture were evident. Her hair was always neatly plaited with black thread. She loved tying a head tie, and her head was always covered, probably as protection against the sun as well.

Biggie dressed in an interesting way, and we, her grandchildren, always took the mickey out of her dressing. Underneath her wrapper and "buba" she wore a dress, and underneath the dress, she wore stretch shorts. She never wore any other undergarments. She was talkative and was a little "busybody," in contrast to her husband.

Despite her age at the time, I came to know her well. She radiated an infectious youthful energy. Her spirit was unbreakable, forged through a lifetime of hardship and struggle under an ever-scorching sun and challenges from a polygamous family where the wives were disunited. She had weathered storms that would have broken lesser women, and yet she still stood, like an impenetrable pillar of strength and resilience. To see her was to be reminded of the beauty and power that lies within every woman, no matter her age or background. She was a testament to the strength and resilience of Manyu women and women in the region.

Without fail, in the evenings, around 4 p.m. on her way

home from the farm, she always carried her firewood or harvest or woven basket on her head. It was always food to eat daily. Sales in the market were only made during harvest periods, when produce was abundant. This was not farming for income. It was for survival. It was a relaxed way of life, and every other household was the same.

Despite the physical demands of farming, Biggie was tireless, and her daily routine had given her an unwavering determination to work. Her daily schedule kicked off before the first light of dawn, followed by a full day on the farm. Upon her return home, her routine would shift to cooking, distributing food, enjoying her own meal, and then preparing for a well-deserved night's rest. This was the rhythm of life that had shaped her into an individual of unyielding determination.

There were many challenges when she arrived at her marital home, including cultural differences, as she came from a different geographical area with distinct customs. The language was different as well. She spoke Boki and Menkea, but she quickly learned to speak Kenyang and Keyaka fluently. Many women spoke many languages. It was common to learn your husband's language if you were not from the same area.

Biggie's life alongside my grandfather was far from easy. To begin with, she was the second choice, brought into the picture when Mami Susanna, the first wife, faced fertility issues. Her primary role was to fulfill the pressing need for offspring, a responsibility that weighed heavily on her right from the very start. Remarkably, she swiftly demonstrated her capability to bear children.

At the tender age of thirteen, Biggie became the spouse of an already well-established businessman in his late twenties. The decision about marrying or not was not hers to make, but she held little concern for it at the time. She possessed a striking beauty, characterized by her petite stature and delicate features. Her husband loomed above her both physically and mentally, a presence that could be quite intimidating. Her veneer of vulnerability, however, masked a reservoir of strength that she did not even know she possessed until much later in her marriage.

Like her husband, Big Mami came from a family of farmers. Growing and nurturing crops for the love of farming and food. She was a busybody, a high-voltage woman obsessed with hard work as well as putting things in order. In her late thirties, she started a tradition of drinking at least one bottle of Guinness stout a day. She did that pretty much for the rest of her life. By the time I knew her, she was also smoking a pipe ("esikong," as she called it). She relished the sensations created by both these habits, and no one could take them away from her. The bitter taste from the bottle and the freedom to exhale her smoke. She made you want to drink and smoke!

It was quite the experience, one cool evening sitting outside and enjoying the warm breeze from the sea in Limbe, when Biggie decided to pass down her cherished smoking pipe to me. At first, I was quite excited to give it a try. The pipe, worn smooth from years of use, rested so comfortably in her hand, a natural extension of her. I thought I could handle it; that it would be easy. With a nod, she encouraged me, watching as I put the pipe to my lips.

As I took a puff, the smoke curled into my mouth, cool and smooth at first. But when I tried to inhale, the thick smoke hit the back of my throat, and it felt like I'd swallowed a cloud of dry leaves. My lungs rebelled, and I instantly gagged, coughing as the acrid taste coated my tongue and throat. The sensation was overwhelming, like breathing in something too thick and foreign, and I struggled to catch my breath as my chest tightened.

My grandmother watched me with a soft chuckle, amused

but not unkind. She had known what would happen, just as it had happened to her once long, long ago. With a smile, she took back the pipe, her eyes sparkling with understanding, leaving me coughing but a little wiser about her world. It was a comical scene, really. There I was, gasping for air and making all sorts of ridiculous noises, while my grandma just sat there, calmly puffing away on her pipe, giving me a knowing smile.

Needless to say, I quickly learned that smoking "esikong" was not for me, as I promptly handed the pipe back to her with a sheepish grin. From that day forward, I stuck to more traditional methods of relaxation, like playing "gombe gombe," Tabala, Ray Ray in or reading a book.

Apart from her face, Big Mami's hands always struck me. During holidays, I would gaze at them and caress them for long periods, even though she would occasionally get upset and shout at me. They were beautiful but rough, calloused, and stained with the dirt of the earth—evidence of her ceaseless toil on the farm. Half the time, she was barefoot and often had no protection against the mud, rain, and biting insects on her farms.

Her toes painted a different picture and were the ugliest I had ever seen. Sadly, she passed this trait down to me as well. They were a stark contrast to the youthfulness and beauty of her face and the rest of her body. They were flat, hard as nails, wrinkled, and calloused, appearing to be in a permanent snarl. The toenails were so hardened that only a sharp kitchen knife or penknife could be used to trim them.

9

The Tiger

***

Biggie had this magnetic charm that made everyone love her. It was a competition to please her with her favorite bottle of Guinness—or a "guinnie," as she called it. With "Anya Bar" conveniently located nearby, even her Nigerian neighbors, like Chukwu and the "Shoe Mender," ensured she received her daily dose of this beloved drink.

Even though she was no longer her husband's favorite, she had an uncanny ability to ease people's stress and bring laughter into their lives. Most of this she did by laughing at herself. She had a bucket of water outside, exposed to the sun. In this bucket, she would steep her bottle of small Guinness for a few seconds, then take it out and drink it in four quick gulps. That was her way of drinking Guinness.

Guinness and smoking brought out her fiery spirit and feisty character. She was always primed for a fight with the other wives. They often poked fun at her petite stature and taunted her about her rural origins, branding her village Eshobi as uncivilized. This irked her immensely. I vividly remember witnessing her in action once. She would pounce as swiftly as lightning, thrusting her forearms forward to grab her opponent's head and slam them onto the floor, followed by a flurry of blows until someone intervened to separate them.

Her eyes, resembling those of a cornered animal, were the telltale sign that she was ready to take on any challenger. A crack of her knuckles, a forward lunge, and a grab for her opponent's knees were her other customary responses to even the slightest provocation. She exuded defiance and intensity, which invariably left her husband—never one to support her in an argument—feeling somewhat embarrassed by her physical and mental tenacity. Unlike other wives, she refused to be subservient to him, yet her culinary skills remained unrivaled. Her meals were served with laughter, but were consistently served behind schedule.

As for her fighting, once, in a blazing moment of fury, she delivered a resounding slap to one of the other wives, her "mbanya," with the force of her open right palm.

The slap came swiftly, like a crack of thunder breaking the stillness. My grandmother's hand, toughened by years of labor, struck her "mbanya's" face with a sharp, cutting sound. The blow landed with brutal precision, snapping the woman's head to the side as if hit by something far greater than human strength. A dark red welt rose instantly on her cheek, the skin flushing where the hand had struck. My grandmother's fingers left a vivid imprint as the shock turned into throbbing pain. The woman's lips quivered, her face momentarily frozen in disbelief, as though her body hadn't yet processed the blow.

Her jaw tightened, swelling at the joint, making it difficult for her to close her mouth. Her left eye twitched as if the force had rattled something deep within—her vision blurred, and the world around her briefly became a swirl of indistinct shapes. She blinked rapidly, trying to clear the dizziness that now clouded her senses.

The Tiger

The pain, sharp and radiating, began to creep down her neck and into her shoulder. Even her cheekbone looked strained, the muscles in her face pulling tight as if the skin couldn't quite relax from the impact. The slap had left its mark, not just on her skin, but in the seconds of silence that followed—an echo of my grandmother's strength and the unspoken tension between them.

The anguished screams that followed reverberated throughout the entire neighborhood. This incident marked a turning point in the relationship between her and her other "mbanyas."

It became abundantly clear that Big Mami possessed the strength of a tiger and the swiftness of a cheetah. None of the other wives dared to cross her path again. From that day on, even when they attempted to provoke her, they did so from a safe distance. At the first sign of her potential response, they would flee and seek refuge, understanding that the tables had irrevocably turned.

Big Mami emerged as an extraordinary force of nature, and her daughters inherited the legacy of her physical strength, self-reliance, and unshakable confidence, ensuring her indomitable spirit would endure through generations.

My grandfather, Big Papa, was deeply upset with my grandmother for many reasons. In a moment of anger, he decided to relocate her to a less favorable part of the house. He relocated her room to the rear of the courtyard, adjacent to her kitchen. For several years, she and her children lived there, quietly enduring the discomfort—the smoke, the heat, the mosquitoes, and the isolation.

Her new quarters were far from ideal. It was a place where the daily activities of the household and the noise of the courtyard constantly intruded, a far cry from the more comfortable rooms upstairs. The frustration simmered for a long time, and though my grandmother rarely voiced her discontent aloud, the tension was palpable. Eventually, her grievances reached a breaking point, and after years of being confined to that cramped space, she was finally relocated to a more spacious room upstairs.

The catalyst behind this change was Mami Susanna, Big Papa's first wife, the original Mrs. Enotanya, who had named my mother at birth. She took it upon herself to have long, heartfelt conversations with her husband, gently reminding him of all that my grandmother had done for him. She spoke of how my grandmother had lifted the stain of disgrace from him and bore him children before any of his other wives had even come into his life. Mami Susanna pressed the point that, regardless of Big Mami's offenses, her children did not deserve to suffer alongside her.

It was one of the few times in her life that Mami Susanna was seen as "good" in the eyes of Big Mami, who rarely held her in high regard. Big Mami often suspected that Mami Susanna instigated trouble within the compound. She believed that, because Mami Susanna had no children of her own to care for, she had less work to do and more time to meddle. Despite these long-standing suspicions, Mami Susanna's efforts paid off. My grandmother and her children were finally moved back upstairs, restoring some peace to the household, if only temporarily.

10

Mami Susanna, the Matriarch

Mami Susanna, my mother's stepmother, held a unique place in our family history. Her journey to my grandfather's side marked the beginning of another chapter—one that transitioned from a monogamous union to a polygamous household over time. Their courtship was long and arduous, filled with trials and triumphs, yet it culminated in a bond that defied societal norms.

This change happened because Mami Susanna, despite her many good qualities, had trouble having children. In a culture where a woman's value was often tied to her ability to bear children, this was a significant challenge. She visited many traditional doctors. Some told her she was cursed. Others said her family had used witchcraft to block her from having children because her father was a bad man. Most of those who tried to help said they couldn't undo what had been done. In the end, she and her husband stopped trying and chose polygamy. Even so, her lasting influence on our family was clear.

Physically, Mami Susanna was a petite, portly woman, with a stature that belied her immense strength of character. She had a distinctive way of walking, with both hands gracefully tucked behind her back—a gesture that became a permanent part of her presence. Her union with my grandfather, Big Papa, was rooted in love, and they aspired to build a life together, nurturing both their bond and their future children.

Regrettably, their dream of a small, harmonious Catholic family was not realized. Despite this, her calm and composed nature remained unwavering. In a heartwarming display of trust and respect, my grandfather entrusted her with the responsibility of naming my mother at birth. Even though she had no prior experience, she was made a mother by my grandfather.

When my grandmother gave birth as a teenager, her baby was given to Mami Susanna to raise. Mami Susanna was much older and more experienced than my grandmother. Despite the age difference, their relationship was strong. When my mother was born, it was Mami Susanna, with her wisdom, who was chosen to care for her.

Big Mami's journey as a mother was both challenging and filled with strength. She was married at just 13 and had her first surviving child, my mother, at 17. The years leading up to this moment were fraught with heartache, as the children she had previously brought into the world had either not survived beyond birth or passed away within weeks of their arrival.

Against the backdrop of these heartaches, the household was often fraught with tension and conflicts. It was during these challenging times that Mami Susanna, my mother's stepmother, played a complex yet touching role. The tensions occasionally boiled over into quarrels and insults, and Mami Susanna was not always willing to yield when it came to caring for the newborn child. She would, at times, hurl insults at my grandmother, questioning her competence and trustworthiness in caring for the baby.

My grandmother, Big Mami, did not shy away from these verbal battles. She would, in retaliation, also cast hurtful words, often targeting Mami Susanna's inability to bear children of her own—a source of great pain for her. She would ask Mami Susanna if she knew what it meant to breastfeed a child, to have that child gazing into her eyes and solidifying the bond between mother and child. These clashes, marked by harsh words and invective, created a complex and tense atmosphere within the household.

Despite these occasional clashes, Mami Susanna displayed unwavering care and devotion to my mother during her infancy. Her love transcended the tumultuous moments, providing a nurturing presence that my mother cherished. In the intricate family web, these moments of tension, contrasted with Mami Susanna's maternal care, painted a complex and touching picture of family life during those early years.

In our culture, there is a strong belief that when you give a child a name, that child will inherit not just physical traits but also the spiritual qualities of the person they are named after. It's like passing down a piece of one's essence to the next generation. As fate would have it, my mother was named after Mami Susanna, a respected elder known for her calm demeanor, maturity, forthrightness, and honesty.

These were qualities deeply admired in our community, and as my mother grew up, she seemed to embody them naturally. She carried herself with quiet confidence, approaching life with a sense of maturity that was beyond her years. Her actions were always thoughtful and sincere, reflecting the virtues of the woman she was named after. It was as if Mami Susanna's spirit lived on in her, guiding her every step.

Mami Susanna's heart found fulfillment in the role she played in raising my mother. Her maternal instincts, previously untapped, found a profound purpose. She relished the opportunity to provide guidance, love, and care to my mother, helping to shape her into the remarkable woman she became.

In her unique way, Mami Susanna left a lasting legacy in our family, not through her own biological children but through the nurturing and guidance she bestowed upon my mother. Her influence lives on, passed down through the generations, as we continue to embody the strength, wisdom, and love that defined her character.

My mother was loved and cherished by her three-parent family: her father, her mother, and her stepmother. Ma Susanna took care of my mother, clothing and feeding her, ensuring she had everything a baby, toddler, and young lady would need to grow up well. Pa Enotanyah was overjoyed to finally have children. Suzy was the first of twelve children who survived.

11

Weathering the Storm

* * *

My mother chose to tread a path similar to her father's, even though neither she nor her sisters had any direct involvement in his business ventures. Big Papa primarily worked independently, occasionally collaborating with one of his sons, although such partnerships proved to be less reliable. However, his daughters were unequivocally excluded from any business affairs, with their roles primarily confined to farm work. They were expected to lead lives as second-class citizens, their main duties revolving around the farm, kitchen, child-rearing, and contributing to the population growth. Given this context, it is truly remarkable that my mother managed to glean so much knowledge from a distance, relying solely on her observational skills.

The only occasion when Big Papa enlisted everyone's help was during a somber incident involving the offloading of salt. It happened when a ship had docked in the river popularly known as "Doctor Mamfe River." Ships and all sizes of boats docked there quite frequently. While the salt was being offloaded, a fierce thunderstorm suddenly erupted.

It started with the wind that came from nowhere, crying as

if to predict impending doom. The howling raised dust, rustling dried leaves in its wake, picking up debris and losing steam as it rushed towards the river. In its quest to reach the river, it physically assaulted the elephant grass, which refused to break but bowed its head majestically to make way for the wind. The other tall, thin grass seemed quite drunk or possessed. The wind was dancing in one spot like one of Big Papa's friends who always came to beg for "white mimbo" but who could not hold his drink after just one "tuskful."

Everyone sensed the oncoming storm. Even though it was only the wind that was gusty, people were running helter-skelter in the hope of avoiding the rain and taking cover under sheltered shop verandas. Shopkeepers hurriedly gathered their goods, sitting on verandas, and packed them inside to prevent them from developing a life of their own and flying away with the wind or getting wet. As the storm approached, cumulus clouds rushed forward, displacing nimbus clouds, and with this, the sky grew darker.

Suddenly, there was a crackling like the sound of dried whips on the backs of enslaved people on farm plantations in the West Indies. The sound sent shivers down everyone's spine. Some instinctively crossed themselves, while others hastily traced arcane symbols in the air, seeking supernatural protection in this moment of dread. The dark sky was blindingly illuminated for a split second before the flashing lightning passed.

Swiftly thereafter, thunderclaps followed suit, a cacophony that deafened the ears. The sound felt primal, as though the sky itself was splitting open in a dramatic prelude to the coming downpour. Each clap reverberated through the humid air, building in volume and force, sometimes rolling on for what seemed like minutes before fading out somewhere else. It was a thunder that commanded attention—an unmistakable herald of the powerful, cleansing rain that was soon to follow. Its force, coupled with the charged atmosphere, filled the air with a sense of anticipation, as nature geared up for its dramatic release. The rain came down, pelting the ground with the ferocity of hailstones, causing rooftops to tremble perilously under the weight of each raindrop. All of this took place within a few minutes. The streets had emptied—empty, except for the people trying to save the salt.

In the absence of weather forecasts, the last thing anyone anticipated was a rainstorm, let alone a ferocious thunderstorm. The majority of the salt had already been expertly unloaded from the ship and thoughtfully arranged away from the shores. All part of a clever strategy to facilitate the arduous trek up the steep hill to the warehouse. But then, out of nowhere, the heavens had unleashed their wrath. Raindrops pelted the earth, catching everyone completely off guard.

Pandemonium ensued as men, women, and even children erupted into a cacophony of screams that echoed through Main Street and Hausa quarters. Their shrill cries acted as an impromptu summons for all hands to rush down to the beach and join the frenetic efforts to salvage the cargo.

Snippets of conversation flew back and forth between them, their voices barely audible above the roar of the wind and the pelting rain, as they rushed in different directions, actively engaged in their tasks.

"Grab that bag and cover it tight with this plastic!"

"Watch out for those barrels, they're rolling!"

"We need more hands over here, the salt's getting soaked!"

"Quick, someone pass me another plastic!"

"Keep pushing, we can't let it wash away!"

"We need to get it all out of here!"

"Careful, don't slip on the wet sand ooo!"

"Has anyone seen Tira?"
"Watch your step."
"The water is rising."
"Keep moving, we can't afford to lose any more salt!"
"Quick, Quick."

And so, through the tumult of the storm, the urgent cries (in Kenyang language and in broken pidgin English) and commands of all hands helping echoed against the crashing waves. In the chaotic rush to unload under the relentless downpour, countless bags of salt met a watery demise.

Dozens of them later transformed into stubborn, rock-hard clumps, like rebellious children refusing to obey. Desperate measures followed as these salt formations were carefully laid out under the unforgiving sun, in a race against time. But even then, the road to redemption was paved with hard labor, for these stubborn clumps had to be "beaten" back into shape before they could be deemed fit for sale. It was a day of unexpected challenges and incredible resilience on the salt-soaked shores of Mamfe.

As quickly as the storm had come, it disappeared. The lightning became a small flashing light far on the horizon. The rumbling thunder became a purr and a whimper. The rain, having achieved its goal, subsided. Big Papa later brought all the women who had helped that day together and gave each of them a half-bag of salt—a wonderful gift and a gesture of appreciation.

12

The Dance with Devils

* * *

Despite having multiple wives, Big Papa, known for his affable nature and considerable wealth, enjoyed a surprisingly favorable relationship with the Catholic Church—a fact that seemed at odds with the church's apparent disapproval of polygamy. Yet, Big Papa's charm, generosity, and standing in the community softened the church's stance. It was his amiable spirit that ultimately led the church to convince him to enroll his eldest daughter, my mother, in the newly established Queen of the Rosary Secondary School, Okoyong, Mamfe, in 1956.

This school, a beacon of education to this day, stood four miles away from their home, at a time when public transportation was scarce, and the journey required much more than simply walking. For a fourteen-year-old girl, it was an arduous trek over uneven terrain, but one that carried her toward the promise of something greater. As the sun dipped below the horizon, casting a golden hue over Mamfe and its surrounding hills, my mother's journey began—not just along the dusty roads leading to school, but into a world of learning and possibilities. Each step she took felt heavy with the weight of change and hidden fear. But the quiet determination of a girl ready to embrace an unknown future carried the day.

Big Papa spared no expense in commemorating this milestone. Just before she was about to go to school, Big Papa hosted a special lunch at his home on Main Street, Mamfe. He invited all 26 new students, along with the priests, reverend sisters, and other religious figures, to celebrate his daughter's journey to boarding school. Some of our curious neighbors watched from a distance.

Among the throngs of spectators, many had never laid eyes on white people before. Their presence, a stark contrast against the backdrop of the bustling African town, elicited a sense of wonder and awe. Whispers rippled through the crowd as they watched the fair-skinned guests mingle with the local community, their attire and mannerisms seeming very different and beyond their own. Many had only heard that a set of people with pale skin had arrived, but this was the closest they had ever seen them. Some in the crowd thought my grandfather was mad. Others said he was too daring, while others described him as an enlightened man.

In those days, the belief in the devil's nocturnal wanderings was deeply ingrained in the fabric of the community. It was said that the devil appeared as a spectral figure, draped entirely in white, his form a chilling apparition that haunted the darkest corners of the night.

This fear of encountering the devil in disguise led people to be wary of anything white after dusk, for it was believed that even the faintest glimmer of light could herald his presence.

Countless tales circulated among the villagers, passed down through generations like whispered secrets, each one recounting encounters with the devil's white-clad form. Many a time, individuals were witnessed fleeing in terror, their hearts pounding with dread, as they claimed to have come face to face with the dreaded apparition. These chilling accounts served as cautionary tales, instilling a deep-seated fear that lingered in the minds of all who heard them.

In the depths of the African night, where shadows danced and secrets whispered on the breeze, the veil between earthly things and the supernatural grew thin. It was here that imagination took flight, conjuring visions of ghostly apparitions and malevolent spirits, their presence a constant reminder of the delicate balance between light and darkness.

For my mother and her peers, embarking on their educational journey amidst such superstitions was both exhilarating and daunting. As they navigated the halls of academia by day and the mysteries of the night, the specter of the devil loomed large, a cautionary tale woven into the fabric of their existence. As my mother stepped into the unknown, her heart brimming with anticipation, she carried with her the whispers of generations past, a reminder of the unseen forces that shaped their world.

It's essential to recognize that various Manyu cultures have their own distinct beliefs and superstitions, each with its unique significance. While the idea of associating white with the devil may seem unusual to some, it was deeply rooted in the cultural traditions of the Mamfe community.

Here is one such tale my grandmother told us. In a village just outside Mamfe, called Banya, tales of mischief and mayhem often found their way into the hearts and minds of its inhabitants. Among the many legends that permeated the air, one stood out above the rest—the legend of Ta-gbe, the Trickster.

My grandmother, a master storyteller in her own right, often regaled us with the story of a young man, Ta-gbe, who had earned notoriety for his cunning exploits. He was a master of deception, with a knack for fooling unsuspecting victims so he could pilfer their precious palm wine. His weapon of choice? A simple white bedsheet—a rare commodity in those days, but a potent tool in the hands of a skilled trickster.

Ta-gbe's escapades were the stuff of legend, sending ripples of fear through the hearts of all who crossed his path. In a region where superstition reigned supreme, the mere mention of the devil was enough to send shivers down the spines of even the most stoic individuals. No one wanted to meet an untimely death at the hands of the supernatural, and Ta-gbe knew just how to exploit this fear to his advantage.

With his co-conspirator Ebot by his side, Ta-gbe would embark on his mischievous adventures, donning the white bedsheet like a cloak of invisibility. They would stealthily approach unsuspecting homes or gatherings, where friends and neighbors gathered to unwind after a long day's work. Ta-gbe would appear suddenly, his ghostly figure sending a chill down the spine of anyone unfortunate enough to catch a glimpse of him. This advantage was skillfully employed when someone died.

Then, like a flash of lightning, Ta-gbe would disappear into the night, leaving behind a trail of confusion and terror in his wake. His co-conspirator, quick on his heels, would burst onto the scene, shouting warnings of impending doom – "Devil di cam ooooo! Run! Run! Whona run oooo. Jen-tied oooo"

The effect was instantaneous. Panic would grip the crowd, sending them fleeing in all directions as their hearts pounded with fear. And while they scrambled to escape the imagined threat, Ta-gbe and his partner-in-crime would swoop in like vultures, seizing the opportunity to snatch their coveted prize—a stash of kegs of palm wine, left unguarded in the chaos of the moment.

It was a game of cat and mouse, played out against the backdrop of an evening filled with laughter and camaraderie. Yet, beneath the surface, a sense of unease lurked—a reminder that in Mamfe town, where superstition and reality often blurred together, one could never be too careful. And that's how the story of Ta-gbe, the Trickster, continued. It was a warning about being greedy and lying. It reminded everyone that the scariest dangers might not be what you expect. Sometimes, it's the people around you, pretending to be your friend.

But soon enough, the image of white people as devils started eroding fast. In addition, my mother's stories about the kindness and humanity of the Reverend Sisters in Okoyong gradually dispelled some of the superstitions and changed people's perceptions of the white man. My grandfather gained in stature as one who was brave and neither afraid of the devil nor sending his daughter to a school run by the so-called "devils."

13

Secondary School at QRC Okoyong

*　*　*

Soon it was time to sever the bond, take the bull by the horns, and head out to Okoyong and away from her family. It was a crisp morning in Mamfe, and as my mother approached Queen of the Rosary College in Okoyong, her heart was racing with a mixture of excitement and anxiety. She wasn't alone; a whole band of her siblings and cousins had come to accompany her on this journey. Silence hung in the air as everyone was lost in their thoughts, though their excitement was palpable.

All you could hear was the sound of footsteps on the dirt road. The dry earth crunched under their weight, kicking up small clouds of dust as they rushed along. For a young girl who had never ventured far from the comfort of her family's embrace, the prospect of leaving home was daunting. Occasionally, someone would shout, "We don reach!" even though they hadn't. They had never seen this school before, so the opportunities on this trip were numerous.

In the 1950s, boarding schools were a rarity, not only in Mamfe but throughout the country. Thus, my mother's departure marked not only a significant milestone in her own life but also a momentous event for her family and the entire community.

Secondary School at QRC Okoyong

As she approached the school, nestled amidst the lush green landscape, she couldn't help but feel a surge of fear and nerves. The towering trees and the gentle flow of the nearby stream offered a tranquil backdrop to the bustling energy of the school compound. It was a world unlike any she had known before.

Stepping onto the grounds, my mother's eyes darted around, taking in the sight of other young women clad in various garments, their voices echoing in the air, speaking of everything and nothing. She felt a pang of uncertainty, a sense of being out of place amidst the throng of unfamiliar faces. But she steeled herself with a deep breath, reminding herself of her father's expectations and the opportunity that lay before her.

The nuns, who ran the school, greeted her with warmth and kindness, their gentle smiles putting her at ease. They led her to a dormitory—a simple building filled with rows of beds and lockers, each awaiting its occupant. This would be her new home, shared with twenty-five other girls, all of whom were embarking on the same journey of discovery and growth.

As my mother settled down after many tearful goodbyes, she found herself surrounded by a sea of eager faces, each brimming with the same mixture of excitement and apprehension. Despite the initial awkwardness, she soon realized that they were all in this together, bound by the common experience of facing the challenges of boarding school for the first time. They started asking her questions. Some told tales of their trek from Bamenda. Their chatting and stories comforted my mother a great deal.

In the days and weeks that followed, my mother forged friendships that would last a lifetime, learning from her peers and discovering her own strengths along the way. Though the transition from home to school had been daunting, it was also a journey of growth and self-discovery, shaping her into the resilient and independent woman she would become.

And so, as the sun set on her first day at boarding school, my mother looked ahead with a sense of anticipation, ready to face the challenges and adventures that lay ahead. It was the beginning of a new chapter in her life, filled with promise and possibility, and she was determined to make the most of every moment.

The next day was a beehive of activity, with orientation sessions and meetings with teachers. She was struck by the kindness and generosity of the nuns, who made everyone feel welcome and supported. As the sun set and the day came to a close, she lay on her bed, feeling exhausted, though she couldn't understand why, since she had not gone to the farm that day.

Her father had prepared everything she would need for her stay, meticulously following the school's instructions. As careful as he was, everything was packed in a very orderly fashion. Among her provisions was a sturdy metal box brimming with bedding, toiletries, and various essentials.

The dormitory was meticulously organized, with each bed accompanied by a locker measuring about half a square meter. These lockers served as personal storage spaces, where everyone kept their essentials: toothbrushes, toothpaste, a stash of underwear, hair lotion, a comb, towels, and bras. At the head of each bed stood an open wardrobe, with hangers neatly arranged at the top, ready to hold freshly pressed uniforms. The trunk box, however, was stored in the box room, just beyond the row of beds. These trunks contained essential supplies. If you ran out of toothpaste or toilet tissue, a trip to the box room was necessary. Typically, such replenishments were made over the weekend when formal classes were not in session.

I am not entirely sure what kinds of things my mother and her school sisters kept in their trunks. For instance, I don't know if they had actual toilet tissue to use with their water system

Secondary School at QRC Okoyong

toilets. However, I do know what I kept in mind when I, too, attended QRC twenty years later in 1977.

The school had its electrical generator, which provided lighting but was only operational in the evenings. Water was sourced from springs and streams scattered across the campus, and each student had her bucket for collecting it.

Okoyong was a haven. Just four miles from Mamfe town, it was the ideal location for a boarding school. Spanning more than 10 hectares, the school was run by a seasoned Catholic Reverend Sister, Mother Aquinas (Reverend Sister Kelly). Mother Aquinas nurtured the girls, shaping them into fine members of a society that was marching toward independence. Other reverend sisters handled various responsibilities, with the role of House Mother being one of the most significant.

Five years passed very quickly in QRC. School life was special as pioneers. Reverend Sister Mary, one of the Irish Rev Sisters, was the liaison person between my grandfather's house on Main Street and Mami in Okoyong. Mami was a real princess. Everything she needed – and it was not much – one of the Reverend Sisters would bring back from Mamfe when returning from Mamfe town.

School was a captivating experience. Beyond the standard academic curriculum, the campus offered a rich array of subjects, including art, music, typing, shorthand, housekeeping, food and nutrition, and sports. What truly stood out was the library, a treasure trove of diverse books that fired my mother's and her classmates' imaginations. It was a sanctuary of knowledge and exploration.

In the afternoons after siesta, as they stepped through the doors of the library, they were greeted by calmness, quiet, the comforting scent of old books, and the soft rustle of pages turning. The shelves were lined with a diverse array of literary treasures, each waiting to be discovered by young minds. From timeless classics to thrilling adventures, the library held a world of possibilities within its walls.

For my mother and her classmates, the library was more than just a repository of books – it was a portal to new worlds and new ideas. They eagerly lost themselves in its pages, immersing themselves in stories of far-off lands and daring escapades. With each book they devoured, they embarked on a journey of discovery, expanding their horizons and enriching their minds.

They learned about politics and becoming politicians. They learned about lawyers. They learned about doctors and the urgent need for all the professionals in a young country on the verge of independence. Their role models were more in the books than in real life. They did not feel it at the time, but the burden was heavy. By the time they graduated, they soon learned that their education was not just for them, but for their communities as well. They learned about different types of sacrifices and that many had left their countries thousands of miles away for the sake of their education. Some of the reverend sisters were barely adults themselves.

But the library was not the only place of wonder in the boarding school. The science lab beckoned with its promise of experimentation and discovery. Here, my mother and her classmates delved into the mysteries of the natural world, conducting experiments with simple products that left their minds reeling with excitement. They were introduced to vinegar and baking soda. When the mix was shaken, they excitedly observed the fizzy reaction that occurred without understanding. They grew beans in jars to learn about plant germination, growth, and photosynthesis.

And then there was the cookery lab, where they felt more at home. It brought out their creativity and culinary delight. In a culture where sweets were a rare indulgence, the prospect of learning to make cakes was met with eager anticipation. My mother and her classmates eagerly rolled up their sleeves, relishing the opportunity to explore the art of baking and the joy of creating something sweetly delicious from scratch. Flour and butter were strange new things. Eggs they were used to, but eggs were a luxury and not many had eaten them regularly before.

During their studies and exploration, my mother and her classmates were surrounded by a culture that celebrated the pursuit of knowledge and the cultivation of upright morals. They were encouraged by all around them to embrace learning with enthusiasm and curiosity, to strive for excellence in all they did.

Looking back on those days, there is a sense of nostalgia – a longing for a time when young people were encouraged to read voraciously and explore the world around them with open minds and eager hearts. It was a time when the library was not just a room filled with books, but a gateway to endless possibilities and endless adventures. And though the years may have passed, the memories of those days remain etched in my mother's heart, a testament to the transformative power of education and the enduring joy of learning.

14

The School Grounds

* * *

The school grounds were embellished with an abundance of fruit trees that seemed to be everywhere you looked – behind classrooms, near the dormitories, on the convent grounds, and even on the school farm behind the kitchen. There was even a designated orchard. While fruits were not an uncommon sight, the trees on campus were subject to stringent regulations. It was strictly forbidden to pick any fruit from the tree, and any violation could result in a student "working punishments" or being excluded from classes.

The trees bore a tantalizing array of fruits, including mandarins, pears, tangerines, oranges, coconuts, guavas (in sour, sweet, red, and white varieties), pawpaw, berries, mangoes, and soursop. In April, as the planting season rains began with a lot of breeze and the sun climbed higher, hiding beneath the clouds, the mango trees that dotted the campus started to bear fruit, their branches heavy with clusters of green mangoes ripening. Each morning, as the girls woke up with the rising bell, the air would be filled with the tantalizing aroma of over-ripening mangoes.

The mangoes in Mamfe were a sight to behold, with their vibrant, smooth, and green exteriors hiding the luscious, deep orange flesh within. To bite into one was to experience a burst of sweet, irresistible flavor that danced on the taste buds and left a lingering sweetness on the lips. This sweet taste is primarily attributed to the mango species known as "Number One" (scientific name: Mangifera indica). It is the most common species in Cameroon and holds a special place in the hearts of all who have gone to QRC to date. There were at least three other species on campus.

For my mother and her classmates, mango season was more than just a time of indulgence – it was a time of adventure and camaraderie. Armed with baskets and eager hearts, they would set out, their laughter echoing amidst the rustling leaves as they stood under these trees in search of juicy mangoes. They would call out to each other, trying to find out who had picked the most from the ground.

But mango season was not without its challenges. As the afternoons wore on, swarms of persistent flies would descend underneath the trees, drawn by the irresistible scent of ripe fruit.

There were girls from different English-speaking parts of the country, and all 26 of them became friends. As the years passed, other girls joined them, and the Okoyong family grew larger and larger. The stories of what girls could do spread far and wide, and the school population increased each year. More and more fathers were getting easily convinced to send their daughters to school.

Life on campus during the 1950s presented its own set of distinctive challenges. While the reverend sisters did not impose strict rules against discussing the opposite sex, the girls, out of a sense of self-censorship, and mainly from cultural practices, refrained from engaging in such conversations. Many of the students deeply admired their parents and the reverend sisters alike. The sisters espoused the values of goodness towards humanity and the notion of saving the world through benevolent actions and prayer. Consequently, a significant number of students harbored aspirations to follow in the footsteps of the reverend sisters and become part of this noble calling.

Letters from the boys at St Joseph College, Sasse in Buea, the only boys' secondary school established seven years earlier than QRC Okoyong, were a rare and cherished occurrence. Sasse, as it was referred to, was more than one hundred miles away from Mamfe, but it was another Catholic school. So, it felt like twin schools where the girls in Okoyong could find partners and friends in Sasse. There were numerous songs about Sasse boys and Okoyong girls.

Here is a sample letter. It shows the excitement the young adults had about learning. The use of big words, even if the meanings did not usually fit the concept. The excitement of adolescence and the hopes for a loving future.

My Dearest Rose,
I hope this letter finds you in good health, my sweet flower. Since the day I first laid eyes on you at the inter-school games, I have not been able to stop thinking about you. You are the apple of my eye, the sunshine that lights up my days.

Time and ability plus double capacity have forced my pen to dance automatically on this benedicted sheet of paper. I hope you're swimming in the wonderful pool of Mr. Health there. I am also perambulating in the cool breeze of wellness here.

Each day, I find myself counting down the hours until I can see your radiant smile again. Your beauty is like the blooming hibiscus, and your kindness warms my heart like the morning sun after a cool night. I write this letter to let you know that

The School Grounds

you are always on my mind.

By the way, I was bamboozled, scintillated, exhilarated, and left in a state of prolonged euphoria by the contents of your missive which was quite edifying and exalting. It left my biochemistry in a paradise-like equilibrium.

Empirically speaking, I love u chemically... I don't ever want to see gloom and doom looming over your angelic live portrait. Let my appellation be scribbled across your heart, with indelible ink.

Please do not forget me, sweet Rose, for my heart beats only for you. Until the next time our paths cross, I will hold you close in my thoughts.

Yours ever-loving Emmanuel (Sasse College)

And at the back of the envelope, the words SWAK. Sealed With a Kiss.

Being teenagers, the students from both schools couldn't resist a bit of mischief. Many of the girls and boys were going through physical changes, and they had no parents to discuss these changes with, except by talking amongst themselves or going to the Reverend Sisters for those in Okoyong. They encountered challenges related to underarm hair, acne, and pubic hair. They played light-hearted pranks on each other. Occasionally, they even managed to sneak contraband foods from Okoyong village onto the campus. Despite these youthful escapades, the majority of the girls were dedicated to their education and adhered diligently to the school rules.

For my mother, Suzy, and her two moms, as well as her family, holidays were very special times. Big Papa was proud of her progress. He was a strong and proud man. He loved telling others confidently that he had sent his daughter to school with the missionaries, even though many of his contemporaries made a mockery of it. At the beginning or end of the holidays, Big Papa would slaughter a large pig or goat and host a grand feast with plenty of rice, stew, and palm wine for the elders, just as he did for Christmas Eve and Christmas Day. When word spread about such a lavish meal, many people would gather to partake in it. No one needed an invitation, and no one questioned any guest. They knew that as a wealthy man, he had access to the finest things. They would expect and receive venison in Big Papa's house, not beef, unlike most people.

My mother had an abundance of stories about the white reverend sisters and the convent situated on the hill overlooking the main school grounds, where they often baked madeira cakes to share with the students. At home, she attempted to introduce her siblings to this sweet new taste. To create a makeshift oven, she got her mother to buy a large iron pot that she filled with sand, forming a layer at the bottom to insulate the heat. The sand served as a buffer to distribute the heat evenly and prevent direct contact between the pot and the food being baked. Once the pot was filled with sand, it was placed over an open firewood fire in her mother's kitchen or hot coals, allowing the sand to heat up. The cake, put in a smaller pot, would then be placed inside the pot of sand on top of the sand.

The lid of the pot was quite heavy, which was good because it was necessary to trap the heat inside, creating an enclosed environment similar to that of a traditional oven. The hot sand surrounding the food would effectively cook it through, resulting in evenly cooked and flavorful cakes. It was a lot of work to bake these cakes at home, and needed a battery of assistance. Initially, everyone looked forward to baking and eating. Then the interest died down considerably, and finally no one was really interested in working so hard just to eat a piece of cake.

The cakes may not have caught on to become a tradition, but my mother's stories about life in QRC were always fresh and always found an audience. The questions were often the same and endless. What were the reverend sisters like? Did they marry the priests? Why did they not marry? My mother did her best to answer even those questions for which she didn't have the correct answers.

Going back to school after the holidays was very sad. All her family would trek 4 miles to accompany her. Back home, there would be laughter for the week following her departure, then everything would return to the boring grind and routine, counting the days to the next holiday when she would be back from school.

15

Bamenda to Mamfe

* * *

The journey to Okoyong was especially arduous for students coming from outside of Mamfe, particularly from Kumba and Bamenda. The roads were in such poor condition that many students from Bamenda had to endure days-long treks just to reach Mamfe. Along the challenging roads, concerns arose about encounters with wild animals, and vast stretches of land devoid of villages with no respite or places to stop and rest. When rain poured down, it turned the roads into muddy and treacherous terrain, intensifying the fear that even accomplished teenagers, carrying loads like trunk boxes or suitcases on their heads, could slip and sustain injuries.

My mother matured very quickly in Okoyong, developing a distinct personality and displaying leadership qualities. She continued as an athlete, and for this she won many prizes.

As a teenage student and adolescent, she attracted many suitors. Some of them were turned away by Big Papa, while others she rejected herself, often with her father's discreet support. She had developed a sharp sense of independence during her time at school, but after completing her studies at Okoyong, Big Papa decided that enough was enough. In his view, she had received all the education she needed for a young woman in their community. Her junior sister, Mary Ndip, who had not been sent to school, had already been married off and had begun to raise children. With her younger sibling now settled, Big Papa believed my mother had enjoyed more than enough freedom and time for herself. The moment had come, he declared, for her to shift focus and prepare to settle down with a suitable life partner, marking the next chapter of her life.

Big Papa, a man of traditional values and patriarchal beliefs, saw my mother's education as a means to an end rather than an end in itself. While he took pride in sending her to secondary school, he viewed it as a stepping stone toward finding her a suitable husband. In his eyes, marrying off his daughter to one of his friends, a prosperous businessman, was not only a matter of familial duty but also a source of pride and social standing.

Despite the pressure from his peers and societal expectations, my grandfather's decision to marry my mother off was not without contradictions. On one hand, he valued education and recognized its importance in shaping his daughter's future. On the other hand, he succumbed to the pressures of traditional gender roles, denying some of my mother's sisters (his daughters) the same educational opportunities simply because they were girls.

It was a bittersweet irony that my mother, the only daughter to receive a secondary education, would now be expected to forgo her dreams and ambitions in favor of marriage. Yet, in the face of adversity, my mother remained resilient and resourceful. Despite the obstacles she faced, she managed to pave the way for her younger, unmarried sisters to receive an education, ensuring that they, too, would have the opportunity to pursue their dreams and aspirations. Tradition and progress were undeniably complex.

For my mother, the attention from suitors was both flattering and overwhelming. She had always been aware of her worth, but the sheer volume and influx of suitors served as a stark reminder of the expectations placed upon her as a young woman in that era. Despite her age and her aspirations for education, the suitors persisted in their pursuit, with their parents acting as emissaries in their quest for a matrimonial alliance.

Yet, my mother had already learned the value of education. She understood the importance of pursuing her dreams and aspirations before settling into the role of a wife and mother. But the suitors, blinded by tradition and societal norms, failed to look beyond the facade of her beauty and pedigree.

As the parade of suitors continued, my mother found herself torn between her desire for independence and the pressures of familial expectations. Each visit from a suitor's parents brought with it a flurry of emotions—excitement, anxiety, and a lingering sense of unease. Yet, through it all, she remained steadfast in her resolve to chart her own course in life, despite the whispers and murmurs that followed in her wake.

In the end, it was my mother's unwavering determination and resilience that allowed her to weather the storm of suitors knocking at her door. Though the path ahead was fraught with uncertainty and challenges, she remained committed to education and self-discovery, refusing to be swayed by the whims of tradition or societal expectations.

And so, as the sun set on each day and the echoes of suitors' footsteps faded into the distance, my mother stood firm in her conviction that her destiny lay not in the arms of a suitor, but in the pursuit of knowledge and empowerment. For her, the greatest love of all was the love she held for herself—the boundless possibilities and the excitement that lay ahead.

Even though her father initially supported her love for

education, his resolve began to waver under the weight of societal expectations. Soon enough, he too started echoing the sentiments of the suitors, insisting that my mother needed to settle down. He emphasized the importance of finding a life partner and starting a family, repeating the age-old beliefs ingrained in their culture. As the parade of suitors continued, my grandfather took a more active role in the matchmaking process. Those suitors he favored were welcomed with open arms, and their gifts were dutifully accepted as tokens of their intentions. It became evident that my grandfather's priorities had shifted, and he had succumbed to the pressures of tradition, overlooking his daughter's dreams in favor of fulfilling societal expectations. Despite his initial support, my mother found herself increasingly alone in her quest for independence and self-determination.

16

Settling Down

* * *

In 1961, after five transformative years in boarding school, my mother and her classmates achieved a significant milestone by successfully passing the prestigious West African Certificate of Education Exam. This accomplishment marked not just the completion of their academic journey, but also symbolized their readiness to step into a world filled with new opportunities and challenges. It was a moment of immense pride, signaling the end of a rigorous educational cycle and the beginning of their futures as educated young women, poised to make their mark on a society on the brink of political and economic independence.

It was during this time, in 1964, that her path crossed with a dashing, young, up-and-coming civil servant named Peter Moki Efange, while she was enrolled at the Clerical School in Buea. Peter, the first son and heir to the throne of the Small Soppo Wonganga chiefdom, also known as Longstreet, possessed the elegance and refinement of a true prince. He had been raised in a world of luxury, educated at the University of Ibadan, and was intelligent, quick-witted, wise, and possessed a delightful sense of humor. His generosity only added to his appeal, and it was no surprise that my mother, among many other women, fell head over heels for him.

My father, Peter Moki Efange, didn't hold much respect for women. Before meeting my mother, he had already "let go" of two wives. In his case, "letting go" meant marrying them and then simply moving on without any formal divorce. If he grew tired, he would leave and find someone new. His relationship with my mother never led to marriage, and he went on to marry someone else, only to "let go" of her as well. This pattern repeated itself more than five times throughout his life.

My father worked with the United Nations Economic Commission for Africa in Addis Ababa and would often come home on vacation. During one such trip, he returned with his wife, and everything seemed normal—until the day they were supposed to leave for Ethiopia. That morning, as preparations to head back were underway, my father calmly informed his wife that she would not be returning with him. Though she had sensed something was wrong in the days leading up to their departure and had tried to talk to him, he had refused to engage.

The shock hit her hard. She cried uncontrollably, falling into a state of near hysteria. I watched as her anguish deepened—she vomited, and her health quickly became a concern. Family members, both women and men, who had come to say goodbye gathered, some trying to console her, others urging her to stop crying and reminding her to prioritize her health. But her heartbreak was beyond words; no amount of soothing could stop her despair.

By the time the sun set, my father boarded the car that would take him to the airport in Douala. His luggage, packed with food for his trip, was loaded into the trunk. Without a second glance, he left, leaving his wife behind. As a teenager, I watched it all unfold. A few months later, I heard through the grapevine that my father had already married someone else—continuing a pattern of abandoning wives that I had seen before and would see again.

17

The Wedding Feast

***

For my mum, things took an unexpected turn when her father informed her that she would be marrying a young man with apparently less education than her. Someone she had never met before.

Papa kept saying, "E no get big book like ya own."

Naturally, she didn't take the news lightly. She became withdrawn, but despite her reservations, she went along with the arrangement, and soon an official engagement was in motion. She didn't want to defy her father and secretly hoped the man would pass away before the actual wedding day. The bride price negotiations were underway between the two families in preparation for both the traditional and church weddings. Aunties and uncles had been notified through the showering of gifts from the groom's family—an attempt to curb their greed when it came to the final bride price.

You see, during events like this, extended family members often demand a lot from the groom's family. When the bride is educated, they tend to ask for even more, almost as if education makes someone a better wife. In our culture, once the bride price is paid, the woman is considered a wife by tradition. However, my grandfather disagreed. He insisted that only a church wedding could make the marriage legally binding and officially complete the union.

As the wedding day approached, my mother found the courage to have a heartfelt conversation with her father—something quite unusual for that era. Back then, family dynamics were typically one-sided, with instructions flowing from parents to children, rarely the other way around. However, my mother shared a unique bond with her father, and he usually listened to her. But this time, he was resolute. Sitting firmly in his grand chair in the living room, his expression unwavering, he gently explained that they had already turned down numerous suitors. He felt a deep responsibility to ensure her future by arranging a marriage with a responsible and ambitious businessman. Despite his pride in her education, he believed that QRC Okoyong had instilled a sense of independence that he saw as somewhat negative.

He sincerely believed he had chosen the best path for his eldest daughter and took great pride in his decision. Besides, the bride price had already been paid—there was no turning back. Big Pa proceeded with plans for the church wedding. My mother would complete her clerical studies in Buea and then return home to get married.

After completing her studies at the Clerical School, she was assigned to the Public Works Department (PWD) in Kumba, where she began her career as a clerk. With her new job secured, she traveled to Mamfe for her wedding, hoping to be swept up in the excitement of the preparations. However, her plans took a heartbreaking turn. On the eve of the wedding, she quietly slipped away, making her way back to Kumba.

The weight she carried in her heart was unbearable—she was pregnant. It was a secret she couldn't bring herself to reveal

The Wedding Feast

to her father, especially in the rigid societal norms of 1964. She was trapped in a daunting predicament. But she was about to learn that in life, the things we choose to ignore don't simply disappear; instead, they linger, casting long shadows over our existence.

Back then, weddings were nothing short of grand festivals. They didn't just unite two people—they brought entire villages, even whole clans, together in joyous celebration. These events were dense, tense, and intense. The air buzzed with excitement, and news of upcoming nuptials spread like wildfire through word of mouth. Formal invitations, as we know them today, didn't exist. Instead, guests arrived from distant places, drawn by the sheer thrill of the occasion, guided only by hearsay and informal communication.

My Big Papa, the master orchestrator of such festivities, announced the wedding to the village elders and other esteemed members of the community. From there, the news rippled through the grapevine, setting in motion an event unlike any other.

Weddings in those days were more than just unions; they were extravagant, vibrant communal experiences. Depending on the family's wealth, these events could become lavish affairs lasting for days. It was a time when the entire community came together to celebrate with feasts, dances, and a variety of entertainment. Wealthier families, in particular, could extend the festivities over several days, fostering a sense of togetherness and joy that left a lasting impression on all who attended.

In Mami's case, the Bayangi traditional wedding sequence was strictly followed. The *"knock door"* ceremony had taken place long before anything else—without my mother's presence. In Bayangi tradition, *"knock door"* is the customary practice where the groom's family visits the bride's family for the first time. This visit serves as a formal declaration of their intention to propose a union between the two families. The phrase *"knock door"* metaphorically suggests that the groom's family is figuratively knocking on the bride's family's door to express their interest in marrying one of their daughters.

The expression *"seeing a ripe fruit in that family that they want to pluck"* symbolizes the groom's family's recognition of the bride's desirable qualities, likening her to a ripe fruit ready for harvest. This metaphor reflects the cultural belief that marriage is not just a union between individuals but between entire families, emphasizing mutual respect and consent.

Big Papa was a happy man. He hadn't had the chance to throw such a lavish celebration for his already-married daughter, Mary Ndip. But Susan was different. With her completion of school in Okoyong, her father was immensely proud. For his beautiful daughter, the future had never looked brighter.

The occasion was treated with the utmost seriousness and solemnity. Every individual involved approached it with unwavering dedication, and any attempt to disrupt even the smallest aspect of the process was met with stern disapproval.

Preparations were meticulous, with gifts procured well in advance for parents, uncles, aunties, cousins, and even distant relatives. These gifts ranged from yam tubers and goats to vibrant wrapper fabric, Schnapps (a popular liquor at the time), hunting guns, and various other offerings. Crates of beer, pipes, snuff, cutlasses, walking sticks, long-sleeved shirts, basins filled with cassava, bush mangoes, and bowler hats were just some of the items on the extensive list. In particularly indulgent families, these lists could stretch on for two full pages. For my mother, the level of preparation for her wedding was nothing short of remarkable. Big Papa was delighted with his choice of a husband for his daughter, and the future seemed full of promise.

The Wedding Feast

The night before the bridewealth event, the home buzzed with excitement and activity. For many relatives, this was the first time they were meeting my mother—the educated one who had attended a prestigious school with white people. Her presence commanded both reverence and admiration.

Several visiting groups had arrived the previous night, following the customary practice of gathering at least a week in advance of the event. The hosting family graciously provided food and accommodation, with mattresses laid out on the floors of various rooms after nights filled with dancing and drinking. Staying in a hotel was out of the question—such an idea was met with disapproval. In those days, hotels were primarily reserved for government workers or strangers without relatives or friends to host them. Come morning, relatives sought permission to use the bathrooms of neighboring households to avoid the long queues at Big Papa's compound.

Two significant events were set to unfold in succession: the bridewealth ceremony and the church wedding. What made traditional weddings—or bridewealth events—particularly memorable were the lively interactions and entertainment shared among families and friends.

Behind the scenes, a barter system was often at play—shirts were exchanged for tobacco, cutlasses for snuff, and wrappers for hats and scarves. These informal trades added an element of fun and camaraderie to the occasion, though they sometimes led to stress and misunderstandings. Regardless, they kept everyone engaged and infused the atmosphere with energy.

Palm wine tappers, fabric vendors, and other traders eagerly anticipated such gatherings, as they presented lucrative opportunities for them. Palm wine flowed abundantly throughout the festivities, while feasting and revelry began at the crack of dawn and continued until twilight each day.

It was neither strange nor unusual for a bride or groom to be absent from their own traditional wedding. Marriage was fundamentally an interaction and union between two families, rather than just the couple. The families would meet, exchange greetings, and uphold tradition. However, the bride was expected to be present at the church ceremony and on the day her family escorted her to her husband's home—an event that typically took place seven days after the wedding. There was no such thing as a honeymoon; in this cultural setting, the modern concept of a honeymoon simply did not exist.

As my mother sat perched on her mother's bed on the eve of her wedding, a cacophony of sounds and spirited singing filled the air, echoing through the night. The tantalizing aroma of ceaseless cooking served as a comforting backdrop. Palm wine flowed as freely as the laughter, joy, and occasional drunken insults of relatives. Someone would break into song, and the rest would instinctively respond, while a few got up to dance. There was no better definition of happiness and communal togetherness than that.

"*Ekinirobo robo ey e bot ani ba.*"
Response "*O Biri yoyo.*" And
"*Nambokini kanda, ey ya ya, eh nambokini kanda, ey eh ehh Nambokini kanda.*"

Occasionally, voices would rise, and tempers flared—an inevitable occurrence at gatherings of this magnitude. Misunderstandings often arose from the simplest mishaps, such as an errant purchase of mushrooms or *ebanga* plantains. Disputes could arise over who should send a child to fetch more water or firewood, or even over the delayed delivery of smoked bush meat—two days late!

The Wedding Feast

As the night deepened, the focus shifted from the bride and groom-to-be. The event had taken on a life of its own, evolving into something far greater than the individuals it was meant to celebrate. It transcended them—it became about the clan, the entire community. It symbolized unity, an unwavering commitment to tradition, and the collective pursuit of what was deemed right. Eventually, a serene hush descended upon the gathering as everyone retired for the night, awaiting the cock's crow that would signal the arrival of the long-awaited *D-Day*.

At the break of dawn, as people stirred from their makeshift beds, all thoughts turned to the feasting ahead. With or without a bride and groom, there would be new drunks that day.

The rhythmic drumbeats began early, reverberating throughout the compound. The energy had shifted into high gear. Amidst the bustling crowd, a shared sense of purpose filled the air. This was the moment everyone had been waiting for—the feast that would surpass everything that had unfolded in the past week. Merriment was inevitable, and the anticipation of an opulent, extravagant wedding celebration was palpable. The sheer thought of it was enough to stir excitement, prompting bursts of spontaneous dance steps amid the joyful chaos.

Various meeting groups, each adorned in their distinct wrapper uniforms, had already gathered well before the festivities commenced. Women wore short-sleeved cream lace blouses, paired with two wrappers and elaborate headgear. Their ensembles were further enhanced with chunky beaded jewelry, matching earrings, and either gold or glistening slippers.

Meanwhile, the men donned long-sleeved white shirts adorned with gleaming buttons. Beneath their shirts lay their meticulously wrapped *nkwen*, a garment of cultural significance. Some men, members of the secret *Mgwe* cult, wore small skull caps, while others carried walking sticks. Many came prepared with small hand towels to combat the relentless heat, sweat, and the ever-present nuisance of flies and mosquitoes. Those not affiliated with any particular meeting groups dressed in matching fabrics, a symbolic gesture of belonging, unity, and support.

As the noonday sun approached, the esteemed elders of the clan began to arrive, their presence unmistakable amid the already bustling crowd. Draped in long-sleeved shirts, they wore velvety wrappers that exuded regal elegance. Many wrapped scarves around their necks, and their dignified look was crowned with the iconic red cap adorned with a single feather.

Yet, it was the jewelry that added the final touch of grandeur to their attire. Among these adornments, the necklace stood out as the most ubiquitous piece, worn by nearly everyone present. The men's necklaces were distinct, featuring miniature horns that lent them a bold, commanding presence. In contrast, the women's necklaces, though equally striking, were more delicate and lacked these horned embellishments, allowing the men's accessories to assert their unique masculine flair.

Each elderly gentleman carried a walking stick, while some contentedly chewed tobacco or puffed on their pipes. As if nature itself acknowledged the importance of the day, the sun had risen early, casting its golden light before 7 a.m. By 6:30 a.m., its warm rays were already illuminating the morning, hinting at the buckets of sweat to come, thanks to the endless dancing and jubilations ahead. The stage was set.

Though the event was officially slated to begin at 3 p.m., everyone knew it would not truly commence before 7 p.m. Big Papa began his search for my mother in the late morning, eager to present her with the exquisite outfit he had meticulously chosen for her wedding. The ensemble consisted of a cream lace blouse trimmed with golden accents, a matching shorter, darker cream-colored wrapper, and a head tie. To complete the

The Wedding Feast

look, he had selected a set of red beads, elegant earrings, and a pair of gold slippers. He could already anticipate the murmurs of admiration from the guests—especially the familiar refrain:

Yes, Banyangi pipo like shine shine.

My mother held a special place in his heart, unlike any other. The significance of this wedding, particularly after her education under the white reverend sisters, weighed heavily on him. As the hours passed with no sign of her, a storm of emotions overtook him. Fear gnawed at his heart—what if something terrible had happened to his beloved daughter? Anger simmered just beneath the surface—why was she hiding, keeping away at such a crucial moment? Frustration mounted with each passing minute, and sadness loomed over him like a dark cloud, threatening to drown him in the realization that this day might unravel into disaster.

Yet, he fought to suppress these emotions, willing himself to remain steadfast in the face of uncertainty.

It was then that my mother's friends, who had become her confidants, approached Big Papa with trepidation. Heads bowed, their voices trembling and stammering, they recounted her heartbreaking tale. They revealed that she had embarked on a clandestine journey back to Buea under the cover of night, driven by the heavy burden of an unplanned pregnancy coupled with a dislike for the groom. It was a moment fraught with emotions—a profound sense of disappointment, a crushing weight of embarrassment, the bitter taste of self-pity, and a searing rage coursed through Big Papa. He did not make a scene.

The old man paced relentlessly up and down the corridor of his private quarters, muttering to himself and occasionally erupting with insults and curses directed at Big Mami, holding her responsible for their headstrong daughter's actions. In his tumultuous thoughts, he shifted blame onto himself for having sent her to school and then onto the reverend sisters for "spoiling" her. The room echoed with his blame, ricocheting off the walls as he vented his frustration. He cast blame upon everyone and everything. The situation was unprecedented in his family. It seemed like an unfathomable quagmire of deception. How could he possibly face the other family? What would he tell them? How could he craft a narrative that held any semblance of credibility, knowing that, for once, the truth was utterly inadequate?

18

The Bond is Broken

* * *

Big Papa withdrew to his room alone and sat on the bed, feeling pulsating anger at this personal affront. My mother had challenged her father. In addition, Big Papa found out later that her younger sister Ebai Nyor was gone with her, too. He had refused to send her to school after she completed primary school, and her sister Suzy, my mother, had said she would educate her. The early socialization process for young girls in those days meant that the eldest children could easily perceive themselves as caregivers, responsible for their younger siblings. My mother had arranged for her younger sister to start teacher training school in Buea, and, to crown it all, her last sister, Tembi, followed her to Buea soon after.

Ironically, this single act of defiance, foolhardiness, or disobedience was responsible for my mother's success in life. She was more successful as a single parent than all her married friends and siblings. She had serious relationships with other men during her lifetime, but she had made up her mind that none of the relationships would ever culminate in marriage, and they never did.

For my mother, the wounds of rejection ran deep. The sense

of abandonment she felt when her father seemingly and silently cast her aside for rejecting her groom lingered in her heart for years. Despite her resilience and strength, the pain of being estranged from her father weighed heavily on her, leaving an indelible mark on her psyche.

It wasn't until much later in life, when circumstances brought her back to Mamfe, that the tides of fate began to shift. Accompanied by her daughter Patricia (that's me), my mother returned to the town where she had spent her formative years, hoping perhaps to find closure or solace in the familiar streets and faces of her childhood.

As they traversed the bustling streets of Mamfe, memories both bitter and sweet flooded her mind. She couldn't help but feel a pang of longing for the warmth and acceptance she had once known from her father, Big Papa. Yet, both remained guarded, wary of opening themselves up to further disappointment.

My grandfather had aged by now. Even though he had traveled out of Mamfe to Tiko, he did not check on his daughter, who was next door in the city of Victoria. But the force of nature pulled and beckoned him home at the same time, guiding him back to the place where his daughter and granddaughter now stood.

As they crossed paths once again, amidst the bustling market stalls and now less crowded streets of Mamfe, something shifted within my grandfather. Perhaps it was the sight of his daughter, now a grown woman with a daughter of her own, that stirred a long-dormant sense of paternal love within him. Or perhaps it was the realization that time was fleeting and that reconciliation could no longer be put off.

Whatever the reason, my grandfather began to soften, his icy exterior thawing in the warmth of his daughter's presence. Slowly but surely, he began to reach out, extending tentative gestures of affection and reconciliation. The years of distance and estrangement melted away, replaced by a newfound sense of connection and understanding.

And so a fragile bond began to form between father and daughter once more. Though the wounds of the past still lingered, they were slowly healing, one tender moment at a time. And as they stood together, united by love and forgiveness, my mother knew that she had finally found the closure and acceptance she had been seeking for so long.

However, as with human nature, forgiveness is often a complex and nuanced process, marked by ebbs and flows that can span years. Despite my grandfather's initial efforts to reconcile with my mother, their relationship remained a delicate balancing act, marked by moments of reconciliation followed by periods of tension and estrangement. It was a journey filled with highs and lows, with the wounds of the past never quite fully healed.

In the final analysis, even though my grandfather had ostensibly forgiven my mother and professed a belief in the value of education, his actions spoke louder than words. Despite the apparent success and accomplishments of his daughter, he still harbored a lingering resentment that seemed to cloud his judgment. In a stunning act of betrayal and vindictiveness, he made the calculated decision to exclude my mother from his will as he neared the end of his life.

It was a devastating blow, a final act of revenge that seemed to defy all logic and reason. Despite my mother's best efforts to mend their fractured relationship, my grandfather's decision to cut her out of his will felt like a cruel twist of fate, a vindication of all her deepest fears and insecurities.

Instead, he chose to bestow his inheritance upon her younger sister, a move that seemed to prioritize marital status over education and accomplishment. It was a humiliating turn of events, a stark reminder of the vengeful side of my grandfather's character that had remained hidden for much of his life.

As my mother grappled with the fallout of her father's betrayal, she was forced to confront the harsh realities of familial discord and the fragility of trust. Despite her successes and achievements, she was ultimately left to reckon with the painful realization that even the strongest bonds of family could be shattered by pride and resentment. And in the end, it was a bitter lesson learned at great cost, a testament to the complexities of human relationships and the enduring power of forgiveness. To add to the injury, Big Papa held a strong conviction that, despite her evident success, she could not single-handedly manage his estate due to her unmarried status.

Despite the heavy burden of grief and disappointment weighing on her heart, my mother remained steadfast in her determination to provide the best possible future for her children. As she returned to Victoria, her mind was consumed with thoughts of her newborn granddaughter, Ayamo. The reading of my grandfather's will had been a crushing blow, a stark reminder of the fractured relationship that had persisted between them until the very end.

Alone in her sorrow, my mother found solace in the familiar routines of her daily life. She threw herself into her work, channeling her pain and frustration into a relentless pursuit of success. Despite the tears shed in the quiet solitude of her bedroom at night, she refused to be defined by the circumstances. Instead, she embraced her role as a single mother with unwavering resolve, determined to defy the odds and carve out a better future for her other children, who were still struggling to lift their heads above water.

In her grief, my mother's determination burned bright. She knew that no amount of sadness or disappointment could stand in the way of her dreams for her children. With unwavering conviction, she set out to ensure that they would receive the best possible education, sparing no effort or expense in the pursuit of their future success.

As the days turned into weeks and the weeks into months, her resolve grew stronger. With each passing day, she became more determined to honor my grandfather's memory by building a legacy of her own. And though the road ahead would be fraught with challenges and obstacles, she faced the future with courage, knowing that her unwavering resolve would carry her through even the darkest of times.

She knew that doubts in the minds of other family members lingered regarding her resolute character and occasional impulsiveness. She had been acutely aware of her father's opinions, and even while he was alive, she felt an unyielding determination to follow in his footsteps, striving to earn his pride at any cost.

This fervent desire propelled her towards a love for real estate. She diligently accumulated properties while simultaneously pursuing a career as a seamstress and managing her farms. Before Big Papa's passing, her portfolio included a four-apartment residence in Mamfe town, a duplex on Kalla Street in Limbe, a standalone house on Mbende Street, and another property she had started developing in Mile 4, Limbe. Additionally, she owned two undeveloped plots of land, which she would later sell.

Thanks to her unwavering acumen and vigilant guardianship, all her children received an education from prestigious secondary schools and either completed or were enrolled in esteemed universities. Those under her care, like her sisters, did not miss out, and soon everyone was standing on their own feet, having gone through some form of higher education. My mum loved her sisters and wanted the best for them.

19

Clerks' Quarters Set the Foundation

***

My mother moved from Mamfe to Buea, then to Kumba, and later to Victoria (now called Limbe), where she settled first on Mbende Street, then in Clerks' Quarters, Kalla Street, and finally at Mile 4, Bonadikombo. Growing up under my mother's nurturing care was an experience that resembled the childhoods of many during the 1960s and 1970s. Mami never really talked about herself or her past unless she considered there was a lesson to be taught. It was all about teaching, inspiring, educating, and enlightening. She was extremely secretive otherwise and spoke very little about her past, present, or future unless it was related to some achievement, prospect, or event.

Limbe was, and still is, a beautiful city located in the Southwest region of Cameroon, at the foot of Mount Cameroon. In the 1970s, it was a relatively small but thriving coastal city with a rich cultural heritage, abundant natural resources, and a population of around 20,000 people. It was renowned for its fresh fish, and people came from far and wide to purchase it. Growing up, we ate fish almost every other day. My mum would leave work and go to Down Beach to buy the fish fresh from the Atlantic Ocean before coming back home.

Clerks' Quarters Set the Foundation

We loved walking along the black sandy beaches. We had no idea beaches could be any other color. We loved harvesting fruits around the Botanic Gardens. All kinds of fruits with various names: Banga school, four-corner yellow, belle fruit, and kuluba. There were also mangoes, guava, tangerines, pawpaw, soursop, berries, and sugarcane.

We loved swimming in the Limbe River, which was just by the Atlantic Beach Hotel. We ran away from strangers, especially white people, because it was rumored that they would take our photos and then we would disappear mysteriously. We loved life and wanted to live. We loved to fish in Jengele Water behind Clerks' Quarters with our baskets. My grandmother was a champion fisherwoman. Each time she was around, we would catch fish, roast, and eat them with roasted cassava, cocoyams, plantains, or roasted yams with red oil.

The Botanic Gardens in Limbe, now known as the Limbe Botanic Garden, is a beautiful and fascinating place that spans approximately 50 hectares. It is home to a diverse collection of plants and trees, many of which are native to Cameroon and other parts of West Africa. It has various sections, including the medicinal plant section, the orchid garden, the fernery, and the palm garden. As children, we had no idea of the importance of this garden. We absolutely loved the place, especially the jungle village with its lush tropical vegetation and towering trees, which created a serene and picturesque setting.

Jungle Village is a large open-air amphitheater located in Limbe, Cameroon. It is a popular venue for hosting a variety of cultural events, including traditional wrestling (palapala), and dance performances. The amphitheater is situated in a beautiful natural setting. The natural stones serve as the theater seats, and the tropical flora adds to the ambiance of the events that take place there. Additionally, the Jungle Village was sometimes used as a venue for community gatherings and meetings of various natures.

When we were growing up, the Jungle Village was a very important place and played a significant role in the cultural and social life of Limbe and the surrounding region. Today, some inhabitants of Limbe are unaware of its existence, and many have never visited it. Unlike many other parts of Cameroon, we had running water in Clerks' Quarters. But life in Clerks' Quarters was not without its challenges. As kids, we loved the dry season because we could play outside for long periods and sing at night while telling stories. Clerks' Quarters was a low-lying area that easily flooded during the rainy season. However hard my mother tried, she never succeeded in preventing water from coming in and flooding our house.

The sound of raindrops falling on rooftops is a soothing lullaby that many people find comforting. However, one night of heavy rainfall brought a catastrophic flood, destroying property and leaving many feeling helpless. During the day, everything was business as usual. However, as the sun began to set, the skies darkened, and heavy clouds loomed overhead. Soon after, the rain started to pour down, steadily at first and then with increasing intensity.

As the night wore on, the rain became more relentless, and the streets of Clerks' Quarters began to flood. Water gushed down the small backyards and courtyards of houses, rapidly rising and sweeping away everything in its path. The sound of rushing water was deafening, and the commotion woke up people.

The floodwaters quickly entered homes and businesses, causing extensive damage. Furniture and other personal belongings that were left outside were swept away by the raging waters. Many residents tried to salvage what they could by piling items on any high surfaces, such as tables and beds. But water soon reached some beds. The flood continued throughout the night, causing widespread devastation. Parts of buildings were destroyed, businesses were ruined, and lives were uprooted.

The flood in Clerks' Quarters was a sobering reminder of the power of nature and the importance of being prepared for emergencies. The resilience and determination of the community in the face of such adversity are a testament to the human spirit and serve as an inspiration to us all.

Nobody could sleep that night. I was perched on top of the fridge, just sitting up. Dozing off from time to time. My two sisters were on top of a cupboard, and my brother, the youngest at the time, was sleeping on a wider space on the dining table, where he was stretched out comfortably by one of my aunts who lived with us. I didn't like the fridge. It was high up and near the ceiling. This meant I was closer to where the huge rats lived. It was scary. So, the insomnia was not simply due to discomfort and mosquitoes, but also out of fear of rats. Surprisingly, the rats were quiet. The chomping and grinding of teeth, squeaks, and hisses that characterized their ascent and descent up and down the roof had quietened considerably. However, it still didn't lead to any sleep. I am not sure where the older people were. My mum was certainly watching the rain from her bedroom window, knowing the water was already inside her room.

As dawn broke on the distant horizon, we were reminded of the promise of a new day. It was August 15, 1976, and my mother hurried to find a canoe owner who could ferry us to church. We held leaves from our cocoyam farm over our heads as makeshift umbrellas. Wearing white dresses may not have been the best choice for a canoe ride after a night of heavy rain, but we followed instructions to the letter—my mother had said to wear white, and so we did. All we wanted was to be in church. It was a special day—our First Holy Communion and Confirmation. We arrived just in time, and the priest was understanding.

As the sun rose on that beautiful Sunday morning, Holy Family Parish in New Town buzzed with excitement. Holy Communion was a significant event in the lives of young Catholic children, and everyone was dressed in their finest clothes.

Many children arrived late. The priest asked for reasons, listened attentively to the answers, nodding his head in understanding. He knew the floods had affected many areas, and he could see the disappointment and embarrassment on the faces of those who had struggled to get there. With a reassuring smile, he welcomed everyone, making them feel at home before beginning the Mass. His powerful, majestic voice rang out as he led the congregation in *Ave, Ave, Ave Maria*.

At the end of the Mass, the priest addressed the congregation, sharing news of the floods and asking for their support and prayers for those affected. He also expressed his gratitude to the children for making it to their First Holy Communion despite the challenges.

As they left the church, the children felt a deep sense of relief and gratitude. They had been welcomed into a community that cared for them, and that was a reassuring feeling.

In those days, white priests had a reputation for impatience, so Sunday felt particularly special. The priest—who was often known for scolding parishioners, even during service—seemed to have changed, perhaps touched by the solemnity of the Assumption of Our Lady into Heaven.

Many priests serving in different parishes came from European countries. Their tetchiness often stemmed from cultural differences, an intense sense of duty, poor coping mechanisms for unfamiliar environments, and unrealistic expectations. To them, punctuality was essential. But for many people in Limbe on a Sunday, it was not a priority. The priests had come from a faster-paced way of life, which often clashed with the more relaxed and unhurried rhythm of Cameroon and much of Africa.

Some priests were also driven—often mistakenly—by an overwhelming sense of purpose and urgency to spread their message and convert as many people as possible. They believed time was of the essence and that any delay in their mission could mean lost souls. This urgency sometimes led to impatience, especially when they faced resistance or obstacles. Many of the European priests sent as missionaries were young men, assigned to remote and unfamiliar regions where they had to navigate new languages, customs, and traditions. This could be frustrating and overwhelming, and their irritability was often a coping mechanism for dealing with their sense of disorientation and displacement. At the time, of course, we didn't understand their outbursts. To us, they were simply *strange whiteman dem*.

That Sunday, by the time the three-hour service ended, much of the floodwater had receded, allowing us to wade back home safely. Despite the floods, a feast awaited us. We rushed home to find neighbors already gathered, the music from the radio cassette booming in celebration.

We posed for photos before finally taking off our beautiful white dresses and veils, which by then looked more like a mix of white and dark brown. We spent the afternoon eating and dancing, but also drying everything under the scorching sun that had appeared out of nowhere, as if challenging the rain. The neighborhood children eagerly helped.

The aftermath of the flood was devastating. Streets were littered with debris, and many homes, once inundated with water, lay in ruins. Countless people lost their possessions.

Happily, though, neighbors came together, helping one another clean up homes and clear away the rubble.

Our house in Clerks' Quarters was at the start of a row of terraced houses—low-cost housing built to accommodate the growing population of low-income government workers. It was a stark contrast to the Government Residential Area (GRA), which housed senior government officials. Ours was an end-terrace house, part of a pattern where four houses stood in a row, followed by a break, and then another row of four.

We had slightly more space inside, and the land beside our row belonged to us. My mother used this 500-square-meter plot as a farm, growing plantains, vegetables, yams, and corn. She also kept a few chickens—old layers that roamed freely by day but instinctively returned to the back kitchen each night. It was fascinating how they always knew where home was.

Occasionally, the hens laid eggs, and when they did, we all enjoyed omelets—sometimes just four eggs shared among eight of us. It was a treat. On days when we had pancakes for supper but no eggs, we made them with just water, flour, and sugar. *Yumm!*

20

Happenings at Clerks' Quarters

* * *

One fine Saturday, my aunt Gloria Tembi and another woman were plaiting my hair outside the house under a mango tree. I was about nine years old. At the time, plaiting was a popular method of styling hair. Three other girls hovered around; each assigned a task. My sister, Elizabeth Ekumanka, measured and cut the black thread with her teeth before handing it to Aunt Gloria. Metem, a neighbor's little girl, held the combs and hair oil. Meanwhile, I clutched a piece of broken mirror, watching the process—not to ensure it was done to my liking, but simply out of curiosity. My mother had already given strict instructions on how my hair should be styled. Even if I had objected, no one would have paid any attention. *She who must be obeyed* had spoken, and her word was law.

Plaiting involved taking small sections of hair and wrapping them tightly with thread, starting from the roots and working upwards toward the tips. Once a section was fully wrapped, it was then braided into the rest of the hair. This process was repeated until the entire head was plaited. The style was both fashionable and practical. It helped protect the hair from damage and breakage, and with proper maintenance, it could last for weeks. Many women loved to plait their hair, appreciating both its beauty and durability.

It was a typical hot Saturday afternoon, with someone's radio blasting *Saturday Afternoon Request*, a program on Radio Buea where people sent in request cards for the songs they wanted to hear and dedicated them to loved ones.

Though the heat was intense, cumulus clouds had been gathering on the far horizon for days. Everyone kept predicting rain, but despite four days of anticipation, the only change was the rising temperature. No rain fell.

Then, the first clap of thunder before the downpour was preceded by a blinding flash of lightning. Ordinarily, a thunderstorm wouldn't have been a cause for concern, but as we continued plaiting hair and hurriedly packing up to go inside, what followed was nothing short of spectacular.

The next thing we knew, my aunt was flat on her back in front of the back door. My sister was screaming for my mother from a shallow hole that had just appeared beneath an uprooted pear tree. I was inside the house, bleeding profusely from my right leg and screaming hysterically.

No one could immediately explain what had just happened. My mother, who had been in her room, rushed out in a frenzied panic. She had witnessed part of the unfolding chaos, but even she couldn't piece together a coherent story. She tried to explain something about the lightning but could only stutter. The immediate concern was the blood—the effect, not the cause.

Eventually, we pieced together what had happened and were better able to understand the events that had unfolded so quickly. When the lightning flashed, a supernatural force seemed to propel everyone into motion at the same time. We all leaped up and ran toward the house in a frantic rush. My aunt was thrown backward, landing flat on her back. The mirror in my hand shattered into pieces, and one of the shards fell on my leg—that was the source of the bleeding.

No one could explain how my sister ended up in the plantain farm, in the opposite direction from where the rest of us had run. The other children were later accounted for, safe in their home next door. Fortunately, my leg injury was the only one sustained that day.

Electrical equipment around the house was smoking, despite the surge protectors. Later, as we recovered from the shock, we each shared our version of events—describing the intense, blinding light and the deafening whip, whack, and crack of the lightning and thunder. What had initially been a terrifying experience soon became a humorous story, recounted with excitement and laughter.

The belief that thunder could be "sent" to punish or harm individuals was deeply ingrained in our community, passed down through generations as a cautionary tale about the consequences of wrongdoing. That day's thunder and rainstorm became part of that lore.

Our neighbor—the one to whom the thunder had supposedly been sent—narrowly escaped, as he wasn't home at the time. But the message reached him loud and clear: it was time to pay his debt. It was said that had he been home, he would have met his demise at the hands of vengeful thunder. But fate had intervened, sparing him from nature's wrath.

The incident was a stark reminder of the power and unpredictability of forces beyond our control. It was a hard-learned lesson for our neighbor, who wasted no time settling his debt once he grasped the gravity of his situation. His narrow escape from death served as a wake-up call, prompting him to reevaluate his actions and take responsibility for his obligations.

As children, we listened wide-eyed to these stories, our young minds struggling to grasp their full implications. Were these tales merely cautionary fables passed down to teach moral lessons, or were they rooted in a deeper truth beyond our understanding? It was difficult to say, as the veracity of such stories remained shrouded in mystery and speculation.

Nevertheless, the stories served their purpose. They instilled in us a deep respect for the forces of nature and the consequences of our actions. They reminded us that even the most minor transgressions could have far-reaching repercussions—and that it was our duty to heed the warnings of those who came before us.

As we grew older, we came to appreciate the wisdom embedded within these tales, recognizing them as valuable lessons in morality and accountability. Though we may never know the whole truth behind the stories of thunder sent to punish the wayward, their impact on our collective consciousness endured, shaping our understanding of the world and our place within it.

My mother ran several small businesses simultaneously in Clerks' Quarters. She planted and sold fresh vegetables, made and sold *moi moi* and fish pies, and sewed men's "jumpas" (ready-made garments). After completing a batch of about 40, she would send them out for sale, usually with one of her children or a relative living with us—most often the older aunties. I don't ever recall selling *jumpas* myself, but we all played a role in helping with other aspects of her business.

For me, after selling vegetables in the market in the mornings before school, the after-school chore was picking coffee at the Produce Marketing Board agency, not far from our house. These tasks became routine for us children—a way of lending a helping hand to our mother and contributing to the financial well-being of our single-parent household. And we did it with joy.

After school, we would eagerly make our way to the Marketing Board agency, ready to tackle the day's work. With enthusiasm and keen eyes, we meticulously sorted through coffee beans, separating the good from the bad with practiced efficiency. Each bean was scrutinized to ensure only the finest made it into the bag. Once our task was complete, the bag was inspected, and if it passed rigorous quality control, we were rewarded for our efforts.

Though our financial contributions may have seemed small in the grand scheme of things, they reflected our commitment to supporting our family and easing the burden on our hardworking mother.

We sold vegetables in the nearby New Town market. Every morning before heading to school, we carried greens, *okongobong*, and waterleaf in oversized, overflowing aluminum basins to sell. We dealt with wholesalers, so our time at the market was brief—usually, by 6 a.m., we had finished our business for the day. The market was only about a 10-minute walk from our house. From there, we would head to church—another 10-minute walk—just in time for the 6 a.m. service.

On the way back from church, the meat market would just be opening. The market consisted of several blocks of stalls, shops, and open-air vendors, all packed tightly together in a bustling, vibrant atmosphere. As you approached, the air filled with a cacophony of sounds—from the blaring music of street speakers and the honking of cars to the shouts of vendors vying for customers' attention. The atmosphere was lively and chaotic, with people of all ages and backgrounds moving through the narrow paths between stalls.

Cows were not slaughtered daily at the abattoir, so on the days they were, meat sellers arrived early. By the time we were heading home from church, the market would be a hive of activity—hustling and bustling with vendors shouting and hawking their wares to passing customers. In the early morning, the sellers were not as loud, but the energy and anticipation were still palpable in the air. To an outsider unfamiliar with African open markets, it might have seemed chaotic. Later in the day, under the scorching sun, when exhaustion set in, only the blaring music would remain—a steady, unrelenting backdrop to the day's commerce.

I found the markets fascinating and admired the vibrant entrepreneurial spirit. Even when I grew older, I continued to visit markets whenever I could or listened to stories about them with a sense of nostalgia.

As I navigated the market back then, vendors hawked everything from traditional fabrics to trendy Western-style clothing, all at competitive prices. There was an array of accessories—jewelry, bags, and shoes—along with electronics and gadgets, creating a bustling atmosphere filled with endless possibilities for discovery.

Everything imaginable was on sale: soap, brooms, slippers, breakfast items like *"make me well,"* meat pies displayed in glass cases, onions, smoked fish, plastic bowls, mortars, cooking oil, spices, groundnuts, and more. The aroma of cooked food filled the air as vendors crouched over charcoal fires, fanning the flames with scraps of paper to get the fire going or waving away thick clouds of smoke. The market was an explosion of color—vivid displays of goods, the press of bodies moving through the narrow paths, loud voices bargaining, and the constant soundtrack of music blaring from the stall where a man recorded songs onto radio cassettes for his customers.

We sold our vegetables to wholesalers before heading to church. On the way back, we collected our money and then walked home before heading to school. The concept of wholesale marketing was deeply ingrained in my mother's psyche. Later in life, she expanded her business to include selling cartons of

Ovaltine, which she sourced at a lower price from some Igbo traders.

She also sold cooked food. One of our weekly chores was grating tins of Peak milk on rough concrete floors to remove the lids—an agonizing task, but necessary so she could prepare *moi moi* (ground bean pudding) for sale. The *moi moi* was cooked over an open fire, sometimes inside the "firewood kitchen" and sometimes outside. Cooking with firewood was already a challenge, but when the wood was wet, it became even more difficult. It was hard to ignite, producing thick smoke that stung the eyes and made breathing difficult. Wet wood did not burn easily, which prolonged the cooking process.

One day, my mum came home with a kerosene stove. We were all overjoyed, but our excitement was short-lived when she explained that, for commercial purposes, firewood was still the cheaper option than kerosene. Despite this, the arrival of the kerosene stove brought other significant changes to our lives. Soon, it wasn't just us—our neighbors also started using kerosene stoves, which made cooking easier, more efficient, and less time-consuming. With less time spent cooking, more time was freed for other activities. Kerosene stoves were a safer and more efficient way to cook, and they reduced our 100% dependence on firewood—a far more problematic option. Firewood smoke was harmful to the lungs and eyes, especially for children, who were often tasked with fanning the flames.

Clerks' Quarters was a quiet neighborhood. We played *tabala* and *dodging* on the roads and rolled tires with two sticks in the rain on pothole-filled roads with water. Athlete's foot, which we called "water-rain," was common. School was just a stone's throw away, and even if it had been farther, there weren't many cars, and no public transportation to worry about.

The biggest outing, aside from going to church and school,

was visiting "Short Ibo Man's" store, a small grocery shop run by a Nigerian. The owner of the corner store had quickly earned the nickname "Short Ibo Man." It's said that he threw a fit when he found out what people had been calling him. Standing just over a meter tall, he was indeed short—whoever gave him the nickname certainly wasn't mistaken.

On the way to the store, we passed the home of a Creole patriarch. The father, it was rumored, was a *"nyongo"* man, meaning a wizard. He was friends with a car owner with the number plate 9090, who was also reputed to be a wicked man. They were part of a shadowy group whose presence was felt but rarely seen—an obscure, sinister, and mysterious cult driven by the desire for wealth. No one could prove anything, of course, but the legends spoke of their clandestine gatherings under the cover of night, where whispered incantations and eerie rituals sent shivers down the spines of anyone brave enough to listen.

For decades, the *"nyongo"* society cast a pall of fear over the land. Members were rumored to possess dark powers and were suspected of engaging in unspeakable acts. Tales of sudden wealth and unexplained misfortune were often attributed to their malevolent influence, instilling a sense of dread in the hearts of many.

Rumor had it that young people were killed and taken as spirits to work as enslaved people in farms far, far away in other countries. As children, we believed all this and would not go past that Creo man's house if the father was sitting in front on a stool, as he often did. If we had to go, we would naively cover our faces with paper or walk on the opposite side of the road to avoid being detected. We would accelerate our steps and run across very quickly.

Despite efforts to unravel the mysteries surrounding the *"nyongo"* society, its true nature remains elusive, veiled in secrecy and obscured by the mists of time. Yet, its legend endures, woven into the fabric of our folklore as a cautionary tale of the dangers that lurk in the shadows.

We loved the Clerks' Quarters. All our neighbors were married couples; two of them were polygamous families. One of the monogamous homes was noisier than the other, with constant loud quarreling between husband and wife. But the polygamous homes were at another level. The noise was not just between husband and wives. Children also joined in fights and shouting matches. There were many children, and daily quarreling and fighting were common.

Because her kids were so different, my mum commanded respect, and other parents would sometimes approach her for advice. It also meant that we did not envy any of these families. In those days, people were friendly, and neighbors were neighbors. There was warmth. There was joy. We ate freely from fruit trees. We were obedient but opinionated, focused, emphatic, and somehow rebellious too. "Grumblers" is what my mom used to call us. Anything we did not want to do, we grumbled about all day. We had opinions, but we tended to lean toward what we were told.

In school and in the community, there were no Francophones among us. Those who had migrated genuinely wanted to be Anglophones and spoke only English. This meant that in school, it was very difficult to understand that families like Njawe, Njomo, Mbarga, Esso, Shalo, Eloundou, Lottin, Nkuo, Dikuba, were migrants whose great-grandparents or grandparents had come from French-speaking Cameroon. Much later in life, we learned, through the force of circumstances, to sadly read names and assign them geographical origins.

There was a lot of unspoken fear that we sensed as we grew up, which had nothing to do with our parents or neighbors. In the evenings, especially, people rushed home and went to bed early. We were told to be quiet at night because people were listening outside, and what we said could be overheard, potentially reaching Yaoundé, where the president would punish the family. My mother was often the first to ensure everyone had supper on time, and by 7 p.m., we were all in our rooms, ready to sleep. If you made a noise, she would threaten you with the whip.

There was a prevailing language barrier and limited educational opportunities among the country's regions. There was no university with English as the base language. A significant proportion of high school graduates from the 1970s sought further education by either attending universities in Nigeria or venturing abroad to countries such as the United Kingdom and the United States (commonly referred to as "USA" back then). This trend persisted despite the passage of time since my mother's generation, underscoring the enduring challenges faced in accessing quality education.

During this period, the educational landscape reflected historical norms, with persistent disparities between genders. It was evident that more young men pursued academic achievements compared to their female counterparts, highlighting an ongoing issue of gender inequality. This disparity not only reflected societal norms but also underscored the limited opportunities available for girls to access education and pursue higher learning. Girls were made to believe that they were better off getting married than getting further education.

Despite efforts to promote educational equity, including governmental initiatives and international aid programs, structural barriers continued to impede progress. The lack of accessible educational resources and inadequate infrastructure in local communities further exacerbated disparities, particularly for marginalized groups such as girls and rural populations.

In this context, the migration of high school graduates to Nigeria or abroad for further studies represented a pragmatic response to the limited opportunities available locally. While these experiences undoubtedly provided valuable opportunities for academic and personal growth for individuals, they also highlighted the broader systemic challenges facing the education sector in the region.

To date, the pursuit of quality education remains a fundamental aspiration for communities, transcending generations. The government has since made efforts to address the entrenched barriers to educational access and promote gender equality. There is a recognition that education is a critical imperative for fostering inclusive development and unlocking the full potential of future generations. Today, the region boasts government institutions of higher learning, and the private sector has also taken up education, making many more institutions available.

21

Mami Waka Waka

* * *

My mother's passion for travel was an intrinsic part of her adventurous spirit, and she seized every opportunity to explore new horizons. Twice, she embarked on journeys across the seas to visit me in the United Kingdom. After succeeding in the General Certificate of Education (GCE) Advanced Level examination, I was awarded a scholarship to study Journalism and Mass Communication in the UK. On her second visit, she brought along my brother Eric, then just ten years old, adding a touch of youthful exuberance to the adventure.

London, with its rich history and vibrant culture, served as our playground as we delved into its myriad wonders. With visas easily obtained in those days, we traversed borders with ease, embarking on unforgettable escapades without fear of rejection.

Many of the places we visited were new to me since my arrival in the UK. Our days were filled with exploration, from the iconic Buckingham Palace and Tower of London, where we marveled at the Crown Jewels, to the majestic Westminster Abbey, steeped in centuries of history and tradition. Strolling along the banks of the River Thames, we gazed in awe at the imposing facade of the Houses of Parliament, its iconic clock tower standing tall against the London skyline.

The bustling streets of Covent Garden beckoned with their eclectic mix of street performers and bustling market stalls, while the serene beauty of St. James's Park provided a tranquil oasis amidst the urban hustle and bustle. And of course, no visit to London would be complete without a trip to the world-famous British Museum, where we immersed ourselves in the treasures of ancient civilizations.

But it was the London Underground that captured Eric's imagination, igniting his curiosity about its origins and purpose. As I shared the history of the Tube during the world wars, he was filled with awe, envisioning the bustling network of tunnels beneath the city's surface. He wondered why there was no city built underground as well. I did not have answers to his many questions.

Our evenings in the bustling West End were often spent sampling what could only be described as the simple pleasures of British cuisine, though at the time, it felt like a grand adventure. We would immerse ourselves in the lively atmosphere, surrounded by the hum of the city, with streetlights flickering on as the sun set. But when it came to the food, it was anything but elaborate. More often than not, our meals consisted of the quintessential fish and chips—crispy on the outside, tender on the inside, and wrapped in newspaper as we strolled through the vibrant streets.

The mornings followed a similar pattern, marked by hearty but straightforward breakfasts. Baked beans, sausages, eggs, bacon, and thick slices of white bread greeted us each day. There was nothing sophisticated about British cuisine, but its simplicity had its own charm. It nourished us as we went about our explorations, offering a taste of the local life, even if the menu remained the same. My mother always made light of it, commenting that the food may not have been fancy, but it filled us up and kept us going—just like everything else she did for us in life. For my mother, the ability to afford such travels was a testament to her hard work and determination. She took immense pride in being able to provide not only for herself but also for Eric, ensuring that he, too, could experience the wonders of the world beyond our Cameroon borders.

As I bid the two of them farewell from London as they returned home, our hearts were filled with cherished memories of our time together. Though the journey may have ended, the laughter, camaraderie, and shared experiences would remain etched in our hearts forever. Years later, as we reminisced about our adventures, we always treasured the joyous moments we shared, united by our love for travel and the world's boundless wonders.

Another one of my mother's traits was a cleverness that was both puzzling and charming. Her skill in handling situations with ease amazed and entertained those around her. She had a special way of facing life's challenges with a sly smile, and this was evident in many ways, especially in how she managed her finances.

Her approach to finances was like a well-orchestrated dance, where every step was over-calculated and then executed with precision. While some saw money as a means to an end, she viewed it as a game—a game she played with expertise, believing she should always win. One of her favorite tactics and her knack for negotiation was well known by all in her household. Nothing was ever taken for what it was. Whether it was haggling with street vendors for a better price or negotiating with block molders, tilers, or diggers, she approached every transaction with a strategic mindset. With charm as her weapon and wit as her shield, she could talk her way into getting what she wanted, often leaving the other party wondering how they had agreed to her terms so easily.

But her cleverness extended beyond mere negotiation; she was also a master of resourcefulness. She always told us that things were difficult, so financial constraints were a permanent part of our family. She could always stretch a little bit of money further than anyone ever thought possible. From creating meals out of leftovers to finding creative ways to save on household expenses and buying in bulk, she was always one step ahead when it came to making ends meet.

However, this character trait was not just limited to saving money; she also had a talent for making money grow. While others played it safe with traditional investments, she wasn't afraid to take calculated risks in the pursuit of greater wealth. She had a keen eye for spotting opportunities that others overlooked. Everyone in her office at one time or another bought something from her. All her neighbors had at some point bought something from her. Everyone was always awed that she always seemed to have money. She had ready cash to buy a house, a car, and her plots, even though, as a civil servant, she really had very little.

But perhaps what made her approach to money so intriguing was the way she balanced shrewdness with generosity. Despite her savvy financial tactics, she was always willing to lend a helping hand to those in need. Whether offering financial advice to a friend or anonymously donating to a charitable cause, she understood the value of using her wealth for good.

In the end, her financial acumen wasn't just about accumulating wealth; it was about using it to navigate life's obstacles and make a positive impact on the world around her. And while her tactics may have raised a few eyebrows along the way, there was no denying that they were part of what made her truly unique.

Later in life, when she traveled to visit my brother in

California, my sister in London, or my other sister in Georgia, USA, it became customary for her to return home laden with cheap souvenirs, countless stories, and, without fail, foreign currency.

Often, these notes had been given to her by one or more of her children or friends, depending on whom she had been visiting. But it wasn't merely the possession of these currencies that was fascinating—it was the clever and calculating game she played when converting them from dollars or pounds sterling to Francs CFA.

One might assume that, given her close relationship with me—her only daughter back in Cameroon—and Victor, my husband, she would come to us to exchange her foreign notes at the most favorable local currency rates. After all, we had always been more than willing to assist her with financial matters, as devoted children would. Yet, her crafty nature could not resist the allure of a more intricate dance.

Before making her exchange request, she would first discreetly reach out to the money changers in Limbe. Charlie, the well-known store owner in the New Town market, knew her well, as he occasionally exchanged money for her. It was her way of gauging the wind's direction and the ocean's tides before setting sail. With her impeccable negotiation skills, she would secure the best exchange rates from these local money changers—without ever fully revealing her intentions.

It was a well-choreographed act, one she had perfected over the years with practiced elegance. She knew that Victor or I would offer her a more generous exchange rate, yet she wasn't content with simply asking for our help. Instead, she preferred to engage in these clandestine maneuvers, pretending she had no choice but to trade with the local currency dealers.

Once she had negotiated a favorable rate, she would then

approach Victor, feigning confusion and innocent curiosity, inquiring about the prevailing rates for converting her foreign currency. Her feigned ignorance was an award-worthy performance, for she was already well aware of the rates she had secured from the market.

Victor would offer her the same rate she had previously negotiated. Then, in a lighthearted tone, she would ask if he couldn't do just a little better than the money changers. Without hesitation, he would oblige, as though it were the most natural thing to do. It was her artful character in action—a calculated move to maintain the illusion of self-sufficiency while secretly embracing the warmth of family bonds.

These repeated interactions showcased her ability to navigate life with a clever grace that was uniquely hers. They were a testament to her innate shrewdness, a trait that added an air of mystery and intrigue to her already captivating personality. While the exchanges themselves may have seemed inconsequential, they symbolized a more profound truth: my mother's shrewd nature was an integral part of her identity. And though we didn't always appreciate this side of her, it added a special kind of magic to our family's history.

22

Our Neighbors

* * *

Against the backdrop of the 1950s and 1960s in Mamfe and later Limbe, where tradition was deeply entrenched and societal norms rigid, my mother emerged as an extraordinary figure—a woman who dared to defy the conventions of her time. This chapter chronicles her remarkable journey through a world shaped by polygamy, limited educational opportunities for women, and the suffocating grip of male dominance, which she refused to accept.

At the time, women made up 58% of Cameroon's population, yet they remained in subordinate positions within both traditional and state institutions. The prevailing belief was that women did not need education, as their primary roles were to become wives and mothers. It was a world where dreams were stifled, ambition was mocked, and young girls' potential remained untapped. Even women themselves often accepted the worth that men assigned to them. But my mother had different ideas—she was determined to chart her own course.

Male dominance was pervasive, as men were seen as the ultimate authority. They could make and unmake, marry as many wives as they pleased (as permitted by law), and treat their wives however they wished. Many women endured wife-beating, verbal abuse, and mental torment with little recourse to justice. Gender-based violence had long been a grim reality in Cameroon.

I recall moments from my time at Presbyterian Girls' School, Limbe, when the harsh reality of this issue became painfully apparent. During break time, a classmate once shared a disturbing incident. She revealed that her mother had been rushed to the hospital after her father had brutally beaten her—striking like a snake—simply because her food was served tepid instead of piping hot. In his rage, he tried to shatter the plastic plates and demanded that another wife bring him food immediately. Her mother's injuries were so severe that she had to be hospitalized. My classmate was visibly shaken. She admitted she had been beaten before, though never as badly as her mother. None of us asked questions—we just listened in somber silence, offering silent prayers that it would never happen to us. As if praying was enough.

Another classmate shared a similarly heart-wrenching story. His father had thrown his entire family out—his mother, himself, and his siblings—after returning home inebriated. In a drunken rage, he had abruptly and callously ordered his wife to leave, blaming her for their children's academic struggles. This appalling event occurred at midnight, leaving them stranded and helpless. It was only thanks to the kindness of a neighbor that they found refuge for the night.

It was common for fathers to vent their frustrations on their families, beating their children mercilessly for no reason. If they failed at work, they took it out on their children. If their boss were cruel, they would come home and lash out at their wives. If they weren't paid enough, their children bore the blame.

Fighting between couples was rampant. Some women fought back, often with their children taking their side. In many cases, however, the woman was overpowered and "taught" a lesson. A man's word was law, and women were expected to obey without question.

This was the world we grew up in, and for my mother, these experiences only reinforced her belief that she had made the right decision. I never heard her express regret, even as she became a grandmother in her fifties and sixties. However, she never discouraged her siblings or children from getting married.

One of our neighbors, who had three wives, frequently beat his least favorite wife. One Sunday morning, a commotion erupted in his house—something we had come to expect. Mr. Tako-re was fighting with Mami Rose Tako-re. This time, Mami Rose's three teenage sons, dressed in their Sunday best for church, joined in, pouncing on their father. Realizing he was outnumbered, he screamed for his other two wives to come to his rescue.

What followed was a chaotic free-for-all—everyone fighting without really knowing who they were hitting or why. When the dust settled, Pa Tako-re stood there, breathing hard, cursing, and pulling at his torn shirt. Furious, he ordered Mami Rose to pack her things and leave.

This, too, was common. A man could decide at any moment that he no longer wanted his wife. It didn't matter if he had paid a bride price. It didn't matter if there was a marriage certificate. The courts would favor him.

But this time, things took an unexpected turn. Instead of siding with their husband, the other wives and their children silently began packing their belongings, preparing to leave as well. Panic-stricken, Mr. Tako-re suddenly found himself begging everyone to stay.

These painful stories were not isolated incidents. They were distressingly common, shining a harsh light on the widespread domestic violence that plagued Cameroon during that era. My mother was acutely aware of these injustices, often remarking that a Bayangi man could never be a true husband.

It is worth noting that progress has been made since then, but gender-based violence remains at unacceptably high levels in Cameroon today. In 1984, political efforts led to the creation of the Ministry of Women's Affairs and the Family. Its mandate included developing, coordinating, and monitoring policies on violence, among other issues. While this ministry achieved many successes, its policies often failed to reach poor and low-income women, who continued to suffer violence at the hands of men, perform degrading jobs, and live in misery.

In 1993, the *International Federation of Female Lawyers Cameroon* (FIDA) was founded, thanks to the hard work of Barrister Miriam Weledji. FIDA empowered women and girls to assert their rights through training, education, and counseling, while also providing them with legal support. Women could now dream of inheriting property and receiving family allowances after divorce.

My mother, however, was cut from a different cloth. Fiercely determined to live life on her own terms, she rejected the confines of both monogamous and polygamous marriage. She refused to be subjugated to any man, envisioning a different destiny for herself. A die-hard feminist, she remained entirely unaware of the global feminist movement gaining momentum around her.

She understood the power of education and wanted her sisters to have the opportunities she had been given. To ensure their schooling, she sacrificed her own studies. Unlike her female siblings, she was fortunate—her father had sent her to secondary school. As a clerk, she worked with an unwavering determination to finance their education.

Beyond her professional life, my mother was steadfast in her commitment to discipline and learning—not just for her own children but for everyone under her roof. Every morning, she left for work at 7 a.m. and returned by 2:30 p.m., just as we got home from school. After lunch and a brief moment of play, she would sit at her sewing machine or prepare seeds for planting on the farm. Yet, no matter how busy she was, she always made time to check our schoolwork as soon as we walked through the door.

Each day, she meticulously reviewed our books, correcting our mistakes and adding her own lessons. It didn't take her long to notice if we hadn't paid attention in class. And if we failed her sums or struggled with our English homework, the consequences were immediate. Her cane was never far, and a mistake meant several stinging strokes on the palms. We despised that cane and hid it more than once in hopes of avoiding punishment, but this only made us more determined to stay on her good side.

Once she was confident in our academic progress, she began teaching us lessons beyond our school curriculum. Even though these were new topics, she didn't go easy on us if we failed. Her high expectations pushed us to study harder, knowing full well that discipline was never far behind.

I remember my sister being so good at spelling that it sometimes annoyed my mother. Before she could finish calling out a word, my sister had already spelled it—correctly too!

"Wait until I finish!" she would scream in frustration. We never quite understood her reactions. Even when we brought home good reports from school, we never knew what to expect. At times, it felt like she didn't like us or was angry for reasons we couldn't grasp. But there was nowhere to run.

We laughed secretly behind her back, yet we were often left scarred by her unpredictability. There was a nagging feeling that we were never quite good enough—that we always had to do more, be better. The fear was real, but so too was our sense of progress. She knew we were learning, and that was always her goal.

Dedicated girls' schools were scarce. After QRC was established in 1956, Saker Baptist College in Limbe and Our Lady of Lourdes College in Mankon, Bamenda, followed years later. However, the number of female students in these schools remained notably low. It wasn't just a matter of tradition—school fees were a significant barrier for many families. Determined to secure an education for her sisters, she enrolled them in government schools, and she succeeded.

The influence of colonial authorities shaped Cameroon's educational landscape during this period. The curriculum was designed to serve the needs of the colonial administration, with little regard for the educational aspirations of the local population.

Resource constraints posed additional challenges. Schools lacked adequate infrastructure, trained teachers, and educational materials.

Traditional beliefs and practices further hindered girls' education. Early marriages and societal expectations that girls should prioritize household responsibilities often discouraged families from sending their daughters to school.

Despite these obstacles, individuals and organizations recognized the importance of girls' education and actively advocated for its expansion. Efforts were made to establish more mixed schools and raise awareness of the value of female education.

In the decades that followed, progress was made in improving access to education for girls and women in Cameroon, though gender disparities persisted. Ongoing efforts have led to increased enrollment and greater educational opportunities for women across the country.

23

Entrepreneurial spirit

In the fascinating story of my mother's life, her entrepreneurial spirit stood as a beacon of resourcefulness. A single parent and a government clerk by day, her ambitions extended far beyond the confines of an office desk. She fearlessly ventured into the world of small businesses, where her determination knew no bounds.

For years, my mother effortlessly juggled multiple entrepreneurial pursuits, ensuring a steady stream of additional income. Through sheer dedication, she achieved financial milestones that even combined household incomes often struggled to reach.

In Clerks' Quarters, she nurtured a diverse array of small businesses. However, when we moved to a new home, many of these ventures were either liquidated or phased out. The limited space around our new house made farming impossible, ending her vegetable sales. No more early mornings at the market with basins of *okongobong*, bitterleaf, or cocoa leaves—we had truly embraced city life.

Likewise, the sale of *moi moi*, the white bean pudding that once filled our courtyard in Clerks' Quarters with its enticing aroma, had ceased. The noisy grating of Peak Milk cans

Entrepreneurial spirit

on concrete—our improvised method in the absence of a can opener—was no more. My mother had taken on the task of tutoring my siblings after school, making it impossible to continue that business.

Amidst these transitions, only one enterprise remained steadfast, anchoring our family's financial stability—her trusty sewing machine. Day and night, whenever the opportunity arose, she sat at that machine, tirelessly producing an array of jumpers. Her sales team consisted entirely of her children and sisters, who lived with her. Anyone who came to stay under her roof automatically became a marketing agent. You didn't get a choice!

My mother's entrepreneurial spirit remained unwavering. Through sheer tenacity, relentless pursuit of opportunity, and mastery of her sewing machine, she continued to carve out a path to a better life for herself and all of us. At every stage of her journey, she embarked on a new venture—one of the most remarkable being real estate. Her first step into this world began on Mbende Street in Limbe, where she built a modest two-bedroom house, part of which she rented out. Though she eventually sold the property, it marked the beginning of her real estate odyssey.

Several years after we moved to Clerks' Quarters, opportunity knocked again. A house on Kala Street—just off Church Street—became available. Mr. Kebai, the owner, was preparing to relocate to the UK with his family and needed to sell quickly. Without hesitation, my mother seized the chance and paid for the property in cash. Her years of diligent saving had prepared her for this moment.

The house on Kala Street was no ordinary duplex—it comprised two spacious apartments, larger than any home she or her children had ever known. At the time, I was thirteen and away at boarding school in Okoyong, Mamfe. The thought of returning home for the holidays to such a grand and expansive residence was beyond exciting. More than just a home, the second apartment provided rental income, marking yet another entrepreneurial triumph for my mother.

Real estate had truly captivated my mother's entrepreneurial spirit. While living on Kala Street, she made a bold move by purchasing a duplex in Mamfe town. In time, she sold part of it to a cousin living in the United States, cementing her legacy as a shrewd and visionary investor.

Throughout her journey, she remained a beacon of resilience and adaptability, determined to build a better future for herself and her family—one venture at a time.

Kala Street was a place of constant motion, where an eclectic blend of sights and sounds spilled right into your living room. Music blared from towering loudspeakers on the bustling main road—Church Street—creating an atmosphere that never truly quieted. As the heart of Limbe's business district, the street was lined with shops, mostly owned by Nigerians, catering to every possible need.

Cosmetic stores, tire sales and replacement shops, and provision stores overflowing with essentials filled the area. Music shops offered the latest tunes, where customers could even record their own songs onto cassette tapes. Off-license bars, despite government regulations requiring a 600-meter spacing, stood shoulder to shoulder, capitalizing on the daily revelry that often led to drunken stupors. The unmistakable sight of commercial phone booths only added to the street's electric persona.

Just across Kala Street, on the other side of Church Street, my mother found an unexpected lifelong friend—Josephine, a married Nigerian woman with eight children, including a set of triplets. Like my mother, she defied the odds, juggling multiple businesses to provide for her family. Their bond ran deeper than mere friendship; it was built on shared struggles, unwavering faith, and the indomitable spirit of two women determined to carve their own paths in a world filled with obstacles.

Josephine was an unsung hero in my mother's life. She never sought the spotlight, yet her quiet influence was profound. As I reflect on her story, I realize that wisdom and strength aren't always measured by formal education. Sometimes, they are defined by an unshakable commitment to family and an unrelenting drive to survive.

24

The Journey of the Ibeagha Family

* * *

Sylvester Ikeokwu Ibeagha hailed from Umuonyeka in Ifite-Oraifite, Ekwusigo Local Government Area of Anambra State, Nigeria. Born on December 31, 1932, he pursued studies in secretarial work in Eastern Nigeria. Upon graduation, he secured employment as an Accounting Clerk at the United African Company (UAC) in Jos. Later, he was transferred to serve as the manager of the Obudu Cattle Ranch in Obudu, Cross River State, Nigeria. It was during this time that the Nigerian Civil War broke out, finding him in Calabar.

Josephine Chineze Nwagu was born on July 24, 1942, in Warri. She came from Ibolo, Okponunoh, in Ekwusigo Local Government Area, Anambra State, Nigeria. Her father worked as an engineer at Water Works and was later transferred from Warri to Kaduna. Josephine was the second of eight children—two boys and six girls. She attended Our Lady's High School in Kaduna for her primary education, completing Standard Six and earning her elementary certificate. For secondary school, she went to Queen of Apostles Secondary School in Kakuri, Kaduna, Northern Nigeria, now known as St. Amina Secondary School. At the time, the school was a strictly Catholic institution run by Irish Reverend Sisters.

Josephine and Sylvester first met in Kaduna through the Oraifite Tribal Group, where both were active members. It wasn't long before they realized they wanted to spend their lives together. Their union was solemnized in 1950 at St. Joseph's Catholic Church in Kaduna. They welcomed their first three children—Christian Ogoh, Jane, and Anthony—in Jos. Later, Aloysius was born in Mamfe, Cameroon, followed by Pauline, Peter, and Paul (triplets), as well as Pascal and Gerald, in Victoria (now Limbe), Cameroon.

The Ibeagha family's journey from Jos to Mamfe was fraught with emotion and uncertainty as they navigated the tumultuous landscape of the Civil War era. Sylvester was the General Manager at the Obudu Cattle Ranch when the Biafra conflict erupted in 1967. With his pregnant wife, three children—Christian Ogoh, Jane, and Anthony—along with Aunty Uju, Uncle Jerome, and several others, they embarked on a perilous journey into the unknown, desperate to escape the war.

Abandoning everything they knew, the family and their companions traversed the rugged terrain of the Kaginga Hills, making their way on foot toward Akwaya in Cameroon. There, amidst the looming shadow of war, they found refuge under the compassionate gaze of the Divisional Officer, a man who had once benefited from Sylvester's generosity during his visits to the ranch.

Life in the refugee camp was marked by hardship and adversity, yet the Ibeagha family remained resilient. Their spirits were buoyed by the kindness of strangers as they clung to hope, waiting for an opportunity to continue their journey to Mamfe.

Years later, Josephine—now affectionately known as Mami Ibeagha—recounted the story to my mother, sharing a vivid memory of their departure from the camp and an incident when

Ogoh lost his coat on the way. A faint smile crossed her face, as if the memory still carried a trace of the old tension.

"He just couldn't let it go," she said in Pidgin English, shaking her head. "It had barely dropped, and the water took it away. Ogoh bolted like that coat was his lifeline." Her voice softened as she recalled the scene. "I had to grab him, hold him back with all my strength. 'No, you can't go after it!' I kept saying, but he wouldn't listen. His eyes were locked on that coat, floating away like nothing else mattered." She mimicked the way he had struggled in her grip, arms flailing, feet pushing forward. 'Let me go, Mma! I need to get it!' he kept shouting. "But I knew the water was too strong, too dangerous." She chuckled softly, though her eyes still held traces of the worry she had felt that day. "It was like trying to hold back a storm. He was so determined—my little boy, thinking he could outrun the water." The anguish of his loss, as he cried loudly, mirrored the collective pain and sorrow that weighed heavily on our family's shoulders as we pressed onward.

Their arduous trek to Mamfe spanned two grueling days, each step a testament to their unwavering determination to reach safety. In Mamfe, Josephine engaged in small-scale commerce, selling fried snacks and oranges sourced from Ntenako, Ndekwai, and Ossing villages, while her husband traded in various goods. It was in this environment that they welcomed their fourth child, a son named Aloysius.

Recognizing Sylvester's remarkable abilities, the Mill Hill Missionary Fathers, led by Reverend Father John Molenar, transferred him to Bota in Victoria to manage the Catholic Procure. There, he excelled in sourcing and distributing a wide range of religious articles across the ecclesiastical province of Bamenda.

While Sylvester served at the Procure, Josephine collaborated with the Holy Rosary Sisters at Mount Mary in Buea, successfully overseeing the Vocational Training Centre.

In 1970, Josephine gave birth to twins, and a few years later, to triplets: Pauline, Peter, and Paul. The birth of the twins following the triplets marked a profound chapter in their family's journey.

At this turning point, Sylvester decided to part ways with the church. He left his role at the Catholic Procure to embark on a new venture, establishing the Cameroon Book Centre in Down Beach, Victoria. Meanwhile, Josephine seized the opportunity to cultivate her entrepreneurial spirit and launched her own business as a seamstress. Through dedication and hard work, she not only honed her craft but also mentored numerous young girls, equipping them with invaluable skills for their future.

However, the winds of change swept through their lives in 1989 when an economic crisis forced Sylvester to downsize his bookshop operations and eventually close its doors for good. Undeterred, Josephine courageously shouldered the responsibility of sustaining the family. She diversified her talents, selling a delectable array of fries, pastries, and cakes, becoming a familiar presence not only in the local markets of Victoria but also in numerous schools.

Through her tireless efforts, she ensured an educated and prosperous future for her children, who received a top-tier Catholic education in colleges across the ecclesiastical province of Bamenda. The Ibeagha family's journey took another turn in 1990 when Sylvester made the difficult decision to relocate to Port Harcourt, Nigeria. He felt the need to return home. Meanwhile, after securing a home in Cassava Farms, Victoria, Josephine chose to remain in Cameroon, later relocating to Wotutu, near Bonjongo. There, she adeptly managed her household, overseeing every aspect with precision and care. However, in 1998, she made the significant decision to move to Nigeria and later to the United States, where she joined her children who had relocated there. It was the beginning of a new chapter in her life. Sylvester spent the remainder of his days in Nigeria, eventually passing away on June 10, 1996, in Rumuomasi, Port Harcourt, Rivers State, at the age of sixty-four. As of September 2024, Mami Ibeagha continues to live in the United States.

25

My mother and Josephine, and the Bonds of Friendship

***

Josephine, much like my mother, shared a vision centered on her children's academic success and their independence. Her life was a testament to the enduring power of self-sacrifice, hard work, and the undying love for her family.

She was a remarkable woman, not by society's conventional standards, but by the qualities that truly matter. Standing tall yet small in stature, Josephine embodied toughness and resilience. She had weathered the storm of the Biafran war, like countless other Nigerians, and found herself in Victoria. It was on Church Street that my mother and Josephine's paths crossed.

The Catholic church in New Town, about a ten-minute walk from either of their homes, was the cornerstone of their connection. A place where their friendship blossomed, Josephine was a faithful member of the congregation, and my mother, equally devoted, found solace and strength in the bonds forged within those hallowed church walls.

At the back of Josephine's home, a stark contrast to the brilliant African sunshine, was a dingy and sun-starved area. This is where the magic happened. It's difficult to fathom the transformation that occurred within those walls, from the dark recesses to the world outside.

Josephine was known as the Iron Lady, crafting her own path to success, often under the dimmest of lights—both natural and artificial—in her backyard. In this space, ducks found a home and usually ate from the trash. Because the backyard lacked good drainage, there was often dirty standing water that needed to be regularly swept to eliminate mosquitoes and their larvae.

But with an unyielding determination, she produced and sold an array of products, including fish pies, beef pies, and the iconic "Alaska" lollipops (available in red, yellow, pink, green, and blue) that were beloved by children and adults alike. She was a culinary artist who created delicacies that would tantalize taste buds and warm hearts.

In the same household, Josephine's husband, a man of quiet demeanor and slow, deliberate movements, ran the bookshop. Their partnership was a silent symphony of strength. He provided didactic materials to eager young minds, and together, they sustained their family with hard-earned income.

Josephine's lack of formal higher education didn't deter her from nurturing dreams of academic excellence for her children. Her focus on their education was unwavering, a beacon of hope in a world that often prioritized formal learning. She understood that the value of education wasn't solely confined to textbooks and classrooms; it was also about instilling the virtues of hard work and perseverance.

Her legacy was etched in her children's academic achievements. Their success was a testament to the values she upheld: dedication, hard work, and unwavering commitment to family. They carried forward the torch of resilience that Josephine had ignited, proving that one's worth isn't determined solely by the degrees on their walls but by the love, dedication, and sacrifices

My mother and Josephine, and the Bonds of Friendship

made for the ones they hold dear.

In Josephine, my mother found not just a best friend, but a kindred spirit. The two were inseparable in many ways, often seen trekking together to church, where they spent mornings on the church grounds and evenings at meetings for the Legion of Mary or other church activities. They were both fiercely independent, dedicated to their children, their faith, and their community, though each approached life in her own way.

Josephine, always a step ahead in business, was the more entrepreneurial of the two. She encouraged my mother to get back into petty trading, seeing the potential for her to thrive in it again. But my mother, ever practical, would often respond, "I just don't have the space for it in the house on Kalla Street."

Their friendship, however, was marked by more than just advice on business or family matters—it was shaped by my mother's careful attention to appearances.

Though they shared a close bond, my mother remained conscious of not appearing too intimate with Josephine. As an unmarried woman with kids, she didn't want to give anyone the impression that she envied or admired marriage, despite Josephine's quiet husband always being home after work.

While Josephine was generous with her time and affection, my mother maintained a boundary, careful not to visit too often or spend too much time in conversation. She felt it was important to maintain a certain distance, both out of respect for Josephine's household and to avoid any gossip that might arise from their closeness.

Still, their bond remained strong, and their conversations often revolved around their children's education and which schools would provide the best opportunities for them. Josephine, who was more outgoing in the community, gave my mother advice on navigating both motherhood and business.

However, my mother, with her quiet strength, was determined to set clear boundaries around their relationship.

Despite this cautious distance, their friendship was a cornerstone in my mother's life—two women, strong in their faith and deeply committed to their families, walking side by side through the challenges of motherhood. Their connection wasn't just about companionship; it was about building something bigger—for their children, their community, and their own growth, while remaining steadfast in their individual values.

As I reflect on Mami Ibeagha's life and how she influenced my mother, I'm reminded that sometimes the most extraordinary stories are hidden in the unassuming lives of people like her. With her unflagging determination, she left an indelible mark on the hearts of those who knew her, a mark that continues to inspire and shape the lives of her children and their children's children.

26

A Mother's Triumph
My Wedding Day

* * *

It was in the house in Mile Four that I got married. By then, my sister, Elizabeth, was completing her PhD in Physiotherapy in Ibadan, Nigeria. My brother was finishing his studies at Lagos University in Chemical Engineering. My sister, Vivian, was preparing to join the convent. She did make it into the convent, and my mother, together with us, Vivian's siblings, were there to drop her off in Buea. Later on, she decided that life in a convent was not for her and left. My mom then sponsored her studies in the United Kingdom. My brother, Eric, was a high school student at Government High School in Limbe at the time.

My wedding day wasn't just a significant moment for me—it was a deeply personal victory for my mother. As a single parent, she had endured years of whispers and judgment from those who believed that, because she was unmarried, her children would face difficulties in finding their life partners. But on this special day, she stood proud, putting to shame all those who had doubted her and mocked her in the past. My wedding was more than a celebration of love between my husband, Victor, and me—it was a testament to my mother's grit.

Though she had chosen to remain single, a decision she had never wavered on, the gossip had always circled her. People couldn't understand her independence or how she managed to raise her children so successfully on her own. And yet, here we were, on the day of my wedding, proving that her choices hadn't held us back. If anything, her determination had propelled us forward.

In the weeks leading to my wedding, my mother threw herself into the preparations, with her sisters by her side. They made sure everything was perfect for the little things their side of the family had to do. From my wedding dress, bridesmaids' dresses, and the rest of the bridal train to other small items that would complete the ceremony. She was filled with joy at the thought of seeing me start this new chapter in my life, knowing that despite all the odds, we had arrived at this moment with our heads held high.

Naturally, there was tension between my mother and my future mother-in-law. My mother felt that, given the greater resources on their side, they should handle the majority of the wedding expenses without seeking her contribution. At the end of the day, they found a compromise and came together for a beautiful wedding.

The ceremony was held at the Catholic Church in New Town, Limbe. Relatives traveled from near and far to witness the event. My grandmother, always a strong presence in our family, was there too. My Big Papa was too sick to make the trip from Mamfe. And though my father, who walked me down the aisle, took center stage for that part of the ceremony, my mother didn't mind. She stood back quietly, her heart swollen with pride. After all, this moment was a culmination of her hard work, her love, and her unwavering dedication.

After the church service, Victor and I, along with the rest

A Mother's Triumph

of the guests and family on both sides, moved to the CDC Bota Club grounds by the sea for the reception. The ocean breeze mingled with laughter and music as friends and family joined us in celebration. A gala followed the reception at the same venue, where we danced into the night.

Through it all, my mother remained the pillar of strength and grace she had always been to me. Watching her that day, it was clear to everyone just how proud she was—not just of me, but of the life she had built for us. Her joy was infectious, and her quiet victory over those who had doubted her was evident in the way she carried herself.

My wedding wasn't just the beginning of my new life—it was also a moment of triumph for my mother. A day that silenced the naysayers and proved that her choices, her independence, and her resilience were not only valid but powerful. It was her day as much as it was mine, a celebration of the love and strength that had brought us that far.

My grandmother, Big Mami, Biggie, Eli-Akwa

My Mum, Suzie and my grandmother, Bigmami Elizabeth on vacation in the US

Two inseparable women, my mum, (Suzie) and my grandmum, (Elizabeth)

My mum and her sister, Florence

There were three girls before the two boys were born. Tricia, Elizabeth and Vivian

Reme's children as teenagers. This is what our family photos looked like

Big Papa's siblings and relatives were mostly all giants. He is seated on the left in a suit. He was the most successful and took care of all of them and their children.

House on Main street as it looks today. It's become more of a business location

Big Mami's kitchen. The last door on the left was her kitchen, and at one point served as her primary room where she lived with her children. The photo also shows part of the courtyard.

The stairs at the back of the house and part of the courtyard as is today

Big Papa bought a car, the first in Mamfe.
He traded it later as he aged for a bicycle

Left, Big Papa's statue in front of one of
the houses he built, Ntenako Village,
Mamfe
Top, Some relatives who live in the house
in Ntenako pose behind Big Papa's statue

Some women who lived in Clerks' Quarters at the time. My mom is seated second from the right on the front row

Victor and I at our wedding at the Catholic Church, New Town, Limbe

Cutting the cake at our wedding

My proud mother at my wedding

My mum and I at my brother's wedding in Cocamonga, CA

My siblings, left to right, Vivian and Elizabeth, at Jubilant's wedding (Cousin, Eku Ekukanju)

Mum with her grandchildren, Ekong, Eku, Akap, Ayamo, and son, Jubilant

27

Our House at Kalla Street

* * *

Since Limbe was a coastal town, there was enough sea breeze throughout the day. In the night, the ships coming into berth would sound a longhorn, and we knew there was a new ship coming in.

After purchasing the house on Kalla Street and settling in, my mother immediately began transforming it into our new home. We moved in just before the rainy season, narrowly escaping the yearly floods that plagued our old place in Clerks' Quarters. The new house was a definite upgrade—it had three bedrooms, and both the kitchen and bathroom were inside. My mother wasted no time completing the half-finished wall surrounding the property, determined to make it feel secure and complete.

With only one bathroom, we had to be organized. My mother set up a schedule, or "roster," for us to take turns each morning. If we ever ran out of soap, we used our imagination, pretending to scrub with soap anyway. Charcoal became a makeshift substitute for toothpaste when necessary—one of the many ways we learned to adapt to life's challenges. Despite the changes, much of our routine stayed the same as it had been in Clerks' Quarters.

One noticeable difference, though, was the distance to school.

It was longer now, but at least we no longer had to make trips to the market before heading to class. The new house represented more than just a roof over our heads; it was the beginning of a more stable chapter in our lives.

Air conditioning was a luxury in Limbe and was seldom sought after; most residents scarcely contemplated its acquisition. Instead, doors and windows remained ajar, inviting in the warm embrace of the day and the warm sea breeze until nightfall, when they were dutifully secured, primarily to ward off the intrusion of mosquitoes. In those times, concerns over security and theft were relatively low, offering a tranquil residential contrast to other parts of the country.

Upon completing my studies at QRC Okoyong, Mamfe, I proceeded to the next chapter of my education at Government High School in Down Beach, Limbe. A daily journey to school on foot, extending over a kilometer, was a considerable contrast to the brisk walk of less than half a kilometer from Clerks' Quarters. Our new surroundings were characterized by the presence of brothels, a matter that weighed upon my mother's mind. She took the initiative to erect a protective wall around our home, driven by a genuine desire for peace of mind.

The brothels predominantly operated during the late hours, while we, the residents of the household, remained mostly ensconced in the embrace of slumber. In our home, obedience and decorum reigned supreme, as there was no inclination among us to engage in prying or seeking out untoward pursuits. Our lives were marked by a serene adherence to routine, far removed from the intrigues that unfolded beyond our walls.

Kalla Street was a step up the social ladder. My mother knew where she wanted to be in her life, and she wanted her kids to be as educated as possible. She never put on airs of any kind. She had no personal life. Her life was entwined with that of her kids. Her happiness lay in seeing her children grow up in good health and doing well in school. She constantly strained and stressed herself, willing to do any amount of work to achieve her goals. She raised her five children, as well as her sisters and other external family and non-family. At one point, 13 people were living in a cramped 2-bedroom house in Clerks' Quarters run by a single parent. So, she never really had loneliness or emotional issues. She was so preoccupied with her household and her job.

She had all the right accolades. She was very hard-working, very meticulous, and extremely well-organized. Every project or plan would be written down in detail and followed to the letter. The house was very tightly run. All expenditures were written down daily, weekly, monthly, and even yearly. Written down and strictly followed. Every penny counted and was accounted for. Expenses were strictly tracked, monitored, and often revised multiple times.

She grew most of her food. What she could not grow, she bought in bulk at discounted prices. Milk, soap, Ovaltine, tea, sugar, flour, margarine, etc. She saved every single penny from her meager salary in the bank and kept a savings book till her dying day. At a time when many people never wore used clothing, it was normal for us. She collected unused school uniforms from her neighbors, patched them up neatly, and gave them to us as house clothes. She sewed our Sunday outfits and ensured they became hand-me-downs, progressing from the larger ones to the smaller ones.

On Saturday mornings, we woke up to the sounds of Jim Reeves.

"We thank thee each morning."

"I'd rather have Jesus"

"This world is not my home"

Followed by a series of songs and culminating in "It pays to serve Jesus, I speak from my heart…" There was no other choice. After her series of personal choices, which sometimes included Prince Nico Mbarga and Mary McGregor, she tuned the radio to Saturday Morning Request from Radio Buea.

My mother's love for the radio was palpable, evident in the three sets strategically placed throughout our home. Each radio had its unique purpose, adding layers to the soundtrack of our daily lives.

The centerpiece was the radio in the living room, a versatile device that doubled as a cassette player. It served as the hub of entertainment, filling the air with music, news, and stories. Whether it was the soothing melodies of local tunes or the captivating dramas aired on the radio, our living room resonated with the vibrant sounds emanating from this cherished device.

In the bedroom, a smaller radio held a special place, coming to life only in the early mornings after her prayers. As the soft glow of dawn crept through the curtains, the radio's gentle hum would signal the start of a new day, accompanied by the melodic tunes that ushered in the morning light.

But it was the third radio, the portable one, that truly encapsulated my mother's unwavering companionship with the radio. With this device in hand, she was free to carry music and stories with her, whether bustling around the house or tending to errands just outside. It became a constant presence, weaving its melodies into the fabric of her daily routine.

Weekday mornings were marked by the familiar voice declaring, "This is the BBC in London." As an adult living away from home, this iconic jingle stirred deep emotions, evoking memories of childhood. That simple tune transported me back to the warmth of our living room, where the comforting embrace of family surrounded me.

As evening descended, a certain serenity enveloped our home, punctuated by the melodic strains of songs emanating from the radio. It was a ritual—a time to unwind and reflect on the day's events before bedtime. The radio became more than just a source of entertainment; it was a companion that soothed our souls and connected us to the world beyond our walls.

Despite the advent of television, the picture box never quite found its place in our household. The radio held sway over our hearts, its enchanting melodies and captivating stories woven into the tapestry of our lives. It remained a constant presence—a source of comfort and joy, proof of my mother's enduring love for life's simple pleasures, which quietly concealed deeper emotional struggles.

28

Her Workplace and the Coming of Francophones

* * *

After clerical school, my mother was recruited into the civil service, where she worked for the Produce Marketing Board (PMB) until 1975. PMB was a structure that was later transformed into the National Produce Marketing Board before being shut down. The late 1960s and the 1970s were periods of intense political activity in Cameroon right after independence.

The suppression of the federation in 1972 saw an influx of Francophones from the other side of the Mungo to work in Victoria, which was renamed Limbe. Their arrival had a significant impact on the lives of the indigenous people. Before then, English was the only official language spoken in Southern Cameroons.

Their arrival felt as if the English colonizers had been replaced by other colonizers, only this time they were fellow Cameroonians. They did not come to work and live in Limbe as farmers or petty traders; they were, for the most part, department heads, chiefs of services, and bosses.

Francophones, who had earlier come to Southern Cameroons, were those who had escaped the violence of what came to be known as the time of the "Maquis." This was a period of political instability in the neighboring French territory as the local inhabitants agitated for independence from France. Those who fled the ensuing violence were mainly from the Bassa, Bamileke, and Ewondo communities. They arrived in the region in their personal capacities and integrated well into the local community. They soon learned to speak English and sent their children to English-speaking schools.

However, those who came later as bosses made little or no attempt to speak English, preferring to maintain a haughty attitude typical of a domineering power. No sooner had they settled than they decided that they needed to maintain their identities. They requested French-speaking schools for their children, and the government complied.

With the newcomers refusing to speak English, the local people were thus forced to learn, or at least strive to understand, French, not only to accommodate them but also to qualify for promotions in the civil service. This shift in the social, economic, and political dynamics in the region was very significant and was especially felt in the linguistic landscape, where a considerable communication barrier arose between them and English-speaking Southern Cameroonians. This, in turn, impacted the social and economic interactions between the two communities, leading to mistrust and suspicion. My mother, for example, refused to go beyond the word "Bonjour," and she was not alone. She reasoned that they were the newcomers and should make more efforts in communication, but the balance was in their favor.

The social and political marginalization of English-speaking Southern Cameroonians also had significant political consequences. With the arrival of the Francophones, the political power dynamics in Southern Cameroons shifted, with the Francophones dominating political appointments and government positions.

Her Workplace and the Coming of Francophones

Economically, the landscape of Southern Cameroons underwent significant changes, driven by governmental policies that encouraged businesses to relocate to Douala, which was touted as the economic capital due to its larger population and purportedly better business prospects. This directive, however, was met with resistance by many entrepreneurs who were deeply rooted in their communities and hesitant to uproot their operations.

Despite the government's persuasion, a considerable number of businesses opted to remain in Southern Cameroons, reluctant to abandon the thriving structures they had painstakingly established. However, for those who acquiesced and relocated to Douala, the aftermath was often a stark downward spiral, followed by oblivion.

Once-proud enterprises like Atabong Enterprises and Neba Automobiles, giants of Southern Cameroons' economy, found themselves adrift in a sea of unfamiliarity—new language, new culture, new hurdles at every turn. What had once thrived on familiar soil now struggled to take root in this foreign land, stumbling through the storms of fierce competition, logistical nightmares, and even laws that seemed alien. The familiar touch of English law, once the foundation of business in Southern Cameroons, gave way to the complexities of the French legal system—leaving many business leaders feeling lost in an unfamiliar maze.

The exodus left ripples of loss in its wake, a quiet mourning for what once was. The flourishing businesses that lined the streets of Southern Cameroons, bustling with life and promise, now stood closed or diminished. The mighty Yoke Power Plant, whose hum had lit the lives of so many, went still and dark. The West Cameroon Lottery, once a beacon of hope and anticipation, disappeared without a trace. And the fate of once-vibrant institutions—NPMB, Cameroon Bank, the Wum Area Development

Authority—grew uncertain, their futures dimmed like forgotten embers.

Even the very laws of the land had shifted beneath their feet, as the familiar rhythms of English common law gave way to the unfamiliar cadences of the French legal system, adding yet another layer of disorientation to an already tempestuous transition. The very soul of the land seemed to pause, caught between what it had been and what it was becoming.

The closure of vital infrastructural projects, such as the Powercam and the Santa Coffee Estate, dealt a heavy blow to the region's economy, leaving communities reeling from the loss of employment opportunities and economic stability. Even transportation hubs like the Bali, Besongabang, and Tiko airports, once bustling with activity, became mere relics of a bygone era.

The impact of these closures reverberated throughout Southern Cameroons, leaving a palpable sense of loss and uncertainty in its wake. The once-thriving business landscape had been irrevocably altered, as communities grappled with the aftermath of relocation and the disappearance of longstanding institutions.

Yet, amidst the upheaval, there were also stories of resilience and determination as individuals and communities sought to adapt to the new economic realities. While the scars of this unstable period may linger, the spirit of Southern Cameroons endured. The linguistic barrier, economic domination, and political marginalization led to a decline in the economic status and political power of English-speaking Southern Cameroonians. This initiated a deep sense of mistrust and suspicion between the two communities that continues to impact the region and its people to this day.

Ahidjo's regime was marked by authoritarianism and iron-fisted rule. The English-speaking regions of Cameroon, comprising about 20% of the population, were particularly vulnerable to his regime. The government's policy suppressed any dissent or criticism, often targeting English-speaking Cameroonians, who were accustomed to open expression, for persecution and harassment.

The regime imposed strict media censorship, making it difficult for English-speaking Cameroonians to voice their concerns and grievances. Another tactic was sowing fear and division among the English-speaking population by pitting different groups against each other and creating a climate of suspicion and mistrust. The regime also encouraged false rumors and propaganda, further fueling tensions and anxieties.

Perhaps the most insidious aspect of the regime's campaign of terror was how it made English-speaking Cameroonians fear even their own shadows. The constant threat of arrest and detention, combined with the pervasive climate of fear and intimidation, prevented people from speaking out or organizing any kind of protest against the regime. Even innocuous activities, such as gathering in public places or speaking to strangers, could be perceived as potential threats to the regime's stability and security.

Before independence, reports indicate that Ibo traders from Nigeria berated English-speaking Cameroonians inside Cameroon, causing them to fear going to markets or buying from Ibo traders. Various factors contributed to this situation, including cultural differences, economic competition, and historical tensions between the two groups. People complained about their treatment when they asked for the price of an item from an Ibo trader. Many felt forced to make purchases. Ultimately, a significant factor driving Southern Cameroonians' rejection of joining Nigeria stemmed from their perception of mistreatment and domination by Nigerians. However, the Francophones proved equally disappointing, as their suffocating mindset permeated a larger population and maintained a tighter grip on the region.

With Francophones, there was no fostering of a culture of respect and understanding, nor a desire to build stronger, more resilient communities better equipped to face modern challenges.

In contrasting work approaches, Anglophones and Francophones displayed marked differences in their outlook toward work. Anglophones exhibited discipline and principled behaviors, valuing correctness and moral uprightness at all times as a source of pride. Their communication was straightforward; "yay" meant agreement, and "nay" indicated disagreement. Clarity prevailed in their interactions.

At one of the sub-regional offices of the Ministry of Commerce, my mom encountered Francophones for the first time. She thoroughly enjoyed her job, although we didn't always grasp its intricacies. She told us stories of how she would discuss office challenges with her colleagues and her boss to find solutions collectively. But she said the Francophones, especially her boss, were cunning.

Occasionally, she shared anecdotes from her office. One memorable incident involved a document for her signature, which she refused to sign, insisting it did not meet standards and would compromise her integrity. This decision left her anxious throughout the day, caught between her commitment to following rules and the perceived necessity to bend them for career advancement.

However, she typically compartmentalized work and personal life, with her office just a five-minute walk from our home in Clerks' Quarters. Whether due to proximity or her conscientiousness, she unfailingly arrived at the office by 7 a.m. We often departed together since our schools were merely ten minutes away, and hers was a brief six-minute walk.

Her narratives changed somewhat with new Francophone

Her Workplace and the Coming of Francophones

colleagues. Her stories increasingly included interactions with them, providing vivid anecdotes that highlighted their distinctive behaviors and attitudes. Among the most notable traits she observed was their tendency to arrive late to work, with meetings and appointments often starting later than scheduled, which caused her considerable frustration. This cultural norm of being fashionably late clashed with her own adherence to punctuality, leading to moments of exasperation and impatience.

Furthermore, she noticed a general reluctance among her Francophone counterparts to adhere to structured protocols and procedures. Whether following office guidelines or established rules and regulations, there seemed to be a certain flexibility and adaptability that sometimes bordered on disregard. This laissez-faire attitude towards protocols often left her and her other Anglophone colleagues feeling bewildered, as she struggled to reconcile it with her sense of professionalism and discipline.

Additionally, she couldn't help but notice their willingness to circumvent rules and regulations whenever possible, finding shortcuts or loopholes to navigate around obstacles. While she admired their resourcefulness and ingenuity to some extent, she also couldn't shake off the discomfort of witnessing such practices, fearing the potential consequences for the integrity of their work and the organization as a whole.

This disdain for certain practices prevalent among her Francophone colleagues gradually contributed to her aversion to speaking French in professional settings. She feared that immersing herself too deeply in their culture and way of thinking might inadvertently influence her own mindset and professional demeanor. As a result, she often opted to communicate in English, a language she felt more comfortable with and which better aligned with her own values and principles. She struggled to find common ground as she tried to forge stronger working relationships, but she consistently failed to succeed in this effort.

In the bustling world of commerce and as the chief of the bureau, my mother stood out as a symbol of fairness. Working in an environment dominated by Francophones, she faced unique challenges that required not only professionalism but also a deep sense of community. Many of her French-speaking colleagues, entrenched in their ways, resisted communicating in English despite working in a predominantly English-speaking region. This linguistic barrier created palpable tension with the Nigerian traders, who comprised the majority of the business community.

The traders, particularly shop owners, often voiced their frustrations about my mother's French colleagues. Allegations of extortion and exploitative practices were rife, and these grievances fueled a growing resentment within the community. Yet, amidst this discord, my mother managed to earn the respect and love of the very people her colleagues alienated.

From the very beginning, my mother's approach was different. She treated the traders with respect, making a genuine effort to understand their needs and concerns. Her warmth and openness became her hallmark, setting her apart from her colleagues. As she climbed the professional ladder and eventually became "Chef de Bureau," her leadership style only reinforced her reputation as a fair and approachable leader.

While many of her colleagues sought personal gain through kickbacks and bribes, her steadfastness endeared her to the Nigerian businesspeople. While others demanded envelopes of money to expedite processes or turn a blind eye, my mother didn't. She was rewarded at the end of the year by these traders with bags of rice, cooking oil, sugar, and other daily necessities—a traditional token of appreciation that symbolized gratitude rather than obligation. These items were carefully preserved and would sometimes last up to 4 months before running out.

Her Workplace and the Coming of Francophones

Shop owners who had long been wary of the system came to trust her. They knew that if she handled their issues, they would receive a fair outcome without the need for under-the-table dealings. Her office, often a place of tension and complaints, became a space where grievances were resolved amicably. Traders would line up, not with trepidation but with confidence that their concerns would be heard. Some even brought small gifts of appreciation—not out of coercion, but out of genuine admiration for a woman who refused to be swept up in the corruption that plagued the system.

My mother's unwavering integrity was not without challenges. She faced criticism from her colleagues, who often viewed her as a traitor. Some tried to discredit her, while others attempted to pressure her into their practices. Yet, she remained resolute, her quiet determination unshaken by the storms around her.

Looking back, her role was more than just a job; it was a testament to the power of integrity and empathy in fostering harmony and trust. Her legacy in that business community endures as a reminder that true leadership is not about titles or power but about the values one upholds and the impact one leaves on the lives of others.

The gossip between her and her Anglophone colleagues ran deep. Every day, she returned home with a fresh story, often filled with criticism of their Francophone counterparts. The Anglophones in the office would make fun of the Francophones, mocking their ways without truly understanding the differences in their systems.

Despite this, misunderstandings fueled suspicions on both sides, creating an atmosphere of division. Efforts to find common ground and forge stronger relationships with her Francophone colleagues were not always successful. The divide was too deeply entrenched, and the gap, though acknowledged, remained a barrier that was never fully bridged.

The Ahidjo regime's repressive tactics, censorship, and fear-mongering had cultivated a persistent atmosphere of uncertainty and anxiety in the country. Today, Ahidjo's legacy serves as a poignant reminder of the imperative to safeguard free speech and protect the rights of minorities within any democracy.

My mother remained dedicated to her position in the same office until her retirement. Her astonishment was palpable when she was promoted to Assistant Chief of Service shortly before her retirement. Interestingly, most Anglophones remained in their existing roles, while Francophones were often appointed to leadership positions.

Despite the challenges and the constant complaints about her colleagues in the office, my mother had a full-time job that she enjoyed going to. For many women, paid employment was a far-off dream. Her job did not depend on the whims and caprices of a husband. Neither were there any expectations of her to prioritize family above all else. She believed she could do both and could make a success of both. She challenged the status quo and successfully redefined her destiny in a world that was not yet ready for change.

The employment landscape remained heavily influenced by colonial policies even after the colonialists had left. Traditional norms and societal expectations further shaped the limited opportunities available to women in the workforce. Most formal-sector jobs, including those in public works, plantations, and administrative roles, were typically reserved for men. This pattern reflected both colonial priorities and prevailing gender expectations.

Education and skills were also significant barriers for women seeking paid work. Access to education and vocational training was unequal, leaving many women without the qualifications necessary for certain jobs. As a result, many women turned to the informal sector as a primary means of generating income. This sector encompassed small-scale trading, food sales, and craft-making, enabling women to earn a living while continuing to fulfill their traditional domestic roles.

Urban centers like Buea offered slightly more employment opportunities, but these positions were often low-paying and came with their challenges. Personal connections and recommendations played a crucial role in securing employment. Over time, significant efforts have contributed to changing societal attitudes and policies regarding women's participation in paid employment.

It is essential to note that the landscape for women seeking employment in Cameroon has undergone significant changes since the 1950s and 1960s. In the decades that followed, progress in gender equality led to more women entering various professions and sectors of the workforce. However, challenges related to gender disparities in employment persist, and efforts to promote women's economic empowerment and equal opportunities remain ongoing.

The business sector reflected a similar pattern. While few women engaged in formal business ventures during that era, many were active in the informal economy. For instance, my mother made clothes after work. Markets were filled with women traders who set up stalls to sell a diverse array of goods, including food, clothing, and household items. Market trading provided a crucial source of income, enabling women to support their families.

Many women also honed their craft skills, creating handmade items such as baskets, mats, and pottery. These goods were sold in local markets or directly to individual customers.

Sewing skills were another valuable asset. Women working as

seamstresses and tailors offered clothing alterations and custom tailoring services, particularly in urban centers like Buea and Limbe.

In the area of personal grooming, women managed small beauty salons or offered hairdressing services, often operating from their homes. In rural areas, women played pivotal roles in agriculture and farming, contributing significantly to crop cultivation and food production.

While the number of women involved in large-scale businesses was limited during this period, some entrepreneurial spirits managed small-scale enterprises such as shops, restaurants, hotels, and service-oriented businesses, including laundry and cleaning services.

Though primarily informal and small-scale, these economic activities were vital for the livelihoods of many women and their families. The formal business landscape remained largely dominated by men, with women's roles shaped by traditional gender norms and colonial-era policies. However, over time, women's economic opportunities have expanded, resulting in the emergence of successful businesswomen and entrepreneurs across various sectors.

As we reflect on those times, we honor women like my mother, who defied the norms of their era, proving that there was an alternative to the prescribed path of marriage and subjugation. Their courage and determination paved the way for a shifting society—one that now recognizes women's abilities and contributions beyond the confines of marriage and motherhood.

29

The Abdication

✳ ✳ ✳

The unexpected abdication of the first president, Ahmadou Ahidjo, in 1982 and the coming of the Biya regime were turning points in the lives of ordinary Southern Cameroonians. For my mother, Susan Mbi Enow, this change meant a shift in perspective, and hope that things would improve—and they did. She often remarked that with Biya's rise to power, "People could talk again freely." Having spent years under Ahidjo's tightly centralized regime, she welcomed the fresh air that Biya initially seemed to bring.

Cameroon has always been a mixture of numerous cultures, languages, and traditions (over 250 ethnic groups and as many languages). The Anglophone regions, representing a significant minority, had long harbored grievances against the Francophone-dominated government. My mother keenly recognized this imbalance and would whisper her frustrations in hushed tones, always cautious of the invisible spies of the Ahidjo regime, who lurked everywhere, ready to pounce on dissent—even in her "small" office. She was a firm believer in fairness and equal opportunity, and she saw these appointments as deliberate attempts to stifle Anglophone progress.

The political landscape of Southern Cameroons changed significantly with the transition from Ahidjo to Biya. Ahidjo had ruled with an iron grip from 1960 to 1982, centralizing power and leaving little room for dissent. In contrast, Biya's leadership style, at least in its early years, appeared to embrace decentralization, greater political participation, and representation of different regions. My mother was hopeful that these changes would provide new opportunities for Anglophones, particularly in education. She had children who needed to pursue higher education.

When the multi-party system was introduced in the 1990s, my mother followed the developments with keen interest. She saw this as an opportunity for alternative voices to emerge. She often engaged in animated discussions with her friends and family, debating the possibilities that lay ahead.

Economic policies under Biya also shifted from Ahidjo's heavily muscled model to one that encouraged private sector participation. My mother, ever the practical thinker, was particularly interested in how these reforms would impact the daily lives of ordinary people. She had seen firsthand how economic centralization under Ahidjo had made opportunities scarce, and she hoped that Biya's policies would allow for greater economic empowerment.

She frequently reminded us that economic stability was the backbone of any thriving society. "If a mother cannot afford to send her children to university or put food on the table," she would shrug, "then all means nothing." Unfortunately, like many Cameroonians, she soon realized that economic decentralization did not necessarily mean economic progress. Corruption remained rampant, and the everyday struggles of Southern Cameroonians persisted.

Socially, Biya's regime aimed to expand access to healthcare and education, particularly in rural areas. My mother was a firm advocate for education and understood its power in breaking cycles of poverty and inequality. When schools in the Anglophone regions began to experience neglect, she lamented that the government's promises of educational reforms were merely empty words.

Cameroonians were eager to believe in Biya's mantra of "rigor and moralization," hoping it would bring transparency and accountability to governance. My mother was no different—she wanted to believe that her children's future in Cameroon could be bright.

As time passed, however, it became clear that the promise of rigor and moralization was not being upheld. The tensions that had been simmering below the surface for decades before Biya came to power, finally boiled over in 2016. By then, my mother had already transitioned to the world beyond, having passed away in 2015. Perhaps it was a small mercy that she did not live to see the full eruption of the Anglophone crisis. But had she been alive, she would have watched in horror as the unity she had hoped for crumbled into chaos, fear, and despair.

The crisis left Anglophones trapped between two forces—on one side, a government that dismissed their concerns and identity, and on the other, separatist groups that resorted to extreme measures, including kidnappings and killings. My mother had always believed in peaceful advocacy.

One of the most painful casualties of this conflict was education. Separatists imposed a school boycott, turning classrooms into battlegrounds. My mother, who had sacrificed so much to educate us, would have found this act particularly distressing. She often said, "Even if you have nothing, knowledge is something no one can take away from you." It would have pained her deeply to see children deprived of learning, their futures uncertain and their potential stifled.

The economic downturn that accompanied the conflict further exacerbated the hardships of ordinary citizens. Plantations, which had been vital sources of livelihood, were taken over by separatist fighters, and those who resisted were brutalized. My mother had always emphasized hard work and resilience, but even she would have found it difficult to endure the ensuing economic collapse.

As the separatist movement became increasingly fragmented and violent, the original purpose of their struggle was overshadowed by chaos and lawlessness. My mother, with her unwavering principles, would have condemned the senseless violence while still acknowledging the legitimacy of the grievances that had sparked the movement. She always believed that no matter how just a cause was, it could never be advanced through cruelty and self-destruction.

As we navigate this uncertain era, I find solace in the lessons my mother taught us. Her voice, though silent now, echoes in our hearts, reminding us that real change is built on the foundations of integrity, perseverance, and a steadfast commitment to the truth. She may not have lived to see how this chapter in history unfolded, but her spirit, her convictions, and her unwavering belief in the power of justice continue to guide us.

30

Her Tenants

* * *

Kalla Street was a two-apartment building. From the outset, we had tenants occupying one side of the building, a smaller apartment with just two bedrooms, compared to the three bedrooms on the other side that we occupied when we moved from Clerks' Quarters. The other apartment had more outside space. In our lifetime with our mother, we saw many tenants come and go. First in Mbende Street, then Clerks' Quarters, and then Kalla Street. These were the ones we knew about. For her house in Mamfe, we knew little about the tenants, and we didn't mind that at all. The challenges with tenants were countless.

Often, my mother resorted to self-help tactics and once actually had the local muscle men forcefully evict a tenant. But she learned that it was better to retain professional legal services than to try to do it yourself by force. For one of the early tenants, she was still green to the sector. When the rent was due, she went into his house while he was at work and confiscated the radio set. The "over smart" tenant went ahead and reported her to the police in Cow Fence, a stone's throw from Clerks' Quarters.

When the police came, she stepped out of her house with a heavy sigh, and her head dropped. A single tear rolled down her cheek as the accusation was being read. A tear she tried to choke back. The policeman was confused. Then he asked her to speak, and it was as if she was struggling to swallow something that was either too big or hard to swallow. She was gasping for air, trembling as she attempted to use her vocal cords. Her voice would not come out. It was very inaudible. After a few stuttered attempts, she was able to convey her message and her anger perfectly. When she was finally able to speak, she said she had no idea the tenant's radio was in our house. His son usually brought it to the house to listen to music with her own children. But that was only part of her story.

The greater part composed of her pleading with the policeman to feel sorry for her. An unmarried woman with four kids who was being taken advantage of by a powerful man. She had no work. Just this house left to her by her husband to feed her kids. And the tenant wouldn't pay his rent. Instead, he wanted to make trouble for her and her children, knowing fully well that even food had run dangerously low in her house. As the policeman listened and followed her keenly, it was clear that he could sense her pain. There was my mother outside our house, her countenance fraught with distress.

Her appearance only amplified the pitiable nature of the situation. Disheveled hair framed her weary, sweaty face; she was barefoot, a stark contrast to her usual dignity. She looked as though she had not had a proper meal in days, her wrapper haphazardly tied over her dress.

The policeman, keenly observing the unfolding drama, could not help but feel my mother's pain. Her unhappiness and annoyance were palpable, yet she refrained from lashing out in anger at her tenant. Instead, she employed a technique she had perfected over the years—a compelling display of grace and composure, especially when prayers seemed to fail and offer little or no solace at times.

The policeman was impressed. He was getting sucked in by my mother. He found himself drawn into her narrative, captivated by her resilience and grace under duress. This was clear evidence of her ability to convey her version of truth and win hearts, even in the face of adversity. He became so upset with the tenant that he took him back to the station and locked him up. Needless to say, the rent was paid before the day was over. We were all watching the incident, standing outside and listening intently. Heads turned from one speaker to another as each took their turn. It was another day of great learning. My mother was fearless, possessing unwavering strength and ingenuity. We were all witnesses to her indomitable spirit in the face of adversity.

Over the years, my mother faced numerous challenges with tenants, but she always handled them with unwavering fearlessness. She remained composed in the face of resistance, her calm demeanor masking a fierce determination. In times of confrontation, she knew how to strategically employ her emotions, often using her tears as a powerful tool to sway outcomes in her favor. Beneath that seemingly soft exterior was a woman who knew how to win, ensuring that no tenant who dared cross her would emerge victorious. Her relentlessness in these matters was not just about control—it was about survival.

With children to send to expensive boarding schools, every penny from her rental income was vital. Boarding schools weren't as affordable as government institutions, and the fees were a significant financial burden. So, she guarded this stream of income fiercely, knowing it was the lifeline that kept her children's education afloat. Every extra franc she could secure was precious, carefully saved, and put toward their future, making each battle with her tenants not just a personal victory but a victory for her family's well-being.

31

Sibling Fights and Squabbles

* * *

One thing I admired about my mother was that, despite having a large number of children to care for, she was always completely fair in how she handled and treated everyone. As a baby and the firstborn, I enjoyed certain rights and privileges—until my other siblings arrived. After that, there were no special privileges.

In everything, from the sharing of food to the settling of quarrels, she demonstrated fairness and impartiality. When intervening in the frequent fights among us children, she took great care to determine who was in the right and who was not. Even if you were unhappy with the outcome, you accepted her judgment willingly. She would have made an excellent governor in an idyllic society. A naturally skilled judge and arbitrator, she wielded discipline without hesitation.

It was Sunday evening. We had just finished dinner. One of my aunts had cooked chicken, accompanied by plantains and green vegetables from the backyard. She was still sweaty from the heat of the firewood kitchen outside. Normally, she would bathe before serving our food, but this time, she did not. Her long, tangled hairstyle was a mess, with flecks of ash from the

Sibling Fights and Squabbles

fire visible in her hair. A loose thread dangled on one side of her face, and she kept trying to brush it away.

My sister and I had to share a piece of chicken. I still wonder why my aunt did not simply split it while serving the rest of the food. Forgetting that we were supposed to share, I ate the entire piece. My sister, realizing what had happened, screamed and ran to grab the nearest object that could inflict pain. She picked up a heavy mortar pestle, struggling to lift it, and in her frustration, she prepared to hurl it at me. Just as she was about to throw it, my mother arrived in time, swiftly taking the pestle from her hands as she continued to sob and scream.

She loudly accused me of eating her piece of chicken—again. My mother was displeased with her attempt at violence, but did not jump to conclusions. She listened to both sides of the story. In the end, I was the one whipped for being selfish, but my aunt received a stern warning as well.

Words were often exchanged at home—it was normal. Sometimes, between my sisters and me, conflicts turned physical rather than remaining just words. One day, tensions were running high over something I can no longer even remember. It escalated into a fierce fight, starting with pushing and shoving. Before long, punches and kicks were being thrown. Everyone at home rushed out, and the commotion also attracted some neighbors. Some came for a good laugh, while others struggled to intervene and separate us.

The fight was eventually broken up, but a few days later, we found ourselves laughing about it, realizing the absurdity of fighting over something so trivial. Looking back, there was no better demonstration of the resilience and strength of familial bonds in the face of adversity.

Growing up in the 1960s was a different experience for children, especially when it came to expressing emotions. We didn't have open discussions or the emotional vocabulary that is common today. In fact, expressing emotions openly was neither encouraged nor expected. Saying sorry or asking for forgiveness felt like navigating unfamiliar terrain.

Whether in private or in front of others, tears were our primary outlet for emotions—our default way of communicating what we struggled to articulate verbally. Crying was our unspoken language, the means by which we let others know that something was wrong or that we were hurting. Looking back, it's clear that we had a lot to learn about emotional expression, but at the time, crying was often the only way we knew to convey the depth of our feelings.

I remember when my sister's hair was cut. She remained silent throughout the process, not saying a word as the scissors snipped away. But once the cutting was finished and she saw the final result, she suddenly burst into tears. Whether it was because too much hair had been taken off or simply because she didn't like how it looked, the emotions only hit her after it was done. She started crying, singing her own song:

"Put my hair back, oh."
Another time, she was crying while singing
"Khumba ya, my Lord, Khumba ya.
Someone's crying, Lord, Khumba ya. Oh Lord, Khumba ya.»

My mother had given the instructions for the haircut, but when she returned and saw how much Elizabeth was sobbing, her heart softened. Without hesitation, she took her to her bedroom and comforted her with candy, trying to ease her tears and make up for the distress caused by the haircut. She did not like showing gentleness in front of people, even at home.

32

Health is Wealth
The Triumph of Healing

* * *

As we navigated the tumultuous waters of our childhood, one constant presence loomed over our lives—our mother's health struggles. It often felt as though she was locked in a perpetual dance with illness, frequently in and out of the hospital and absent from work. Malaria was a familiar adversary that occasionally left her bedridden, but it was her right leg that bore the most visible battle scars.

A massive scar, a haunting reminder of her medical ordeals, stretched across her leg. This was no ordinary wound; rather, it was the result of an agonizing procedure performed by traditional healers attempting to extract elusive worms that had plagued her for years. These insidious creatures crawled up and down her leg, causing excruciating pain. We, her children, watched in a mixture of awe and terror as native doctors dug into her flesh to remove the tormentors. As she screamed in pain, we, her children, screamed and cried along with her.

Only as we grew older did we fully grasp the extent of her health troubles. Beneath the scarred surface, my mother also battled a heart condition that cast a long shadow over her life.

Her frequent collapses—sometimes multiple times a week at work—became unsettlingly routine. Each time, her co-workers would carry her home, where she would take her prescribed medication. Neither my aunts nor I understood why she didn't simply bring her medicine to work instead of enduring those repeated collapses.

A turning point came when a medical diagnosis confirmed her condition. Her path to better health was marked by an impending surgical procedure aimed at addressing her heart condition, offering hope for a brighter, healthier future. The operation was scheduled at Manyemen Hospital, where a specialist surgeon had been arranged for the procedure. However, reaching Manyemen posed a significant challenge—it was far from our home in Limbe, and the poor condition of the roads only made the journey more daunting. Despite these obstacles, the urgency of the surgery made the trip unavoidable, as it was the only hope of putting an end to her fainting spells.

With all appointments scheduled and preparations in place, my mother's diagnosis set the stage for the impending procedure. Yet, fate intervened on the appointed day. As her family waited for the surgeon's arrival, his absence cast a shadow of uncertainty. To this day, it remains a mystery whether he simply forgot his commitment or was delayed by unforeseen circumstances.

In an astonishing turn of events, my mother experienced an unexpected healing. Despite the absence of the planned surgery, the ailment that had plagued her for so long seemed to vanish, as if touched by a divine hand. She never suffered from her heart condition again. She later recounted a vivid dream in which a reassuring presence assured her that all was well, dispelling her fears. It was a profound moment of solace, as if a guiding force had intervened to bring about her healing.

This unexpected turn of events not only brought relief but

also deepened her sense of faith and gratitude. She insisted that her family need not wait for the surgeon, and they returned home to Limbe. My mother's journey toward health had taken an unforeseen detour, but the outcome was nothing short of extraordinary. It was a testament to the power of hope, faith, and the resilience of the human spirit.

This chapter in my mother's life stands as a tribute to the extraordinary power of faith—and perhaps even the miraculous. It is a testament to the indomitable spirit that carried her through trials and tribulations, allowing her to emerge victorious against the odds.

She often recounted the story of her healing to anyone who visited our home, her voice filled with awe as if she could hardly believe the miracle herself. Her journey had been one of deep physical struggle—a scarred leg and an ailing heart that had weighed heavily on her every day. Yet, her story took an unexpected turn toward triumph, a healing that defied explanation. This was not just a personal victory but a beacon of hope that illuminated our family's history.

With vivid detail, she would describe the dream that changed everything—a vision that brought her peace and renewal. She often said that from that moment on, it was as though the illness had lifted with the dawn. Her leg felt lighter, her heart stronger, and, most importantly, the fainting spells that had plagued her for so long ceased completely. Each retelling filled our home with gratitude, reminding us that her healing was more than just physical—it was a testament to faith and resilience.

33

Merrily Around the World

* * *

Despite refusing marriage, my mother remained in touch with my father, who had just completed a six-month work assignment in Monrovia. Intrigued by his experiences, she became eager to see that city for herself, but there was more to it than mere curiosity—her decision was deeply personal. The devastating loss of Judith had left an unfilled void, shaking our family to its core. Grief weighed heavily on her, and she longed for a change, a fresh start, a breath of new air.

How she managed to get the documentation and visa requirements, I do not know. What I do know is that, despite never having flown before, she boldly boarded an aircraft for her first flight ever. When she returned, her descriptions of the flight—every detail of the soaring bird—held her audience spellbound. It was as if, for a brief moment, the journey had lifted not just her body but also her spirit. The idea of soaring through the skies ignited a sense of wonder in everyone's hearts.

However, her tales of turbulence during the flight soon followed. As she recounted the bumpy ride, the desire to be back on solid ground became palpable. Every word she spoke held the audience in rapt attention. Flying, even in those days, remained a marvel of human achievement.

Following the questions some asked her, in their innocence, they even believed that you could reach out and touch the clouds from the comfort of your seat inside an aircraft. Such was the enchantment of the skies.

Filled with a mixture of excitement and nerves, she boarded the plane alone, carrying with her the weight of her grief. Yet, her spirit was undaunted. For as long as I could remember, she had been captivated by Africa and its rich array of cultures. This voyage was her opportunity to immerse herself in the wonders of this continent, a dream she was determined to fulfill. "How did other black people live?" She often asked, and it is also one of the questions that drew her towards the USA and other European countries where black people had migrated.

Upon her return from her trip, Monrovia dominated her conversations. The city left an indelible mark on her, a bustling metropolis with a vibrant art scene and a history as rich as the colors of the fabrics she brought back home. As she navigated the bustling airport after deplaning, her apprehension began to wane, replaced by an overwhelming sense of awe at the sights and sounds that enveloped her. The heat outside the airport hit her like a wall, an introduction to the intense warmth that Liberia was known for. It was a climate like what she knew, and my mother welcomed it as a testament to her newfound adventure.

When she arrived in Monrovia, she could not resist the city's lively markets. They were like a magnet, pulling her in with an undeniable charm. The markets were alive with a contagious energy that matched her expectations.

Amidst the hustle and bustle of these vibrant markets, she started building connections with the locals. The people she met radiated warmth and hospitality, embodying the true essence of the city. These connections would soon become an integral part of her journey, shaping her experiences in Monrovia.

One of her other stops was the National Museum of Liberia, a treasure trove of exhibits that unveiled the country's enthralling history, including its ties to the United States. Among the artifacts, my mother found herself drawn to the collection of traditional masks and other relics from Liberia's diverse ethnic groups. They bore a striking resemblance to the artistry she knew back home, evidence of the universal threads that connect humanity.

In the 1970s, Monrovia thrived as a dynamic hub of life and vitality, akin to a motley of cultures. Amidst the lively atmosphere, the women of Monrovia showcased colorful and bold styles in their fashion, echoing the vibrant aesthetics of their counterparts across the continent. The vivid hues and intricate patterns of their attire painted a vivid tapestry of self-expression and cultural richness.

After her memorable sojourn in Monrovia, she returned home, carrying with her a treasure trove of memories and mementos that would forever color the mix of her life. Her journey had been more than just a break; it had been an enriching experience, a journey of self-discovery and cultural immersion.

Among her most prized acquisitions were the traditional Liberian dresses, fashioned from resplendent African fabrics. These dresses, with their long, flowing skirts and fitted bodices secured by lengthy strings or ropes inside, were a showcase of the enduring allure of Liberian fashion, even in the face of sweltering heat.

As she unpacked her belongings, the dresses stood as vibrant symbols of her time in Liberia—a land where fashion was not merely clothing but a statement of identity and cultural pride. Lightweight and comfortable, the clothes whispered stories of the warmth and hospitality she had encountered, the colors of

Monrovia still vivid in her heart.

With these dresses, she brought a piece of Liberia back with her, a tangible reminder of the rich experiences that had enriched her life. Her return marked the beginning of a new chapter, where the memories of her journey would continue to shape her perspective on life and culture.

As I reflect on my mother's journey to Monrovia, it becomes evident that the fashions of the 1970s in that vibrant city continue to inspire and influence the women who call it home. The echoes of her adventure resonate through the generations, reminding us of the legacy she left behind.

In the chapters of her remarkable life, this voyage to Monrovia stands as a confirmation of her boldness in pursuit of a meaningful life. It was a testament to her love for being unfettered and free to go wherever her heart led her. She embraced the world with open arms, eager to explore and experience new cultures, and in doing so, became a more tolerant person.

Monrovia was not just a physical voyage but a spiritual one—a journey of self-discovery, cultural enrichment, and personal growth. The vibrant colors of Monrovia's fashion, the warmth of its people, and the memories she carried back with her enriched her life in profound ways, outwardly making her forget her grief.

As we close this chapter in her biography, we honor her spirit of adventure and her unwavering commitment to living life to the fullest. Her journey to Monrovia remains an enduring legacy. It shows her courage and fearlessness sustained by an adventurous spirit.

34

A New Beginning in Mile 4

✳ ✳ ✳

When we left Kalla Street, my mother, Susan Mbi Enow, envisioned more than just a new address; she was seeking a place to build her dream home and a quieter, more connected life. She had bought our Kalla Street house—a bold and impressive move as a single mother in her time—but her ambitions didn't end there. My mother wanted a place to retreat from the city's hustle and bustle, a peaceful setting where her family could grow closer and thrive. That's how we found ourselves in Mile 4.

It took two years to complete the house in Mile 4. Unlike many others who might move in as soon as the basics are done, my mother had her standards. For her, a home was more than walls and a roof. She wanted a complete, comfortable, and finished house that welcomed family and friends with warmth. She insisted on adding small touches, like the little garden strip in front, so that even our outdoor space reflected her care and attention to detail. By the time we moved, Mile 4 was ready, almost everything done, just as she had envisioned.

Mile 4 marked several milestones in our lives. It was the place I returned to after my studies in the UK, where the familiarity of home offered a sense of belonging. It was from this house that

A New Beginning in Mile 4

I began my own journey of marriage, walking down the aisle from a place steeped in my mother's love and sacrifices. In this house, I grew closer to my siblings. We were adults now. We shared laughter, struggles, memories, and dreams, all nurtured by the safe space she created for us.

For my mother, Mile 4 was not only a home but a testament to her journey. She even purchased a car—a symbol of her progress and her determination to keep reaching for more. I remember the pride she took in that car and how it represented her achievements and independence.

Yet, as time passed, Mile 4 didn't entirely unfold the way she had hoped. Instead of the peaceful, community-oriented neighborhood she had dreamed of, it gradually became a place far from her ideals. The community was not cohesive; it was more divided along tribal lines, and a strong sense of mutual support never really took root. For my mother, this was a disappointment.

The council's neglect of infrastructure made things worse. The roads in Mile 4 were never properly completed; they remained the same narrow, stony roads as when we first arrived, difficult to navigate and barely improved. Makeshift stores and bars piled up along both sides of the road, further crowding the streets and giving the area a rougher edge. My mother had hoped for a nurturing, family-friendly environment, but the neighborhood began to attract a different crowd. As time passed, the area experienced an increase in crime, further eroding the sense of safety and peace she had so eagerly sought.

Despite these challenges, Mile 4 remained our home, a place where my mother's legacy was written into every corner. The dream may not have turned out exactly as she had envisioned, but she poured her strength, love, and values into that home. It became not only a testament to her resilience but a memory that endures for all of us who were shaped by her dreams, her sacrifices, and her unfailing dedication. In Mile 4, my mother's story unfolded, and her love continued to define us—even when reality fell short of her dreams. It was also in this house in Mile 4 that she was laid in state and buried when she passed away in November 2015.

35

Aversion to Politics

* * *

As Cameroon transitioned from colonial rule to independence, the concepts of independence and self-determination gained increasing importance. Some women sought to assert their independence by making their own decisions regarding their lives, including choices about marriage and financial independence.

In the early 1970s, women's participation in politics in Cameroon was still in its infancy. This period marked a time when the path to political participation for women was fraught with challenges. The women knew their roles and were faithful to them, except for a few women who were co-opted into the political game. It is their example that others soon began to emulate as women started to formally organize and advocate for greater representation in politics. However, the representation remained very limited. This was largely due to the persistence of cultural and societal norms of the time, which often viewed women as inferior to men and relegated them to traditional gender roles.

Those who broke through these barriers laid the groundwork for future generations of women to pursue political careers and fight for gender equality in Cameroon. The women in Limbe were fortunate to have someone in their community, Mrs. Gwendoline Burnley, who became the first woman to be elected to the Cameroon National Assembly in 1957. She represented the British Southern Cameroons, which was under British administration at the time. She was a member of the Kamerun National Democratic Party (KNDP), which advocated for the independence of Cameroon from both French and British colonial rule.

My mother had a somewhat ambivalent relationship with politics. She wasn't particularly interested in entering the political arena, mostly because she couldn't quite comprehend what it entailed. Additionally, she prioritized her family over networking with politicians. Despite her initial hesitation, circumstances pushed her in an unexpected direction. Mrs. Gwendoline Burnley, a woman my mother admired for her resilience, found herself unexpectedly thrust into the world of politics. However, her political career wasn't by choice – she was co-opted into becoming a parliamentarian. My mother found this situation somewhat ironic.

Observing Mrs. Gwendoline Burnley navigate the political landscape sparked a flicker of interest in politics within my mother. However, she quickly realized that, as an unmarried woman, earning respect in the political sphere was a challenge. It seemed that without being married, her opinions weren't valued as highly as those of her male colleagues. Discouraged by this lack of recognition and respect, my mother ultimately decided to refrain from participating in active politics.

Despite her initial short-lived foray into politics, my mother remained a keen observer from the sidelines. She admired women like Mrs. Gwendoline Burnley, who blazed trails in the political arena, but she also recognized that perhaps the path of a politician wasn't meant for her. After all, there's more to life than parliamentary debates and political maneuvering – like spending quality time with loved ones and enjoying the simple pleasures life has to offer.

After French Cameroon gained independence in 1960, her mentor, Mrs. Burnley, continued to play a role in politics. She served as a member of the National Executive Committee of the Cameroon National Union (CNU), the then-ruling party. Mrs. Burnley's contributions to politics and her fight for women's rights paved the way for more women to join politics in Cameroon.

Mrs. Eyong was another prominent woman in politics in English-speaking Cameroon in the early 1970s. She was a member of the House of Representatives, which was the Lower House of the Cameroon National Assembly. She was a vocal advocate for women's rights and was known for her efforts to improve the status of women in Cameroon. She also advocated for the education of girls and women, working tirelessly to promote women's involvement in politics and decision-making at the most basic village levels.

Politics, for my mother, was a sector clouded by fear. Even most of the women who ventured into the political arena did so reluctantly, driven by circumstances rather than choice. It was a world thrust upon them, not necessarily one they willingly embraced.

My mother had great admiration for Mrs. Burnley, the member of parliament for Fako, who she considered a trailblazer, not only for women's rights but also as someone who effortlessly championed community causes. My mom's closest brush with politics came in the form of a voting card, a simple yet powerful tool that allowed her to exercise her right to vote. It was a duty she took seriously, a way to make her voice heard within the democratic process.

On occasion, she received a party uniform free of charge.

Instead of pursuing active politics, she became a grassroots member of the then single political party, dutifully paying her dues, donning her party uniform, and attending meetings. It was her own small way of contributing without sacrificing family time.

There were years when she was given the party fabric for free. She proudly wore it as a symbol of her civic engagement, a subtle statement of her involvement in the political landscape, although from a distance. Politics may have been a path she chose to avoid, but her commitment to her civic duties remained unwavering.

Those were days when politics in Cameroon was steeped in fear. People worried that spies were listening to them and would report anyone who said the wrong word or showed disapproval of the regime in power. Violence occurred in certain parts of the country where the opposition was strong. There was widespread intimidation and some corruption. Even though my mom could not verify any such claims, she was fearful and preferred to remain anonymous rather than be seen and potentially get into trouble. The fact that men dominated politics also meant that many women thought their efforts would be futile. No one would hear them or appreciate their contributions in a system that was heavily skewed toward men.

Overall, the general atmosphere surrounding Cameroonian women, who hesitated to actively participate in party politics in the 1970s, was one of cultural restrictions and fear of violence and intimidation. Cameroon was under a one-party system during this period, and there was limited space for opposition parties or dissenting voices.

My mother, who had only completed form five in secondary school, did not pursue higher education for personal reasons and also because access to education was limited, especially for women. Such restrictions on higher education hindered the political participation of women, who were still regarded mainly as objects, and ambition in women was looked down upon and frowned upon.

The patriarchal society and traditional gender roles and norms also hindered women's political participation. As a single woman, society did not encourage her involvement in politics. Women themselves hesitated to join politics, fearing that such engagement would undermine their men, who, for the most part, viewed women as irresponsible and unfit for the complexities of the political game.

Existing political parties provided limited support for women, who were given little or no access to the inner workings of such parties, and often encountered discrimination and exclusion.

Financial constraints also loomed large on the horizon, casting a shadow over women's political aspirations. The lack of financial resources posed significant hurdles, making it difficult for women to launch campaigns, attend political rallies, and engage in various political activities.

Many women were housewives, dependent on their husbands for their livelihoods. In this context, politics often took a backseat in women's lives. Convincing husbands to allocate resources for political endeavors was a daunting task. Men held the belief that their male counterparts would question their priorities if they were seen promoting their wives' political careers instead of their own.

Skepticism ran deep, as many men doubted whether their wives could be taken seriously in the male-dominated political arena. These barriers, a complex interplay of societal norms and structural limitations, added layers of complexity to the already formidable challenge of women's political participation in that era.

In those days, unlike today, there were no legal frameworks mandating a minimum representation of women in political positions. The notion of gender quotas, which today ensures at least 30% of women's participation in political elections, remained a distant dream. The absence of such safeguards made it challenging for women to secure a foothold in the male-dominated arena of politics. Yet, beyond the legal constraints, a more insidious deterrent existed—an apprehension of social stigmatization. The fear of being labeled as "deviant" loomed large in the minds of women contemplating political participation. The prospect of social stigma and ostracization from their communities was a genuine concern.

In the conservative landscape of the 1970s, many women who dared to challenge traditional gender roles or raise their voices against social injustices were often branded as "troublemakers" or "deviants." The weight of these labels was heavy, casting shadows on the aspirations of women who wished to make a difference in their communities.

Above all, there was the palpable fear of discrimination and exclusion from the socio-political sphere. These apprehensions cast a long shadow over the dreams and ambitions of many Cameroonian women during that era, deterring them from actively pursuing a career in politics.

However, it is essential to acknowledge the courage of the women of Cameroon. Despite the formidable barriers they faced in the 1970s, they nonetheless laid the foundation for a new era of political engagement. Over time, they shattered these constraints and became active participants in politics and decision-making processes, heralding a brighter and more inclusive future for generations to come.

36

My Mother Buys a Car
A Single Mother's Car Journey

* * *

Limbe, in those days, was a bustling hub of activity as the nation stood on the brink of gaining independence from colonial rule. There were all kinds of supermarkets, such as Printannia, which sold imported goods ranging from clothing to housewares to canned food. My mum loved Printannia and got all our Christmas dresses from there. It was a time of great change and uncertainty, but also a time when people's spirits were high and dreams of a better future filled the air. During this historic transition, one woman stood out among the crowd: my mother, a single parent determined to make her mark on the world.

At a time when society often relegated women to the background, my mother was a beacon of determination. She was a young single mother raising her five children in the quiet neighborhood of Clerks' Quarters in Limbe. As a clerk, she worked long hours at the Produce Marketing Board and the Delegation of Commerce, dedicating herself to her work and the petty business she ran on the side. But she harbored a dream, a dream that would bring unimaginable joy to her family and friends.

One sunny day, etched forever in my memory, my mother arrived home with a secret she could no longer keep. The excitement that filled the air was palpable, like a sudden rush of adrenaline. We gathered in the small courtyard of our modest home, surrounded by a loving extended family that had weathered many storms with her. My mother was screaming for everyone to come outside, "quick, quick!" And everyone hurried from wherever they were, anxious to see what this was all about.

As the car drove into the courtyard, we all made way. It was not the first time a visitor had come to see us with a car. We did not recognize this visitor. The driver emerged from the vehicle and, with a sense of gravitas, handed the keys to my mother. We were all perplexed, and the anxiety was building up by the second. And then she unveiled it, the source of our collective awe and wonder—she had just paid for the car standing right in front of our house. A Mitsubishi Lancer, glistening in a deep shade of brown.

The car stood there, gleaming in the sun, like a symbol of possibilities yet unexplored, reflecting the promise of countless adventures yet to come. The sheer astonishment on our faces mirrored the feeling of the entire neighborhood, who had come to witness this momentous occasion. Silence enveloped us for a brief moment, a collective breath held. Even the courtyard held its breath, and then it all burst out—there was commotion, screaming and hugging, and all kinds of emotions on display.

We hugged, we danced, and tears of pride and happiness flowed freely. It was a day that would forever be etched in our memories as the day my mother, through her determination and hard work, had turned a dream into a reality, bringing immeasurable joy to our lives and inspiring the entire community to believe in the power of resilience and discipline.

The story of my mother's cherished car had an intriguing

twist that added a touch of serendipity to her journey. It was during one of her regular visits to Bojongo Parish, a small and close-knit community located near Limbe, where she often sought solace. She liked the church there and felt that each time she went up to Bojongo to pray, her prayers were always answered. However, she was not just a devout churchgoer; she was a thinker, always eager to engage with priests and religious leaders on various societal issues. One subject that had often piqued her curiosity was the concept of tithing, a practice she faithfully adhered to, yet one that left her with a persistent hunger for deeper understanding.

One day, as she delved into yet another discussion about tithes with the parish priest, fate intervened. A white priest, who had dedicated years of service to the mission, was preparing to return to his homeland. The news of his departure unveiled an opportunity my mother could not resist. It turned out that the priest's car, the very same car that had carried him through countless journeys in service, was up for sale. It was in this unexpected revelation that my mother found the path to acquire her beloved Mitsubishi Lancer. Negotiations ensued, and she managed to secure the car, a vehicle that would become not just a mode of transportation but a symbol of her staunch independence and the culmination of her curiosity, faith, and pride.

Well, the car was truly standing right in front of us now! With laughter and excitement, everyone clambered to see the inside, to touch it, and to admire its sleek lines. My mother was beaming with pride, knowing that her hard work and determination had brought this symbol of success to her doorstep. She knew, however, that with great power came great responsibility. Her voice rang out through the crowd, attempting to regain some semblance of order.

"Don't dirty my car!" She playfully shouted as we piled into the vehicle. She shot a worried look at my brother Eric, her youngest, and warned, "Your fingers will get trapped in the door!" But her words fell on deaf ears, as we were all caught up in the joy of the moment. We were driving her stationary car, and nothing could dampen our spirits.

My mother's achievement was not just about owning a car. It was a statement, a testament to her hard work and her unyielding commitment to whatever she set her heart to. In a time when many questioned the capacity of a single mother to provide and prosper, she was proving them all wrong.

Word quickly spread throughout her workplace and the community. People couldn't help but wonder how she, a clerk, managed to save enough to buy a car, even if it was a used one. My mother was aware of the curiosity and whispers surrounding her achievement, but she took it all in stride. Instead of dwelling on skepticism, she had decided to take a bold step and dispel any doubts regarding her abilities.

She enrolled in driving lessons and quickly became proficient behind the wheel. Soon, she was on the road herself, a symbol of empowerment, navigating her way from Mile 4 down the hill to Limbe with grace and confidence. She used her car to go to work, run errands, and drive to church, all with the same determination she'd applied to every other aspect of her life.

My mother's journey as a single parent in Limbe during the independence era was a testament to the fortitude of the human spirit. She proved that determination and hard work could shatter societal limitations and expectations. Her Mitsubishi Lancer became more than just a car; it became a symbol of her unbreakable spirit and an inspiration to all who knew her. In an era when women were striving to make their mark in a rapidly changing world, she blazed a trail that others could only admire and follow.

My Mother Buys a Car

When she first bought her car, it was a symbol of status and pride, and she took great care of it. In those early days, she would only allow her own children inside; the car represented a personal luxury reserved for family alone. The seats were always spotless, and the car was treated with reverence, almost as if it were something sacred. It was her private space, a testament to her hard work and determination.

But as time passed, the boundaries around the car softened. Slowly, the back seats filled with more than just her children. The neighborhood kids and her children's friends started joining the ride. What was once a vehicle of personal prestige became a shared resource, and its importance in her eyes began to fade. The car no longer carried the weight of luxury it once had; instead, it became a practical tool for daily life.

Her friends, always aware of her schedule, would eagerly shout for her as she passed by,

"Mami, take we go town oo!" or "Reme, I di go Mile 2!" Her response was always "Straight to Down Beach." She only stopped at her office, and everyone had to make their way to their destination thereafter.

What once was a personal item now bridged her social connections, and her car became a familiar sight on the way to town, filled with laughter, conversations, and the warmth of community. It was the same year she bought the car that I went to college, while she continued to pay school fees for secondary school and mission schools, where my siblings were enrolled. Though outwardly gentle, her strength was deeply rooted. She was always self-reliant, never depending on anyone. She admired those who had more or had help from others, yet she remained determined to prove she could thrive on her own.

37

Parenting Style

* * *

The parenting style my mother and her peers adopted was authoritarian. We have heard stories of children disappearing when their fathers came home or being so quiet that people peed in their pants for fear of making noise by going to the bathroom. Children were not to be seen or heard. It was either the way of the parents or the highway: no compromises or midways. If you stepped out of line by disobeying any rules, you were punished, often by flogging with whips made of cane, rubber, sticks, brooms, or whatever was handy at the time of the crime. We know today that this kind of parenting can easily result in depression and other mental health issues. In the past, the kids learned to be submissive and passive. Internal grumbling was one of the greatest skills developed.

In our household, we were mostly grateful for having someone who, even when she was strict, was also considerate and kind and ready to support our education 200%. Her style was mixed. She was trained by Reverend Sisters, so not being strict was not an option. Sometimes she would cane you and cry with you. At other times, she was just hard and uncompromising. But she was one in a million, to borrow the cliché. Very considerate,

Parenting Style

she took her role as mentor, molder, and head of family very seriously. She knew she was both father and mother to all of us, and her actions demonstrated that she was determined to instill a sense of fairness, responsibility, and diligence in those under her charge. Her love was indeed tough love.

She was so restrictive; she refused her adult sisters, Ebai Nyor, popularly called Aunty by all, and Tembu, any social life. Being seen with the opposite sex was taboo unless you wanted to go to the real hellfire. No interaction with boys was permitted. Thinking of music or sports as a career was unheard of.

But let me spin you a little tale about my vivacious aunt Ebai Nyor, the undisputed music maven of our family! She was the real deal. This woman had pipes that could rival a choir of angels and a passion for tunes that could outmatch any jukebox. She didn't just sing; she belted out hits like a real superstar!

She didn't discriminate when it came to genres either. She could rock the Blues, jam to Rock, soulfully croon to Soul Music, get irie with Reggae, bust a move to Disco, twang along to Country, salsa her way through Pachanga, and basically conquer every popular music trend of her era. From the funky sounds of American legends like James Brown and Ray Charles to the infectious beats of Nigeria's Victor Uwaifo and the mesmerizing melodies of Congo's OK Jazz and Franco, she knew them all.

But here's where the story gets spicy! Aunt Ebai Nyor's musical journey didn't start on a grand stage. No, it began at the tea-time dances, where she and her sister would sneak off in the afternoons for some secret groove sessions. It was here that she quite accidentally discovered her true calling, serenading the teatime crowd with her mesmerizing voice.

One fateful day, as she sang her heart out, an intrigued onlooker dropped a bombshell. "You know," he whispered, "the nightclubs are where real stars are born! Na for dey." Well, that was all the motivation Aunt Ebai Nyor needed. She made up her mind right then and there to chase her musical dreams.

Now, here's the part that had everyone on the edge of their seats. At our house, nightclubs were a no-go, either at night or during the day, due to some strict rules my mom had implemented. So, Aunty, as we all called her, hatched a plan. Every Saturday night after my mother, her sister, and mentor went to bed, which was often before 9 p.m., my aunt would stack pillows on her bed to create a convincing dummy. Then she would strike some secret deals with her sister Tembu and other roomies, and sneak out through the window like a ninja. If only she had been born in the US, she would have auditioned for a spy movie and aced it!

One night, though, my curious mom decided to play detective. She had observed the "Saturday nights, Sunday morning, refusing to go to church because of headache syndrome." She was watching her sister like a hawk. She was convinced she had seen her go out more than once. So, she followed Aunty Ebai without the latter being aware of it, and arrived at Bay Hotel Night Club near Down Beach Limbe. As the music thumped and the nightclub lights beckoned, Aunty unleashed her moves and her vocals on stage while my mom hid in the shadows—the ultimate undercover agent.

But after what felt like an eternity (30 minutes can be pretty long when you are playing hide-and-seek with your own sister), my mom couldn't resist the allure of the dance floor any longer. She decided to swoop in and rescue her sister from this musical mischief. And just as she was about to make her move, disaster struck!

Someone in the club recognized her as she approached. And she stood out because she was clearly not dressed for the nightclub, and she stood out like a sore thumb with her wrapper.

Parenting Style

The alarm bells rang louder than Aunty Ebai's high notes. Our heroine didn't miss a beat. She pulled a Houdini and made a dramatic exit through the back door, leaving my mom in the dust. The night was safe for another round of secret nightclub escapades, and Aunty Ebai Nyor's legend continued to grow.

And that, my friends, is how our family's musical maverick eluded capture in the name of music, leaving behind a trail of melody, mischief, and unforgettable memories! Back on the home front, you would think the nightclub incident would become the stuff of legendary family tales, right? Well, nope! It was like the great unspoken secret that everyone tiptoed around. Life just carried on, and Aunty didn't skip a beat in her Saturday night escapades. Perhaps it finally hit my mom that maybe, just maybe, there was a whole life of music and adventure to be had out there. We could not understand her silence. Of course, with great nightlife comes great responsibility, or so our family thought. There were more talks about the birds and the bees, as well as cautionary tales about not getting too cozy with boys or men. But you know how it is with teenagers, some lessons take a little longer to sink in. Fast forward a few years, and Aunty had a surprise in store – she was expecting!

As you can imagine, that revelation didn't exactly receive a standing ovation. It sent shockwaves through our household. Aunty had to put her school days on pause and return home. In those days, it was a big no-no for a young girl attending school to be pregnant. Tensions in our home hit an all-time high.

But here is where the story takes a heartwarming turn. My mom, Reme, may have been initially furious, but love has a way of softening even the sternest of hearts. When the baby finally arrived and the little bundle of joy was named after my mom, it was as if a magical spell had been cast.

Tensions slowly started to fade away, like the last notes

of a beautiful melody. The baby became a symbol of love and forgiveness, a little beacon of hope that reminded us all that family ties could withstand the occasional off-keynote. And as life continued to unfold, we learned that sometimes, it's the unexpected moments that bring us closer together. Aunty Ebai had been dismissed when she became pregnant in form four at the Baptist Teachers Training Center (BTTC) Soppo, Buea, where she was a boarding student. When she was ready to return to school eleven months after her baby was born, Reme went to St. Francis Teacher's Training College in Kumba and pleaded with the Reverend Sisters to take her sister, and they did. Aunty had an incredible talent, but she never went back to music formally or informally. Who knows if she would have been the first Tina Turner? Despite her unexpected detour into the world of parenthood, my mom was determined that education would be the beacon of hope for her.

In the end, our family's story isn't solely defined by secrets and tensions; the transformative influence of discipline and consequences was very evident in all our lives. It's a narrative enriched by the profound forces of love, redemption, and the enduring bonds that shape our identities. Against the captivating backdrop of Aunt Ebai Nyor's legendary music-filled adventures, this chapter in our family's history becomes unforgettable. Yet, the crowning jewel of our tale is the remarkable woman, my mother, whose actions and reactions charted a path to success that few women of her era achieved.

38

The Strength of Solitude

***

Suzie, my mother, was a woman of incredible resolve. She made a conscious decision not to marry, choosing instead to raise her children on her own terms. Determined to provide us with a good education and instill strong moral values, she worked tirelessly. While her unwavering dedication would ultimately shape our lives for the better, it wasn't without its challenges.

As children, we were blissfully unaware of the extent of her struggles. As a private person, she shielded us from the hardships she faced as a single mother. We never saw any of her boyfriends stay in the house, and she drank only occasionally. However, there were moments when the weight of her responsibilities became evident.

One recurring memory is of Saturday mornings in our house on Kalla Street. Those were typically lazy days, as in most households. My younger brother would bustle around, attempting to carry a large silver pot filled with water from the bathroom for some chore. Little did he know that his innocent activities would lead to a confrontation with our mother.

She emerged from her bedroom, wearing only a wrapper draped across her chest. In a stern tone, she ordered my brother out of the bathroom and instructed him to go to the back of the house.

Another incident comes to mind. We were sitting behind the house, roasting groundnuts and skillfully removing their skins. My mother returned from work and, without explanation, told us to put everything away. It was not the right time to roast groundnuts, she decided. Once again, we exchanged confused glances but complied. It was clear that there was more on her mind than we could understand.

In Mile 4, where we later relocated, there was another incident that left a lasting impression on my memory. My mother had just returned from Down Beach, her usual spot for buying fresh fish, which she would skillfully turn into her famous tomato stew, accompanied by a side of vegetables. But this time, she had returned without any fish and was unresponsive to the greetings that met her at the door. We obeyed without question, though we were too young to fully comprehend the reasons behind her outbursts. Was it transferred aggression from her struggles? We couldn't be sure.

In those days, the doors of homes were often left open when people were inside. The gentle caress of Limbe's sea breeze kept the curtains swirling in all directions. Occasionally, one might find oneself trapped within the undulating fabric, necessitating a flurry of arm movements to navigate the labyrinthine passage that led either into the house or back out onto the open front veranda. The breeze was a fleeting respite from the relentless grasp of the oppressive 30-degree Celsius heat. Some days, the heat in Limbe was truly daunting.

On this particular day, my mum pushed the curtains with more energy than necessary, as though they were heavy with the weight of unspoken sorrows. She walked straight into her room, shutting herself off from the world outside—a world that seemed to hold promises unfulfilled.

Now, as an adult and a grandmother myself, the recollection of those moments is an ache that resides deep within my soul. I often find myself drifting back in time, retracing the steps of my mother's solitude. In the quiet of her room, did she lie on her bed with her gaze fixed upon the ceiling above? The ceiling—a silent witness to the relentless battles she fought daily.

I can't help but wonder, in the stillness of those solitary hours, if tears ever betrayed her resolve. Were there moments when the weight of the world—her world—became too much to bear, and silent tears flowed like unspoken lamentations? It is a secret she kept, one we were spared. For we, her children, would have willingly abandoned the comfort of our innocence to sit beside her on the floor, sharing in the poignant communion of tears.

In those solitary hours, in the sanctuary of her solitude, during the quiet of the night, my mother must have often wondered if she had made the right decision. The decision to forgo the warmth of marital companionship, the choice to bear the burdens of life's struggles alone—these were questions that surely haunted her nights.

With the house quiet and the weight of the day's struggles pressing heavily upon her, she was left alone with her thoughts, her silence her only companion. Every sound—the crickets outside, the toads after rainfall, or even the wind softly blowing—might have seemed like reminders of unanswered questions. What if she had chosen differently? What if she had taken the path of companionship, leaned on someone else to share the load?

But my mother was not one to indulge in regret. She had chosen her path long ago, and once she had made up her mind, there was no turning back. Her refusal to marry, despite the parade of suitors who had come seeking her hand, was not just a rejection of tradition but a bold statement of her independence. She had vowed to forge her own way, even if it meant standing alone in a society where, at the time, a woman's worth was often measured by her ability to secure a husband.

I was told that my grandfather used to question in frustration, "Why is she so stubborn? What will become of her without a man to protect her? Who will look after her children?" He knew little of her resolve to protect herself and her children.

But defying expectations came at a cost. In Mamfe, people considered her conceited, arrogant, and even ungrateful. Some pitied her; others judged her. But she stood tall, shoulders squared against the tide of judgment. She had chosen to walk a path few women dared to tread, and she was willing to pay the price.

Like most, her days were grueling. Her modest salary as a civil servant was never enough, but she found ways to stretch it. She would return home in the evening, her feet aching and her body weary, only to start her second job—being both father and mother. I never once saw her break down. She would just smile—a tight, determined smile—and press on. "God will provide," she would say. And somehow, her God always did.

There were moments when we caught a glimpse of the strain she tried so hard to hide. Sometimes, at night, when she thought we were all asleep, we would hear her in the other room, softly murmuring to herself, the words too quiet to make out. Was she praying? Crying? We never dared to ask.

Once, in the dim light of her bedroom, she sat at the edge of the bed, her hands clenched tightly in her lap. Her eyes, normally sharp and focused, were distant, as though dazed—staring at something only she could see. We often quietly moved away, too young to understand the depth of her burden but old enough to know she was carrying something heavy.

The Strength of Solitude

"God, I am straining," she would whisper over and over into the darkness, unaware that we were watching and listening. "I hope they never see how hard this is."

That was her greatest gift to us—her unyielding shield. No matter how difficult things became, she made sure we never felt the full weight of it. School fees were paid, somehow. Clothes appeared when we needed them. And there was always food on the table.

But the cracks in her armor were visible to my aunts, old enough to know where to look. The way she stared sometimes. The deep sighs she would release at the end of a long day, as though exhaling all the exhaustion she didn't allow herself to feel while awake.

Now, I wonder what she thought about in her quiet moments. Did she ever wish for a different life—one where she wasn't always the strong one, the provider, the protector? Did she ever imagine what it would be like to have someone else to share the load with? Or maybe she found strength in her solitude. Perhaps that's where her true power lay—in her ability to face the world alone and still stand firm.

A few years after my marriage, I asked her why she had never married. I was hesitant, but I managed to find the words.

"One day, you'll understand," she told me. "One day, you'll see that love isn't just about a man and a woman. Love is about giving everything for your children. You just keep giving. You never even think about it again. It becomes a drug—'opium.'"

And she did love us—fiercely. A love so strong it sometimes felt like it could move mountains. But it was also a love that came with sacrifice. A love that meant putting her own desires, dreams, and needs aside so that we could have a better life. Now that I'm older, I see it clearly—the quiet battles she fought, the silent tears she must have shed. And I realize that her choice to be a single parent wasn't just about defiance or independence. It was about love. A love so deep, so profound, that it overshadowed everything else.

In the end, my mother may have walked her path alone, but she was never truly lonely. She had us, and we had her. And then she had God. And that, for her, was enough.

Being a single parent is a formidable journey, one that demands unwavering strength and resilience. My mother didn't have all the answers, and her ways may have seemed enigmatic at times, but her determination to provide for her family never wavered. Her story is a testament to the strength of single parents everywhere—those who face challenges and adversity with unyielding love and determination.

39

The Spirit as Partner

* * *

Life as a single parent can be daunting—a journey filled with numerous decisions and responsibilities that must be navigated alone. Without a partner to lean on for support or guidance, single parents often find themselves carrying the weight of every choice on their own. My mother was one such parent, raising a family without anyone to share the burden. With no one to turn to for a second opinion or advice, she grappled with difficult decisions behind closed doors, shielding us from her struggles and worries.

Her days were filled with challenges—from financial strains to balancing work and family obligations. The weight of responsibility bore down on her shoulders, and at times, her quiet lamentations echoed through the walls of our home. It was evident that the load she carried was overwhelming, yet she bore it with dignity and resilience.

Though my mother didn't have a life companion, she had a constant spiritual one—God. He was her confidant, the one she turned to for guidance and strength. Every night, I would see her on her knees or pacing her room, speaking softly to Him, sharing her worries, hopes, and fears. She didn't need anyone else because, in her heart, God was enough. Though as a family we didn't pray together except for grace before and after meals, her private prayers were an unspoken pillar that held our home together.

She trusted God with everything. When money was tight, she turned to Him. When one of us fell ill or school fees were due, she sought comfort in the solitude of prayer, kneeling by her bedside and finding strength in whispered conversations with Him. I remember the nights I heard her soft voice in the darkness, filled with gratitude even in the hardest times. And sometimes, there was frustration in her words—an open annoyance when things didn't go her way. It was as if she truly believed He was there, sitting beside her, holding her hand through every trial.

40

The Rhythms of our Home

* * *

Keeping our household in shipshape was no small task for my mom. The daily grind of chores was a shared endeavor, with plenty to do—from taming kitchen chaos and conquering bathroom battles to tidying bedrooms and tending to the courtyard. As if that weren't enough to keep us on our toes, she also ran a side hustle, crafting postcards for sale—a sprinkle of entrepreneurial flair in an already bustling life.

A well-ordered routine governed our days. Mornings began promptly at five, and our evening curfew was set at 7:30 p.m.. On occasions when Reme wasn't home early, we followed a different schedule. We would butter our "economic blockade" with margarine, make our sandwiches, and enjoy them with Tole tea or Ovaltine before six. By 6 p.m., the house was locked up for the night.

Unexpected visitors could arrive at any time, day or night. In the evenings, however, the doors remained firmly shut, except in emergencies. If someone had urgent business, they had to raise their voice loud enough to reach us through the iron and concrete gates or the windows. In those days, people rarely notified others before visiting—a custom that, while less common now, still persists.

Some days began with a sense of togetherness as the family gathered for collective prayers, setting the tone for the day ahead. After morning devotion, we embarked on a daily pilgrimage to church—a cherished routine that bathed our lives in faith and community. My mom believed that if we were attending church, there was no need for long prayers at home. So, morning prayers were kept brief: one Hail Mary, an Our Father, a Glory Be, and a request for God's forgiveness.

In those days, even in the darkness of early morning, insecurity was not a major concern. The real fear in the shadows was political—who might be listening or who might be a government spy. Yet, our path to morning service remained a journey of unwavering faith, a testament to the tightly knit community we were part of. From Monday to Friday, we attended school without fail. This consistency reflected our commitment to education and the values instilled in us by our mother.

During the extended school breaks—the "Third Term Holidays"—our daily rhythm changed. We embraced the countryside, where farming became a meaningful occupation. The fields called to us, and we answered, nurturing the earth and reaping the rewards of our labor.

In moments of leisure, we found joy in braiding each other's hair, immersing ourselves in novels, and playing spiritedly with the neighboring children, as our homes blended seamlessly into one another. Running from one house to the next was a common occurrence.

During the rainy season, when the downpour seemed endless, it was the rare sunny days that brought a special thrill. We embarked on tire-riding escapades, transforming old car tires into a source of endless adventure. With two sticks securely placed inside for control, we pushed and rolled the tires along,

The Rhythms of our Home

racing through muddy puddles and standing water. Sometimes, it became a friendly competition, each of us vying for the coveted title of the fastest tire-rider. But not every moment was carefree.

One particular memory still makes me smile, though at the time, it nearly escalated into a physical altercation. It involved a dear friend who would later rise to prominence within the Catholic Church. The incident began with a dispute. My brother, caught up in the excitement of an upcoming tire-riding race, snatched one of our friend's sticks without asking for permission. Tensions flared, and just as the race was about to begin, a confrontation seemed inevitable.

The situation grew heated until we all stepped in, reminding my brother of the importance of fairness and sportsmanship. With a sigh and a reluctant nod, he handed back the stick. Determined to compete, he decided to race with just one stick, even though it was clear his tire wouldn't roll as smoothly. In the end, he finished last—a humbling lesson on the consequences of not playing by the rules.

But wait a minute, there's more! Weekends took hard work to a whole new level, packed with extra-intensive cleaning, deep scrubbing sessions, and backyard farming for good measure. The workload felt like a chore pyramid scheme—the older you were, the more you had to shoulder. It was all part of the grand plan to teach us responsibility, or so we were told.

When it came to education, my mom had a mantra: *"Study, study, study!"* She swore by it as if it were the ultimate life recipe. Music? Nope. Sports? Not a chance. Anything that dared to distract from the sacred textbooks was strictly forbidden. And if you happened to fail an exam, you had better brace yourself for a symphony of family disapproval—you wouldn't make that mistake twice.

Though she tried not to show it, my mom carried a lingering

fear that someone else in the family might follow in Aunty Ebai Nyor's footsteps. But she had developed a toughness of her own—a hard exterior wrapped around a heart of gold—ready to tackle whatever life threw her way. In the end, that resilience kept our household humming: a blend of hard work, determination, and tough love, with a sprinkle of hope for good measure.

And then, there's the tale of my sister's General Certificate of Education (GCE) adventure in May of 1988! A story set against the backdrop of my mom's unwavering dedication to education—and Aunty Ebai Nyor's musical escapades—adding yet another layer to our family saga.

It was the very last day of the GCE. My sister had successfully written all eight of her papers, and this final day was dedicated to the practical exam for Food and Nutrition. Brimming with youthful enthusiasm, she set off early in the morning, determined to conquer the kitchen. Little did she know she had chosen a culinary challenge worthy of a cooking competition—she had decided to prepare koki beans for her practical.

Now, who in their right mind chooses to cook koki beans in an exam? Well, my sister did—driven by a mix of ignorance and a lack of proper guidance from her teachers. She had seen this dish prepared countless times at home, thanks to Aunty's culinary prowess. Confident in her abilities, she dove headfirst into the task.

However, as the clock ticked down in the high-stress exam setting, it became painfully clear that her koki beans bundles were not going to cook in time. The time constraints worked against her, leaving her dish undercooked and far from appetizing.

But the real drama unfolded back at home. For the next two weeks, our household became an echo chamber of reminders and reproaches, with my sister at its center. The infamous koki beans became a lasting symbol of what was perceived as a culinary catastrophe—one that brought nothing short of mortification to our beloved mother.

As my sister grappled with her misery, this story shows the high standards and expectations set by our family, particularly my mom, when it came to education and achievement. Even amid Aunty's musical adventures and my sister's culinary mishap, the underlying theme of striving for excellence, in whatever form it may take, remained a thread that bound our family's narrative together. Even though my sister was an outstanding student and passed the Food and Nutrition subject, she feared she had missed something, and my mom was still not satisfied with the grade she received. She wanted perfection from her daughter.

Miscommunication incidents at home were almost a regular occurrence, often providing a mix of amusement and frustration. My mother, despite her usual composure, tended to give instructions that weren't always clear. But admitting this? That was something she would never do in front of us. One instance that stands out vividly involved my aunts. My mother had left the house early in the morning, leaving us with what we later realized were vague instructions for dinner. When she returned in the evening, my aunts had prepared a completely different meal from what she had intended. The confusion was apparent from the moment she stepped into the kitchen. Her facial expression showed mild disbelief, but instead of acknowledging any lack of clarity on her part, she skillfully shifted the narrative.

"Did I not say fish soup?" she would ask, raising an eyebrow as if challenging anyone to disagree. My aunts, trying their best to justify the rice and stew sitting on the stove, hesitated for a moment. "Well, we thought you meant stew," they stammered, sensing that there was no easy way out. Of course, my mother insisted that her instructions had been perfectly clear, though none of us could recall her mentioning fish, let alone soup. The entire ordeal would turn into a humorous affair once she was no longer on the scene. No one dared laugh in her face.

It wasn't the only time such incidents occurred. There were moments when she'd send one of us to the market with a list that didn't quite add up. "Buy vegetables," she'd say, without specifying which ones, leaving us to navigate through a sea of possibilities. Upon returning, she'd casually remark, "I meant water leaf," as if it was obvious all along. We would grumble behind the house and laugh, knowing full well that the real instructions had never been said. Yet, admitting this in front of us? Never.

Despite the frequent mix-ups, these moments became a part of our family dynamic, where laughter followed frustration, and no one took it too seriously. It became a running joke in our household, a lighthearted reminder that even though communication could fail, we always managed to get by.

There were moments when my mother's anger would erupt like a sudden storm, catching everyone in its path off guard. These moments were rare, but when they did happen, they left an indelible mark on everyone around her. One of the most memorable incidents of this kind was the day the okra soup fiasco occurred.

It all began innocently enough. My mother had asked her sisters to prepare okra soup for dinner, a simple request she thought. The farm, where various crops grew, was located just by the house. Okra was one of the staples we planted and harvested regularly. On this particular day, she had assumed her instructions were clear: harvest just enough okra from the farm for a single meal, cook it, and leave the rest to grow for future harvests. However, things took a different turn.

When she returned home that evening, expecting to find a hearty pot of okra soup simmering on the stove, she was met with something that set her blood boiling. All the okra from the farm had been harvested; every single pod had been picked clean. And yet, when she looked into the pot, only a small amount of soup was cooking. She couldn't believe her eyes—there was no sign of the abundance of okra that had been harvested from the farm. Confused and increasingly enraged, she stormed into the kitchen from the farm where her sisters were preparing the meal.

"What do you want to do with the rest?" she screamed, her voice rising as fury took over her usual calm demeanor. "Why did you harvest the okra if you did not plan on cooking it? Where is the rest of the soup?"

The questions came rapid-fire, her anger palpable, each word stinging the air between them. Her sisters stood there, startled by the intensity of her reaction, mumbling something incoherent, but it was clear no answer could pacify her now. In her mind, the waste of all that okra was unforgivable. She had always been economical, ensuring that nothing went to waste. To see her sisters, who should have known better, carelessly pluck the entire crop without a plan for how to use it all, felt like an act of betrayal.

My mother's face flushed with anger as she slammed her hand down hard on the back table, the sound reverberating through the room. Spittle flew as she continued to yell, her temper rising with each passing second. Her frustration was visible in every gesture, in the way her fists clenched, her lips tightened, and her fast pacing up and down the house. She was a woman who rarely lost control, but in moments like these, her anger was like a force of nature.

She wanted to lash out, to slap her sisters for what she saw as their carelessness and disregard. And for a brief moment, it looked as though she might. But somehow, in the heat of her fury, she managed to hold herself back. She took a deep breath, her eyes burning with rage but her hands steady, and walked away from the confrontation before she did something she would regret.

The tension in the room remained thick long after she had stormed out, her sisters standing there in stunned silence, unsure of what to say or do next. They knew better than to try to reason with her in such moments. The rest of the evening was filled with an uneasy quiet, the remnants of my mother's anger lingering like a shadow over the house.

In the days that followed, the incident became a cautionary tale. My mother never said anything about her outburst, nor did she need to. Everyone understood that her fury wasn't just about the okra; it was about the principle behind it. She had a deep respect for hard work, for the land that sustained us, and for the food we grew on it. Wasting something as precious as an entire crop of okra was, to her, not just a simple mistake—it was a violation of everything she stood for.

That day, we learned an important lesson about my mother's anger. She was not quick to lose her temper, but when she did, it was always for a reason, and it was always righteous.

Sometimes the drama was of a positive nature. It was a good mix. The good, the bad and the... When my sister and I passed the General Certificate of Education (GCE) with flying colors, my mum visited her friends shouting at the top of her voice: "I am gladding the gladdiness!"

Over and over and over, she sang her joy loud and clear, completely oblivious of what was happening in the other houses. It was only later on that she realized not all her friends appreciated this. Some had children who had failed the exam, so you can imagine the reception she received in her state of ignorant euphoria.

41

The Absence of a Father

* * *

Our single-parent family was a mélange woven with love and togetherness. Surprisingly, the absence of a father figure never left a void in our lives, so much so that I cannot even remember a time when I questioned why my mother was alone. It was not until I reached university that I learned the truth: my father had another life, with multiple other women in the picture.

Remarkably, the dearth of male presence during our formative years became a topic my brother and I reflected upon only as we grew older. We came to realize that this absence played a pivotal role in shaping our characters. It fueled an unquenchable drive within us, igniting a burning desire to succeed. We were acutely aware that our mother was carrying the weight of the family on her shoulders, and her happiness meant the world to us. And making her happy was the single goal that brought us all together.

One day, as our mother returned from a meeting, we heard her softly repeating the phrase, "Nkube nya a beke yah," "Nkube nya a beke yah," "Nkube nya a beke yah," which roughly translates from Kenyang to English as "The cowhide is not enough." It may sound like an odd thing to mutter, but it had a profound impact on her.

During that fateful "country" meeting, where the utterances were made, my mother found herself at the center of unwarranted criticism and harsh judgment. The source of the contention? The perceived lack of pieces of meat in the food she had brought. Everyone took turns bringing food every month as a rule.

To some, the absence of ample meat was more than just a culinary oversight—it was seen as evidence of her supposed inability to provide, a subtle jab at her unmarried status. In their eyes, her singlehood rendered her incapable of affording even the basic ingredients to make a meal flavorful and satisfying. It was as if her worth as a person and as a provider was being called into question simply because she didn't have a man by her side to supplement her income.

The insinuations and disparaging remarks made my mother feel small and insignificant, as if her single status somehow diminished her value as a human being. Yet, amidst the sea of criticism and judgment, my mother discovered a reservoir of boldness that she had never known she possessed. Instead of allowing herself to be crushed by the weight of their words, she chose to stand tall and defy their expectations.

In a moment of sheer defiance, my mother rose to her feet, her voice unwavering as she refused to be belittled or demeaned. With unwavering determination, she eloquently defended herself, addressing past comparisons and laying bare her detractors, leaving them with no choice but to acknowledge the injustice of their assumptions.

This episode, though fraught with tension and discomfort, ultimately catalyzed another profound transformation. She greeted each challenge with silent promises to prove to them that she would excel in the future. Rather than allowing adversity to tear her down, she emerged from this experience stronger than before and committed to overcoming all obstacles and thrive despite societal expectations.

Indeed, my mother's bold stand not only challenged the narrow-minded perceptions of those around us but also reaffirmed our belief in the inherent dignity and worth of every individual, regardless of their marital status or social standing. It was a powerful lesson in courage.

This episode, in a strange way, strengthened our family bonds. It reinforced our determination to overcome obstacles and served as a reminder that happiness and success could be achieved, regardless of one's family structure.

In the end, our single-parent family was not defined by what was missing; it was defined by the love, determination, and resilience that flourished in the absence of a father figure. It was evidence of the unbreakable bond between a mother and her children, and it fueled our collective pursuit of happiness and achievement.

Throughout her remarkable life, my mother encountered numerous unjust biases and snubs, many of which deeply baffled and pained us. Even more surprising was the fact that some of these prejudices came from the very women who had once shared the same educational journey from QRC Okoyong in Mamfe. It was disheartening to witness individuals whom she had considered friends and peers look down on her, casting judgment based on perceived social status and marital status.

These former classmates had moved on to pursue higher education, forging successful careers and establishing their own families. Their elevated social standing seemed to grant them a sense of superiority, leading them to view my mother with condescension. It was as if her singlehood and lack of academic achievements beyond QRC Okoyong were seen as marks of inferiority, unworthy of respect or recognition.

Yet, in the face of such unjust treatment, my mother remained steadfast in her determination to rise above it all. She refused to be defined by the narrow-minded prejudices of others, instead choosing to forge her own path with grace and dignity. While the snubs and biases she faced were hurtful, they only served to strengthen her resolve and reaffirm her sense of self-worth.

She would make a comment or two about being a better student at school than this one or that one, but she never allowed herself to be consumed by bitterness or resentment. Instead, she channeled her energy into building a life filled with compassion.

In the end, my mother's journey was not defined by the unjust biases and snubs she faced, but by her unwavering determination to overcome them with grace and dignity. Her legacy serves as a powerful reminder that true worth and value cannot be measured by societal standards or superficial judgments. True worth is found in the strength of character and integrity that shines brightly.

In my own professional journey, I also encountered systemic and institutional bias, but I have managed to persevere largely because I have adopted the same unwavering attitude my mother possessed. It is the kind of attitude that refuses to surrender, that constantly seeks the silver lining in the darkest of clouds, no matter how daunting the challenges may be. You might call it resilience, determination, or sheer willpower. In Nigerian local parlance, it's summed up in the phrase, "I no go carry last" – which roughly translates to "I refuse to be left behind in the race of life, and I won't succumb to circumstances."

Sure, some may have pitied her along the way, but my mother had resolved within herself to shatter every expectation and surpass even the loftiest dreams. She was a force to be reckoned with, an indication of the extraordinary heights one can achieve through unwavering resolve and an unyielding spirit.

Among the many challenges she faced due to stereotypes and discrimination, it was the church that seemed to truly understand her, offering solace in times of uncertainty. While my mother did not adhere to every teaching and doctrine of the church, she held a steadfast belief in a higher, supernatural being. She saw this as the source of power to achieve her goals, the guide of her destiny, and the shaper of her life's convictions.

This belief transcended the church's teachings in her eyes. It was evident in her unwavering faith and her unshakable positive mindset. She possessed a unique ability to will things into existence, and while she faithfully attended church services, she felt that the spirit within her held a power beyond any religious institution's offerings. She faithfully recited the Rosary every day. She went to church daily, unless there was a serious problem that deterred her from doing so.

Yet, she had a different side, a formidable side. She wasn't afraid to use her beliefs as a source of strength when faced with obstacles. Those who dared to stand in her way would receive a warning. She would tell them that she would pray, and her prayers would bring affliction on them.

My mother was an ex-student from Okoyong and remained a devout Catholic throughout her life. Her connection with the church ran deep, and she regarded Jesus as her closest companion. In her eyes, He was the miracle worker who never ceased to amaze. When the pantry and food store were empty, Jesus provided sustenance. When funds for school fees and uniforms were scarce, it was Jesus who came to the rescue. Her devotion to prayer was unparalleled, a continuous dialogue with Jesus that extended from dawn to dusk, sometimes even echoing through the streets as she walked home from work or the market. She would sometimes pray aloud on the road. She frightened some, and some thought it was fun, while others thought she was mental.

Throughout her life, the church and her unwavering faith were inextricably intertwined, weaving a narrative of resilience, strength, and an unbreakable bond with the Divine. Needless to say, many thought she was weird, and others even considered her a witch. She made a choice not to be like others, and making this choice was seen as peculiar, condemning those non-conformists, like my mom, to a life of suspicion, where society viewed them as something of an oddity.

To us, her children, it was abundantly clear that our mother possessed a captivating and formidable power that extended its dominion not only over us but also over her tenants and others she dealt with. This power was nothing short of awe-inspiring, leaving those subjected to its influence quaking with both fear and astonishment. Her unwavering conviction was the bedrock of this authority. She boldly proclaimed that Jesus himself walked in lockstep with her, prepared to dispense divine retribution upon any tenant who dared to falter in paying their rents.

The chronicles of miraculous events that graced her life and ours were nothing short of extraordinary. If she were still alive today, one could easily envision her taking the reins of a Pentecostal church, commanding the stage with fervent acts of exorcism, glossolalia, and spirited, frenzied music that would set the congregation on fire. When she prayed, she could be seized by the power of the Holy Spirit, trembling with the force of divinity, a phenomenon akin to the passionate worship practices witnessed among Pentecostal church members across Cameroon today.

Alas, during her time, the world was a different place, and women often found themselves relegated to second-class citizenry. Many were confined to the role of mere ornamental fixtures within their homes, akin to beautiful potted flowers.

This societal paradigm added an extra layer of complexity to her life, for she was a woman of unwavering faith and undeniable spiritual power.

Moreover, the religious landscape in Limbe, where we resided, featured a few unconventional churches that carried an aura of mystery and even dread. Whispers about some of these places circulated among the townsfolk, painting them as potentially dangerous sects. The Baha'i church and the enigmatic Olumba Olumba congregation were among those that inspired fear in the hearts of the community. No one dared venture within a mile of these enigmatic houses of worship, fearing the unknown that lay within.

Given this climate, the notion of my mother establishing her own church was far from a feasible dream. It was an idea that would not have been well-received in a society where religious traditions were deeply entrenched, and unconventional faith practices were viewed with suspicion.

So, my mother continued her journey, leaving a trail of miracles and unshakable faith in her wake. While she may not have started her own church, she remained an indomitable spiritual force, a beacon of hope and inspiration within her family. Her unwavering resolve and profound spirituality would leave an indelible mark, one that transcended the confines of any congregation or doctrine. We all knew that if we needed anything, our mother could literally conjure it up.

One particular incident showcased her remarkable influence. A tenant, indebted to her for six long months, received a chilling ultimatum: settle the unpaid rent or face the wrath of the Almighty. Two more months passed, and still, the rent remained unpaid. Then, fate took a startling turn. The tenant was diagnosed with a formidable adversary—cancer. Within a few months, he succumbed to the relentless illness, leaving behind a trail of wonder and disbelief.

The tenant's wife, grappling with grief and confusion, confided in her family, convinced that her husband's demise was no mere coincidence. She firmly believed that their formidable landlady had played a role in his tragic fate. Such was the aura of mystique that surrounded my mother, an aura that left a lasting mark on the lives of those who crossed her path.

On another occasion, she faced some stubborn tenants who were causing trouble. Frustrated, she decided to seek help from the local gendarmerie. When she arrived at the gendarmerie, they instructed her to put her complaint in writing. Overwhelmed with anger, she rose from her seat and began to write, not realizing how a whole page poured out of her pen.

The officer in charge was taken aback by the passion in her words and her speed. He was so impressed that he decided to accompany her back to her home to address the unruly tenants himself. It was purely by chance that I crossed paths with this officer long after he had retired. When he saw me, he turned around with a look of astonishment and said, "I know your mother. She is an incredible woman." He then shared with me the remarkable story of how he had visited our house after that incident, gaining knowledge of our mother's kids' names, their whereabouts, and what they were up to. And he only needed to hear one of our names to be happy to recount that incident in his office with my mother.

Her fame went far and wide, and people feared her. No one dared cut her plantain or steal her vegetables on her farm or her mangoes on the huge tree in front of her house in Clerks' Quarters.

42

Maintaining a Closed Book

* * *

It was hard to say for sure if our mother was happy or not. She was a closed book. This means that she was one of those people who tend to keep their thoughts, feelings, and personal information to themselves. The person may be reserved, introverted, or simply private. They may have difficulty opening up to others, even those they consider close friends, and may prefer to keep their thoughts and emotions to themselves.

People who are perceived as a "closed book" may be seen as mysterious or enigmatic, as others are left to wonder what lies beneath the surface. They may be difficult to read, making it challenging for others to connect with them on a deeper level. Despite this, they may still be valued by their friends for their loyalty, dependability, and ability to keep secrets. That was my mother.

She kept her emotions to herself. If she was lonely, it was never evident or obvious. She surrounded herself with a diverse group of people, making it difficult to find time to feel lonely. Unless it was a death or extreme case, it was difficult to read her. When she lost her daughter, Judith, who was born and died a week later, she was inconsolable. Judith never came home.

We later learned that she was yellow all over and soon died of jaundice. However, we learned this only much later. She was inconsolable at this loss, even though she had four living children. That was the time we saw her devour the book "Is Death the End" in her bid to handle her grief and pain.

When her father passed away, it was crystal clear to everyone that she had unequivocally validated his decision to invest in her education. Perhaps, it was her ardent desire to impress him that fueled her relentless pursuit of success. She didn't just achieve; she soared to remarkable heights. Her accomplishments included constructing and or owning impressive houses, enrolling her own children in prestigious secondary schools, and generously funding the education of her sisters. All of this while comfortably residing in her own home in Limbe.

While Big Papa, as we affectionately called him, didn't make frequent visits, his presence was always awe-inspiring. There was an aura of respect and reverence whenever he graced us with his company. He visited all his children. He surprised everyone when he visited Kribi to see Florence in the heart of francophone territory. As Big Papa embarked on the journey from Mamfe to Kribi, his mind churned with a mix of emotions. The bus was crowded, and the distance felt even longer as he pondered the path his daughter, Ebai Nyor had chosen. He remembered her strong-willed nature, which had been a source of both pride and concern for him. Florence had once enjoyed a blissful marriage, but whispers of trouble had reached him—stories of deception, mistreatment, and struggle that weighed on his heart. Hence the trip. He pushed the thoughts aside. Despite his reservations about her marriage to Mr. Ndam Bayard, he couldn't deny the pride he felt in her adaptability and resilience in a world far removed from the familiar Anglophone territory.

When he arrived in Kribi, Big Papa was greeted warmly by

his daughter and her husband, who welcomed him into their home with open arms. As they sat down to share a meal, Big Papa observed the Francophone customs and language that had become second nature to his daughter. Though it troubled him to see her so immersed in a culture foreign to his own, he couldn't help but admire her strength and determination in forging her own path.

As the visit unfolded, Big Papa found himself drawn to Mr. Ndam Bayard, despite his initial reservations. He discovered a man of integrity devoted to his daughter and their family. Although their backgrounds differed greatly, Big Papa couldn't deny the love and happiness that were evident in their home.

Returning to Limbe after his memorable journey, Big Papa carried with him a newfound understanding and acceptance. While he still held onto his roots and traditions dearly, he realized that love and family transcended language and culture. And as he reflected on the achievements of his other children, particularly his eldest, Susan, our mother, he couldn't help but feel a swell of pride for the remarkable individuals they had become, each charting their course in life. Our mother, following in her father's footsteps with a passion for real estate, was a source of immense pride for Big Papa. Her dedication to the world of property investment mirrored his own, and it was a bond that strengthened their relationship even more.

In the grand tapestry of their family history, each member had carved their path to success, but it was the legacy of hard work, determination, and ambition that bound them together. Big Papa's investment in his daughter's education had paid off handsomely, shaping a future filled with accomplishments and achievements that made him proud beyond measure.

When her father died at the ripe old age of eighty-five, our mom still tried to connect with him even in death. When her mother died after struggling with sickness for four years, she was utterly shattered. In the annals of my mother's life story, a pivotal chapter unfolded with the passing of her beloved mother, my grandmother. This chapter, fraught with emotion, had its roots in a bond that transcended the ordinary.

Their connection had been profound, a bond woven with threads of love, understanding, and unwavering support. From the moment my mother drew her first breath, my grandmother had been her guiding light, her source of strength and solace through life's trials and tribulations. My mother relied on her for advice on many things, even though there were things she felt her mother would not understand. They shared secrets whispered in the dead of night, dreams woven beneath the stars, and laughter that echoed through the halls of the home in Mamfe and that of Limbe. They shared not just meals, but the experience of preparing their food together as well. They ventured out to the local market in Mile 4, cherishing their outings until age and sickness slowly confined Big Mami to the comforts of home.

As illness crept into my grandmother's life, slowly stealing her vitality and vigor, my mother's heart grew heavy with the weight of impending loss. For four agonizing years, she watched helplessly as her mother battled the relentless tide of sickness, clinging desperately to hope even as despair threatened to consume her.

And when the inevitable moment came—when death finally claimed my grandmother—it hollowed my mother out, crushing her spirit beneath the weight of grief. The void left by her mother's absence was a chasm too vast to bridge, a gaping wound that bled with every beat of her broken heart. Her mother had been the closest person to her, like a husband, throughout most of my mother's life.

At the burial in Mamfe, as she stood by her mother's

graveside, tears streaming down her cheeks, my mom clung to the coffin for what felt like an eternity—it was pitiful to witness. It was not because she lacked faith that her mother had gone to a better place. As the coffin was lowered into the bowels of the earth, my mother whispered a promise into the wind—a vow to carry on her mother's legacy of love. And though her heart bore forever the scars of loss, it continued to beat with the enduring echo of a mother's love—a love that knows no bounds and transcends even death itself.

In the days that followed, as my mother grappled with the harsh reality of life without her mother, memories of their time together flooded her mind like a torrential downpour. She recalled the warmth of her mother's embrace, the sound of her laughter, the amusing anecdotes, the childhood stories, and even the lingering scent of her presence. These recollections bound their spirits in a solemn promise to remain connected, even beyond the veil of death.

Yet, amidst the pain and sorrow, a glimmer of solace emerged—a faint flicker of light in the darkness. In her mother's absence, my mother found herself drawing strength from their memories, knowing that their bond would endure beyond death.

Big Mami, as we affectionately called our grandmother, shared an exceptional closeness with my mother. Among all her offspring, she visited our mother more frequently than anyone else, and this unique relationship inevitably extended to us, her grandchildren. As Big Mami aged, her final days found her in the embrace of her daughter in Limbe.

Big Mami's departure marked the end of an era. She never returned alive to her house in Mamfe, her lifelong home, choosing instead to spend her twilight years in the company of her daughter. It was in Limbe that she peacefully passed away.

Following the Bayangi Manyu tradition, when a woman

passes away, her body typically returns to her parents' or relatives' village. However, Big Mami had different wishes. She expressed a strong desire not to be buried in Ntenako, my grandfather's village, where he lay at rest. Nor did she wish to be buried in her own village, which she had left decades ago and never returned to.

Instead, she requested—if the elders permitted—that she be laid to rest behind the main house on Main Street, in the heart of Mamfe. It was a house she had built with her own hands, a place she had poured her heart into, and where she had spent the greater part of her life.

It was a quiet, hot afternoon, but the weight of grief in the air made it feel as if the sky had darkened. As the coffin was slowly lowered into the ground, my mother clung to it, her fingers trembling as if letting go meant losing a part of herself forever. Her cries pierced the stillness of the air, raw and filled with such sorrow that it was impossible not to feel the depth of her pain. Her voice broke with every sob as she called out to Big Mami, hoping, perhaps, that her mother might hear her one last time.

Tears flowed freely from everyone around the grave. It was impossible not to cry as we watched my mother—who had been so strong for so long—break down in a way we had never seen before. In that moment, she was not just mourning her mother; she was mourning a lifetime of love, memories, and the irreplaceable safety that only a mother could provide.

As the earth began to cover the coffin, my mother stood frozen in her grief, her hands reaching out as though she could pull it back from the darkness. But there was nothing more that could be done. The finality of death was upon us, and slowly, the grave was filled. The mourners who had gathered began to disperse, their sorrow muted as they shuffled away from the place that now held Big Mami.

Maintaining a Closed Book

After the burial, the house felt empty. Big Mami had not been back for so long. My mother and her siblings gathered to distribute what little was left of their mother's possessions—her old pots, a few pieces of clothing, and some household items. It was a simple task, but its simplicity made it all the more heartbreaking.

Big Mami had been a giver all her life. She had given so much that she had almost nothing left when she passed. Even in death, she left behind only the essentials, knowing that material things meant little compared to the love and care she had shared.

Watching my mother go through those few belongings was almost too much to bear. Each item she held seemed to carry the weight of a thousand memories—a pot that had once bubbled with meals Big Mami had lovingly prepared, a worn loincloth she had wrapped around herself on cold mornings, even used chewing sticks. Every piece told a story, and as they were handed out, it felt like pieces of her were slipping away, leaving only the echoes of a life that had once filled the house with warmth.

In the end, life went on, as it always does. But something had shifted forever. My mother, who had been a pillar of strength for so many, was now navigating a world without her own anchor. The house behind which Big Mami lay remained standing, open for others to use. Yet, it served as a quiet reminder of the love that had once filled its walls—and of the emptiness that grief brings when those we cherish most are no longer with us. It was a fitting conclusion to a chapter filled with love, companionship, and the unbreakable bond between mother and daughter, a bond that endured even in the face of mortality.

When her son died at the tender age of twenty-four, my mother was inconsolable. In the story of her life, my younger brother, Eric, played a unique role. Born as a poignant replacement for Judith—who had tragically succumbed to yellow fever just one week after birth—Eric brought a new light into our family. He was a child filled with boundless joy, finding solace in the company of his siblings. Among us, he shared a particularly special bond with his older brother, Ako Chokobi, and with me. I cherished him deeply, treating him almost as if he were my own child, and I couldn't have been prouder of the intelligent, artistic young man he was becoming.

After successfully completing his A-levels, my mother made the pivotal decision to send Eric to the United Kingdom. While the rest of us had ventured abroad for our education, the circumstances surrounding Eric were different—guided, it seemed, by the power of the Holy Spirit. It was as if a divine message had reached my mother, revealing that she would be responsible for nurturing just one of her children. She embraced that responsibility wholeheartedly.

Eric's time in the UK was marked by his remarkable intellect and his burgeoning artistic talent. However, tragedy struck just a few years into his stay, casting a dark shadow over our family. His sudden and untimely passing left us in shock and profound grief. At the time, my mother was in the United States visiting my sister Elizabeth. Upon receiving the devastating news, she immediately made the arduous journey back home to bury her beloved son.

The scenes that followed were heart-wrenching, as my mother once again found herself drowning in inconsolable sorrow. The anguish was deepened by the cloud of uncertainty surrounding Eric's death, making the loss even harder to bear.

This chapter of my mother's life—marked by the profound loss of Eric—serves as a piercing reminder of fate's unpredictability, leaving our family forever changed by his absence.

Yet, through it all, my mother embraced life's ups and downs with grace, always believing that something good awaited her at every turn. And in the end, she was rewarded.

43

Was there Ever a Love Life?

* * *

In the chapter on my mother's love life, one word rises to the surface: choice. She was, without a doubt, beautiful—strikingly and classically so. With her delicate features, inherited from her parents, she and her sister, Florence, captured the attention of countless young men. From her earliest years, my mother's looks were magnetic, drawing the gaze of eligible young bachelors who found her beauty and spirit captivating. This constant attention even unsettled her father, who grew increasingly wary, fearing she, being headstrong, and Florence, looking up to her sister, might fall into the wrong hands.

My mother, though, was decisive about her life's path, especially when it came to love and marriage. Her approach to romance was marked by a clear and almost defiant sense of independence. She knew what she wanted and, just as firmly, what she did not. While she cherished the idea of motherhood, of raising her own children with her own values, she was adamant about avoiding the commitments and compromises that came with a traditional marriage. It was as though she had glimpsed a different way to live, one where she could love her children fiercely and fully without ever having to share her life or identity with a partner.

Despite her chosen path, she was no stranger to love. My father was her one great romance, a bond filled with the tender vulnerability of young love. She gave herself fully to him, allowing herself to be captivated by his charm and warmth. There was a time when they must have shared dreams and whispered promises, when my mother's laughter rang out in the comfort of his presence. I like to think of her, young and in love, with the radiant glow of hope and possibility in her eyes.

But when my father's actions shattered that trust, it was as though he had drawn a line for her, a line she would never allow anyone to cross again. In her heart, she knew the sting of betrayal, and in response, she made a resolute decision: she would live for her children, pouring all her love and energy into raising us. And although admirers surely surrounded her, she remained undeterred, choosing a life on her own terms. She might have had love again, with her beauty and warmth, but she made it clear, both to herself and the world, that she was content.

This choice, a conscious act of independence, could be seen as an indictment of Cameroonian men, or perhaps on the expectations of men in general. Many would have viewed her as a prize to be won, a beauty to be claimed, but she saw herself as complete, needing no one to validate her worth. Her solitude was not a result of a lack of opportunity; it was a quiet and powerful statement of self-respect, discipline, and control over her life.

As her children, we were part of her unwavering focus. No man's presence ever noticeably interrupted the serene bond she had with us. My memories hold no trace of amorous connections or flirtatious interactions. Her devotion to us was constant and absolute, her love unfaltering. Perhaps there were men who longed to win her heart, but my mother chose to walk a path of independence, cherishing her autonomy and her role as a single mother. For her, romance was an early chapter, a beautiful memory, but one that was closed.

Her love life, then, is not a story of multiple romances or fleeting relationships. It is a tale of an early love that touched her deeply and left an indelible mark, ultimately guiding her to live a life of her choosing. Her life was lived by her own rules, driven by her fierce love for her children and her refusal to be bound by societal expectations. She remains an inspiration, a testament to the strength of self-defined womanhood, a woman who knew her heart, followed its wisdom, and lived unapologetically in the way she felt was right for her.

44

QRC Okoyong ... Again!

* * *

The sun came out early. However, everyone at home was too busy and too sad to notice anything outside. The Common Entrance exam results had just been published, and my name did not appear on either List A (for high scores) or List B (for lower scores). In local parlance, I failed the Common Entrance exams that would have been my gateway to secondary school.

My mom's whip didn't come out that day. It came out about a week later when she lashed out and vented her frustration and anger at me, falling on my small body with a whip. It left me writhing in pain and tears. But as always, in her smart thinking, she had a Plan B: to take me to her alma mater, QRC Okoyong in Mamfe, and plead for my admission into Form One.

I remember the day vividly, the sun beating down mercilessly as we made our way to the school. My heart raced with uncertainty, unsure of what awaited me beyond those gates. Yet, as we approached, I couldn't help but notice the grandeur of the buildings, standing tall and proud against the lush green backdrop.

Inside, the halls echoed with the sound of footsteps, mingled with the chatter of students. I felt small in comparison, overwhelmed by the unfamiliarity of it all. But my mother's reassuring hand on my shoulder gave me the strength to push forward.

As we met with the school administrators, I could see the determination in my mother's eyes. She believed in me, in my potential to succeed even in the face of adversity. And as we left the school that day, I knew that no matter what challenges lay ahead, I would face them head-on, armed with the unwavering support of my mother by my side. I knew that I could not let her down.

Years have passed since that day, and looking back, I realize that failing the Common Entrance was not the end, but rather the beginning of a new chapter in my life. QRC Okoyong became more than just a school; it became my second home, shaping me into the person I am today.

And though the journey was not without its struggles, I am grateful for every obstacle I overcame, for they have made me stronger and more resilient. So here I stand, ready to embrace whatever the future may hold.

The first time I arrived in Mamfe in 1977, as an 11-year-old child, was at 3 a.m., having spent two days on the road. An interminable journey, it was a relief to finally arrive in Mamfe from Limbe.

Mamfe was a small town located in the southwest region of Cameroon, and Kumba was the nearest city from where we had to start our journey. The roads between Limbe and Kumba were not as bad as the road from Kumba to Mamfe.

We set off early in the morning from the park in Kumba, hoping to make good time before the heat of the day became too oppressive. The bus was overloaded, as was often the case, with five passengers sitting on seats meant for four people. As we left the outskirts of Kumba, we soon found ourselves crawling along a dirt track that wound its way up into the hills. The road was rutted and pitted, and our bus bounced and jolted over every bump. Not even one hour into the trip, many passengers were already sleeping despite the bumps.

The road from Kumba to Mamfe in the 1970s was a beautiful, if challenging, route to travel. There were steep valleys on either side of the road. They looked like gullies, and it seemed like one wrong move could send our vehicle tumbling down into the forest below. It was frightening but breathtaking to look out the window.

As we began climbing the famous Kupe Hill, I could see a magnificent cascading waterfall in the distance, with a white veil of mist surrounding the area. It was a stunning view, but I did not appreciate it until years later. Many passengers did not even seem to notice. This hill had many stories told about it. As the driver began to ascend, he warned everyone to remain quiet and not utter a word. He needed all his experience and concentration. It was a single-track dirt road, and he was praying that no other vehicle would come from the opposite direction at the same time. Added to this were the gullies on both sides of the road that made one forget the lush green vegetation. We were going to Mamfe at the start of the rainy season, when the road had a reputation for being treacherous.

People were accustomed to trucks and other vehicles getting stuck on the road, which was slippery and muddy, making it difficult for them to gain traction. Passengers often had to spend days stranded on the road. Everyone had their story to tell about their trip to Mamfe. As we climbed higher and completed the Kupe bridge, everyone relaxed. The scenery also changed, and we passed through mainly forested areas. In many places, the road was narrow, and the driver had to engage the bus's four-wheel drive to navigate some of the more treacherous sections.

As we approached what my mum said was the halfway point, the road began to deteriorate even further. This trip was definitely not for the faint-hearted. We had to cross a river after Konye, which was swollen and rushing with water from the recent rains, making navigation difficult. The bridge that crossed it was little more than a series of planks held together with rusty nails, and the driver had to expertly drive slowly and carefully to avoid slipping off the edge.

There were occasions when passengers had to carry their luggage across muddy areas to find another vehicle at the other end. During these times, the driver would inform the passengers in Kumba that he would not be able to cross. So, they were aware and prepared to cross the deep mud with their luggage on their heads. Sometimes, the local boys were there to help for a fee, moving luggage across and even carrying people on their backs.

After crossing the river, the road became little more than a muddy track, and we had to negotiate deep ruts and potholes. We passed through small villages where people waved and called out greetings to us, and children ran alongside the car, shouting and laughing.

As the day wore on, we grew increasingly exhausted, and the oppressive heat of the day intensified. We had to stop several times to refill the car's radiator and to take breaks to rest and rehydrate. However, despite our best efforts, we were making slow progress, and it soon became clear that we would not reach Mamfe before nightfall.

We approached the village known as Faitock, one I will never forget in my life, because this is where we spent the night. It was getting dark. Coupled with that, the dense vegetation on either side of the road often made it impossible to see more than a few meters ahead. The vehicle began to slow down, and everyone looked out to see what the issue was. We could clearly see a line of trucks and cars, so we slowed down and came to a stop. We soon learned that a truck was stuck in the mud, making it difficult for any other vehicles to go past.

The constant rainfall in the region makes the road surface extremely slick, making it difficult for vehicles to maintain traction and navigate sharp turns. This can lead to vehicles sliding off the road or getting stuck in the mud, causing significant delays and discomfort for passengers. I stayed in the car while some people stepped out to find out the real story, and others stretched their legs after being cramped in the car for hours.

The truck that was stuck was carrying a load of goods from Mamfe to Kumba. The driver, like many others, was aware of the road's condition but had no choice but to brave the journey. The truck was one of the few vehicles that had attempted to make the journey that day. As it made its way along the road, the driver encountered a particularly difficult section that was filled with mud. As the truck tried to navigate through the muddy terrain, it suddenly got stuck. The driver tried everything he could to get the vehicle moving again, but it was no use. The wheels spun uselessly, sinking further into the mud. The situation was made worse by the incessant rain, which had turned the road into a quagmire.

Soon, other vehicles began to pile up behind the truck, and passengers started to disembark from their vehicles. Everyone was agitated and frustrated, knowing that they would be late for their respective destinations. The stranded vehicles and passengers had to wait in the rain for hours, hoping that the truck would eventually be able to get unstuck.

Unfortunately, the situation worsened as time passed. More and more vehicles piled up behind the truck, blocking the road completely. There was no way for anyone to get through. Some attempted to push the truck out of the mud, but their efforts were in vain. I could hear the sounds of animals and insects all around. At night, the forest came alive. An orchestra of sounds filled the air. Cooing, screeching, crying—sounds of nocturnal creatures. The darkness seemed to close in on the road, except for the headlights signaling that another vehicle had joined the queue.

Some people believe that local people come out at night to dig holes in the roads, causing vehicles to get stuck, and that local boys are paid to help dig out the vehicles. The boys worked all night, and by morning, vehicles had started crossing the bad patch with the guidance of locals screaming instructions even at five o'clock in the morning. It was the next day, and we set off early, hoping to make a better time. After some tugging and firing with mud sprayed by the bus turning from side to side, we made it across. The road was still rough, but we were refreshed and determined to reach our destination.

The vegetation along the road was equally impressive, with tall trees that reached towards the sky and formed a natural canopy over the road. The foliage was so thick that sunlight could hardly penetrate it. The variety of trees and plants that grew along the road provided a breathtaking display of colors and textures, making the journey a feast for the eyes.

As we neared Mamfe, the scenery became more rugged and mountainous, and we were rewarded with breathtaking views of the surrounding landscape. We were greeted with a stunning display of greenery that stretched as far as the eye could see. The dense forest canopy formed a natural roof, providing a cool and serene atmosphere. The air was filled with the sweet scent of wildflowers and the sound of morning birds singing, which created an air of excitement.

Finally, after what seemed like an endless journey, we arrived in Mamfe. We were tired, dusty, and hungry. We had survived a challenging journey, and we had seen parts of the country that few people in Limbe who were not from Mamfe had the opportunity to experience. Looking back on that journey, I realize it was a significant experience for me. I could see resilience, determination, and perseverance on the faces of fellow passengers. And it showed me that even in the face of adversity, there is always something to be gained.

It was 3 a.m. when we knocked on the door. After a few minutes of knocking, the sound of shifting feet signaled that someone was coming. The sound was preceded by Big Mami's voice croaking "Chi aha' aa" (who is it?). Even before hearing her daughter's voice, she opened the door, happy but surprised by her guests. As we entered the living room, the smell of tobacco and leather filled the air that had remained shut for more than six hours.

We managed to catch a couple of hours' sleep, and in the morning, I was in the living room waiting. A door creaked, and my grandfather came out. He wore a long-sleeved shirt and black trousers, accompanied by his bowler hat and walking stick. His handkerchief, used mainly for his snuff, was waving away at some invisible sweat. That was the most amusing thing I've ever seen, and the image is still vivid in my mind. He was clearly happy to see his daughter and granddaughter. My grandfather did not hug me. He did not give me a handshake. That was what men did. He rubbed my shoulders one after the other. He had impossibly enormous hands. Big, generous hands. His handshake could have snapped my wrist in two. His hands were hard, with long, broad fingers. His nails were as thick and ridged as little clam shells, and the space between thumb and forefinger was callused.

Despite the challenges, the road from Kumba to Mamfe remained an important transport route, not only connecting the two towns and allowing people to access the markets, schools, and hospitals in the area, but also connecting Nigeria and Cameroon through Ekok. The road was the only means of transportation for the locals, and they had to brave the challenges posed by the weather and the terrain to reach their destinations.

45

Following in Her Footsteps

* * *

In the enduring saga of my mother's life, a pivotal chapter unfolded in my life. One that would echo the themes of discipline, leadership, and resilience that defined my mother's journey. It is a chapter marked by the indomitable spirit of a young girl who would carry her mother's legacy forward in the most remarkable of ways.

For me, the journey began when my mother made a momentous decision. With unwavering determination, she resolved to send me to her alma mater, Queen of the Rosary College (QRC), Okoyong, for secondary education. Unlike in 1956, when she left her house on Main Street, Mamfe, for QRC, which was four miles away, in 1977, QRC was far from my family's home in Limbe. However, she was resolute in her conviction that this was the path her daughter should follow. Thus began another extraordinary five-year adventure at QRC Okoyong. The journey was not without its challenges, but it was marked by moments of growth, achievement, and unexpected leadership.

I thoroughly enjoyed my time in secondary school and created bonds that would never be broken. The convent, perched on a small hill overlooking the rest of the campus, was an attraction, and I believe that at one point or another in the lives of the college students, they aspired to be reverend sisters, too. The sisters had dedicated their lives, talents and energy to educating girls and inculcating in them the virtues of honesty, integrity, self-discipline, and hard work. Preparing the girls to take their rightful place in all sectors of society. Their work was admirable. They were young and incredibly courageous to have left their countries thousands of miles away to Mamfe, where they endured bad roads, mosquitoes, malaria, and everything else.

We attended church services daily and said the rosary every evening. If this world could be healed through prayers, QRC Okoyong girls and their reverend sisters could have healed the world long ago. We had evening prayers and recited our communal night prayers in our dormitories before going to bed. We prayed in the classrooms, in the refectory, and on the playgrounds. Those who were not Catholic were also allowed to pursue their own faith. The Baptists and Presbyterians, for example, had their services on Sundays. We were encouraged to take a siesta every day for at least thirty minutes. Our resident priest was the Reverend Father Stockman, an old Dutch priest, whom we often referred to as "Mon Père." It was only after four years in Okoyong that I learned his name.

I did not know how to study, so I struggled in my first two years. Then, like a flash of lightning, I watched one of my classmates study, and it dawned on me what I was supposed to do to retain the information I had learned, a practice I still use to this day. I would read a chapter, close the book, try to remember what I read, and write it down. And if what I write is incorrect, I redo the exercise. It was not just writing; sometimes I would repeat what I was learning aloud over and over. I loved the library. There were all kinds of books, including Mills & Boon, Nancy Drew, and Charlotte Brontë books.

I was in Fatima House, which was nearest the administrative block. Mount Carmel House was the furthest. The others were Loreto House and Lourdes House. Fatima House had four dormitories: Fatima A, Fatima B, Fatima C, and Fatima D. Each house was supervised by a reverend sister. The lone Cameroonian sister at the convent, Sister Therese-Marie, was our House supervisor. We played all kinds of games and sports. There was even a functioning Lawn Tennis Court that we never used for that purpose. Basketball, handball, and Volleyball were the most prominent sports. I remember that one of the sports supervisors used to call out the then-sports prefect. *"Branch Tima. If the vorreybore prayers are not prepared to pray the vorreybore match. I decrare the vorrebore match crosh."* He had to put the letter r in almost every word he used. It was hilarious, and the girls made fun of him in the dormitories. Another enigmatic figure was the discipline master, Pa Leke. He would try to catch students doing the wrong thing, but this was not always possible, as the students often outsmarted him, to the amusement of their friends and classmates.

In an unparalleled move, I was appointed a school Food Prefect in Form Two. It was a role that typically fell to older students, and I couldn't help but wonder how a junior student like me would address her seniors. However, much like my mother, I possessed a certain magnetic quality that inspired confidence in those around me. The reverend sisters who ran the school saw the potential within me and bestowed their trust on my young shoulders.

As the years passed, I continued to excel in my role as Food Prefect, ensuring that fellow students were well-nourished and cared for. My sense of responsibility extended even further when I took on the additional duty of being the Bell Ringer. Each day, I roused my classmates from their slumber, signaling the beginning of another day of learning. Sometimes, I even assisted the night watchman, ensuring the wake-up bell rang promptly at 5 o'clock.

In Form Four, I reached new heights, being elected as the Senior Prefect by my peers. The moment of my election is etched in my memory—standing before my classmates during the morning assembly, my heart pounding as hands were raised in support. It was an exhilarating affirmation of their trust and belief in my leadership.

As my time in QRC Okoyong progressed, I found myself not only excelling in my official duties and leadership roles but also being recognized for my astuteness and charisma. It was during the transition to Form Five, a period when the senior students traditionally handed over their responsibilities to us, that I truly felt the weight of leadership.

The handover process was a time of uncertainty and turbulence, marked by significant changes in the administration of the student body by our peers. As we assumed our new roles, the challenges became apparent, especially when younger students occasionally tested the boundaries of discipline.

I vividly recall a moment in the refectory shortly after the handover when chaos seemed to reign. It was then that I uttered a phrase that has stayed with me throughout my life: *"Sticks and stones may break my bones, but words can never hurt me."* In that instant, I recognized the value of unwavering resilience—a trait I undoubtedly inherited from my remarkable mother.

This lesson in resilience shaped not only my leadership style but also my approach to life's challenges. It transcended the walls of QRC Okoyong and became an enduring part of my journey.

Upon completing my O-levels, I achieved the best results in my class—a testament to my dedication and commitment. It was then that my mother, Susan, decided I should experience a more liberated life. I transitioned from boarding school to being a day scholar at GHS Limbe for high school, allowing me to bond more closely with my family beyond the holiday seasons.

Two swift years passed, and as my A-levels approached, my mother's strictness reached new heights. Determined to excel, she insisted I study alone, forbidding group study sessions. Even a brief visit to a friend's house for studying resulted in a harsh lesson in punctuality—I was locked out one night for arriving just five minutes late.

Then, one day, my mother shared unexpected news: I could join my classmates for night study sessions at school. Excited, I packed my bag, eager to immerse myself in an atmosphere of academic dedication and shared pursuit of knowledge.

However, upon arrival, I was met with a scene far different from what I had envisioned. The air was alive with activity, but instead of intense study sessions, the focus revolved around food, socializing, and casual strolls along Down Beach. The school grounds buzzed like a lively marketplace, offering an array of tempting snacks—puff-puff, dodo and beans, boiled eggs, and uniquely named treats like "kwili-kwili," "make-me-well," and "gru-gru."

Inside the classrooms, the situation was no better. The few students present followed an erratic routine, frequently taking breaks to eat, chat, or wander around to stay awake. Some succumbed to exhaustion, their heads resting on desks, their loud snores filling the room. Others devised creative methods to remain alert—wet towels were draped over their heads, or their legs were submerged in buckets of water to fight off drowsiness.

Rather than a haven of learning, night school felt more like a carnival of indulgence—an experience that taught me just as much about discipline and focus as it did about distraction. Standing amidst this tumultuous sea of distractions, I realized that this environment—where diligent study had taken a backseat to culinary indulgences and the struggle to stay awake—was not aligned with my academic goals. My mother had high expectations for my exam performance (*she would crucify me otherwise*), and I was determined to meet them. Rather than tempting me, the myriad diversions only strengthened my resolve.

Memories of my time at QRC flooded back, particularly those late nights during our O-level studies. One night remains especially vivid in my mind—we had gathered, ostensibly to study, but in reality, little to no studying was taking place. As the clock ticked on, restlessness and distraction took over.

Then came a surprise visit from the principal, sending shivers down our spines. We feared the repercussions of our apparent lack of dedication, bracing ourselves for the inevitable consequences. The air was thick with trepidation. But, to our astonishment, the principal did not scold us. Instead, she assumed the role of a nurturing mother. Like a protective hen gathering her chicks, she addressed us with unexpected kindness. Rather than punishment, she prescribed something simple yet profound—sleep. In a motherly tone, she instructed us to retire to bed immediately and declared that no one should rise until the bell signaled the official wake-up time.

Relief and gratitude washed over us. Our stern principal had revealed her compassionate side, understanding that even the most diligent students sometimes need rest to rejuvenate their spirits. As we lay in our beds that night, we couldn't help but appreciate her wisdom—a leader who cared not just for our education but for our well-being.

Reflecting on this, I knew there was no point in remaining in this chaotic night school environment when my primary goal was to excel. I had to convey my decision to my mother, even if it meant resisting the allure of evening gatherings and mouthwatering snacks. Success, I realized, required unwavering dedication and a steadfast commitment to my academic pursuits.

46

A Mother's Faith, a Daughter's Flight

***

In those days, one of the most significant events in the lives of Cameroonian students who lived in the Southwest and Northwest Regions was the release of the GCE examination results. It was a national moment. Families gathered around their radios, holding their breath as names were read out one after another. The radio transformed from more than just a machine — it became a lifeline, carrying the hopes and dreams of a young generation.

My mother had several radios at home in each house we have lived in, and when the results season came, all of them were always in use. Everyone in the neighborhood listened to the GCE results. The whole community was involved. In that year 1985, my mother listened with more anticipation than most. Her two daughters were expecting A and O Level Results respectively. For her, these were not just results — they were the fruit of years of sacrifice, stress, shouting, anger, teaching and sleepless nights.

At the time of the results that year, my sister, Elizabeth and I were not home in Limbe. We were in Edea vacationing with our uncle, Peter Ayukegba, who was then the Divisional Delegate for Agriculture. When we heard that the results would be read, we carried a small radio to the back of the house. Together with a few relatives, we huddled close, straining to catch every word. The air was thick with tension. We kept adjusting the volume again and again, as if that could make the journalist's voice come through clearer and faster. Then, finally, the announcer began reading the results for Government High School Limbe. Time seemed to stop. Hearts were pounding, and I held my breath. I had never forgotten the sting of failing my Common Entrance exams, and since then, I had learned never to take any exam for granted.

And then it happened—my name was called. It sounded like music. *"Passed in three papers... Patricia Agbor Efange."* For a moment, I couldn't move. My sister jumped up, shouting with joy, and everyone around us clapped and hugged. I felt a rush of joy, shock, and profound relief all at once. Moments later, my sister's name was also announced among the O Level results. We had both made it.

At the end of the results, they read out the Honor Roll, and my name was among the first five. I can't remember exactly what position I held—second or third, I really can't say—but what I do remember is the confidence it gave me. That moment filled me with a sense of pride and self-belief that carried me all the way to the UK. I travelled with the attitude that I could do anything I set my mind to, and that no one was better than a hardworking Patricia Efange.

We tried several times before finally reaching my mother on the phone that evening. When she answered, she was still breathless from excitement. She had been screaming at the radio, cheering and crying all at once. Her voice trembled, but her words were full of pride. "God never forgets hard work," she said. That was all she could manage before emotion took over. That night, she told us that she cooked pepper soup and shared

A Mother's Faith, a Daughter's Flight

it with family and neighbors who came to celebrate. It was her quiet way of giving thanks.

As for me, the idea that I might one day be plucked from obscurity and given a scholarship to study abroad had never crossed my mind—and it certainly had never crossed my mother's. In those days, students who excelled in the sciences often went on to study overseas, but for arts students like me, the path was uncertain. Most of us ended up at the University of Yaounde, the only university in the country at the time. It offered mainly History, Geography, English, and Law. The idea of studying abroad was a far-off dream reserved for others.

After my results, I began the procedure to register at the University of Yaounde. My aunt, Mrs. Ekobena, and my cousins were helping me navigate my way through the endless paperwork and queues. It was my first time in Yaounde, and it was a challenge getting around and speaking to people only in French as opposed to English, where I came from.

Then, one afternoon, something extraordinary happened. A stranger I didn't know came to us with a newspaper. I can't even remember what he looked like. He simply handed it to my aunt, pointing out her maiden name, "Efange." The name said Patricia Agbor Efange.

I saw my name printed in black and white. I had been selected for a scholarship to study journalism in the United Kingdom. I could hardly believe my eyes. My aunt looked at me in shock. We both sat still for a while, then she said, "You have to call your mother."

At her office in Yaoundé, I picked up the phone and dialed the number I knew by heart—332103. It rang several times before she answered. When I told her the news, there was silence. Then she laughed, then cried, then asked me to read the lines from the newspaper again. She could hardly believe it.

From that moment, she began asking questions everywhere — from family friends to people she thought might know something about how my name had appeared on that list. But no one could explain it. Everyone congratulated her, but nobody claimed any connection to the scholarship. My mother simply concluded that it was God's doing. She often said after that, "When God decides to bless a child, He doesn't need permission."

A few weeks later, I received my scholarship letter. It stated that my tuition and living expenses would be fully covered. It felt unreal. My mother read it over and over again, holding the paper close to her chest as if afraid it would vanish.

When the day came for me to leave, she accompanied me to the airport in Douala. She was dressed simply, as always — a dark brown skirt paired with a light polka dot blouse and a slim belt around her waist. Her shoes were her usual flats, practical and modest. Her face was calm, but her eyes heavy with emotion. She did not say much, but there were a thousand words in her mind. Before I walked away, she held my hands tightly and whispered, "Pee, go and make your mark. But don't forget where you come from."

As the plane took off, I could see her in my mind's eye standing by some rail, small, tall but strong, waving and smiling through tears. That image stayed with me for years. It was the picture of love, sacrifice, and faith — the foundation on which every step of my journey was built.

I arrived in London to a cold October. I was one of many students who had received the scholarship that year. One of six on that flight. It was the start of a new chapter — one filled with discovery, challenges, and growth. But in every phone booth, every letter I wrote home, and every quiet moment abroad, my mother's voice remained the sound of home.

47

Retirement and Old Age

*　*　*

Many years had passed since my mother, Susan Mbi Enoh—affectionately known as Reme or Suzie—had completed the noble task of raising her children. She had entered a new chapter of her life, one filled with globe-trotting adventures. From her home base in Limbe, she embarked on journeys to the United States, where her children had built their lives. One moment, she would be crossing the Atlantic to visit my sister in the U.S., and the next, she'd be off to see my other sister and brother in the UK.

In Gainesville, Georgia, she set her anchor for a few years, dedicating herself wholeheartedly to supporting Elizabeth, who had endured the emotional turbulence of divorce. Now a single mother, my sister was raising two tall and handsome young boys—Michael, named after the Saint of the same name, and Mbi, named after none other than our beloved mother, Susan Mbi Enoh. Despite the whirlwind of raising two spirited and active children, life in the United States often felt solitary for her.

My sister would head off to work, the boys to school, and my mother would frequently find herself alone in the house, gazing out at the towering trees that framed the backyard. In those quiet moments, she would drift into reverie, yearning for her home thousands of miles away in Mile 4, Limbe. The vastness of America and its unfamiliar way of life presented her with a significant learning curve—one that profoundly reshaped her perspective.

Back in Cameroon, social customs held immense value, and hospitality was a way of life. Neighbors were not merely acquaintances; they were an extension of one's family. It was perfectly normal for a neighbor to offer guidance or discipline a child, and such gestures were embraced with warmth and understanding.

However, America introduced my mother to a different reality—an individualistic society where the sense of community differed starkly from the tightly knit bonds she had known. While she was aware of the Christian presence in America, the sight of congregations in church pews was rare. Even on the streets, she was perplexed by the absence of people. Cars were abundant, yet the roads felt eerily empty. She soon realized that people cocooned themselves within their homes, immersed in private music sessions, television, online shopping, or indulging in retail therapy at shopping malls. Even children were seldom seen outdoors in neighborhoods, a stark contrast to the vibrant communal life she had left behind.

Amidst this stark contrast, my mother fondly reminisced about her life back home, where neighbors dropped by unannounced, and family visits were spontaneous affairs. In Cameroon, the sense of community and interconnectedness was profound—family members not only lived together but often chose to reside nearby, fostering enduring bonds.

She yearned for the lively off-licenses just 500 meters from her home, where vibrant music played, and camaraderie flowed freely. There, people greeted one another warmly, exchanging pleasantries in a relaxed and unhurried atmosphere. It took my mother several years to acclimate to the American way of life. Loneliness and anxiety occasionally gripped her, prompting heartfelt conversations with the trees that lined Elizabeth's backyard. She gave each of them a name and, during the harsh winters, communicated through the sanctuary of her windowpane.

Her journey to adapt to her new surroundings was a testament to her resilience. Through moments of solitude, reflection, and connection with nature, she discovered the strength to embrace cultural differences and carve her place in the tapestry of American life. She worried more about her two children in the U.S. than those in Europe. Despite the laws, she had learned of the deep-seated discrimination and prejudice against immigrants—especially black people. This awareness weighed heavily on her heart.

Determined to gain some independence, she soon obtained her driver's license. This newfound mobility enabled her to attend church independently and interact with others when her family was not at home. She even took the boys to soccer and other extracurricular activities. One sunny afternoon in Gainesville, after dropping the boys off, she was heading back home when she was involved in an accident. She was traveling eastbound on Interstate 285. The sun was glaring, making it difficult for her to see. At one point, uncertain if she was veering off the road, she panicked, slammed on the brakes, and came to a sudden stop.

It was a busy morning, and her abrupt stop nearly caused a multi-car collision. Other drivers were forced to react quickly, swerving and braking to avoid a crash. Fortunately, no one was injured, but the incident triggered a significant traffic jam, delaying several commuters.

The glare from the sun in Atlanta, compared to Limbe, can be blinding, making it difficult to see the road ahead. Many drivers combat this by wearing polarized sunglasses, using a sun visor, or adjusting their mirrors to minimize reflection. My mother, either unaware of these precautions or caught off guard, had a momentary lapse in judgment. Thankfully, the consequences were not severe—a reminder of the challenges she faced adapting to a new and unfamiliar world.

As my mother embarked on her journey from Cameroon to the United States, the stark contrasts between these two worlds began to unfold before her. It was a journey that revealed striking differences in culture, landscape, and scale.

When she arrived in Atlanta, she was awestruck by the sheer enormity of everything around her. The streets stretched endlessly, dwarfing the narrow, winding roads of Cameroon. Cars were massive in comparison, and even the people—hailing from diverse ethnic backgrounds—seemed taller and more robust. From the grandeur of houses to the towering skyscrapers and sprawling shopping malls, the built environment in the U.S. stood on a scale she had never encountered in her homeland.

The expansive American highways, with their multitude of lanes, felt overwhelming at first, especially when contrasted with the modest roads she was accustomed to navigating. The rapid pace of life, the abundance of consumer goods, and the intermingling of different cultures fascinated her in those early days.

Beyond the cultural and physical contrasts, my mother also saw the U.S. as a place where she might finally reconnect with her long-lost brother, Peter Enoh. Years before, Peter had left home with his American girlfriend, Josephine, a Peace Corps volunteer he had met in Mamfe. She had facilitated his visa and paperwork, and together, they had set off on a new life abroad.

I was just two years old when my uncle, my mother's immediate younger sibling, departed Mamfe with Josephine. His decision had deeply saddened my grandparents and the entire family, but Peter had promised to stay in touch, even in an era when access to telephones was scarce, especially in Mamfe. Yet, as time passed, his communication dwindled and eventually ceased altogether. Rumors began to circulate, suggesting that he had met a tragic fate.

Years later, when my family finally reestablished contact with Josephine, her response was heartbreaking. She explained that their relationship had ultimately unraveled, and Peter had left her. She did not know his whereabouts, leaving my mother and her family with the enduring mystery of his fate.

Although she had anticipated cultural differences upon arriving in America, witnessing them firsthand was a revelation beyond anything she had imagined. The sheer magnitude of the American experience—from its vast physical landscape to its cultural diversity—was both a world of opportunity and a challenge she would have to navigate in her new home.

In hindsight, she often reflected on how the descriptions she had heard about America had not adequately prepared her for the monumental reality she encountered with her own eyes. She, in turn, found it difficult to convey the vastness, scale, and profound differences between her homeland and her newfound American life. What was certain was that her experiences had forever etched themselves into her consciousness, serving as a poignant reminder of the transformative power of travel and the mysteries that lay beyond the horizon. It was after her grandsons had grown up that she decided she would split her time between Mile 4 in Limbe for part of the year and the US for the rest.

She received a new car, which my brother in California bought for her about four years before she died. It was in that car that she traveled around with a chauffeur in the driver's seat whenever she returned home to Limbe from her travels around the world.

48

CANCER, The big C!

* * *

It was one of those stretches in Cameroon when, with her grandchildren now grown, she could afford to linger longer in her home in Mile 4. During this time, she decided to give her beloved house a fresh touch. She put in a new staff ceiling, changed her furniture, and breathed new life into the place she had worked so hard to build. But even as the house transformed, something was shifting within her—a silent battle she was unaware of.

At first, it was a nagging abdominal pain, something she brushed off as a passing stomach bug. It was not unusual for her to feel a little under the weather after eating something spicy or heavy. There were also bouts of diarrhea, followed by periods of constipation. They felt unpleasant but manageable. Concerned enough to seek medical advice, she visited her doctor. The diagnosis was dysentery, a common ailment, particularly in tropical regions. She was prescribed antibiotics, and she took them faithfully, expecting the symptoms to subside.

Months passed, but her symptoms grew worse. There was rectal bleeding now, coupled with an unrelenting fatigue that drained her strength. Her once steady frame began to shrink;

the weight loss was stark, and it left her looking frail. Those closest to her were at a loss. She had seen the doctor several times already, and yet, her condition continued to deteriorate.

She didn't want to worry us, her children, and close friends, so she kept the details vague when we called to check on her. She assured us she was fine, that it was nothing to be alarmed about.

Then fatigue set in like an uninvited guest. She would wake up feeling tired, her energy drained before the day had even begun. It was unlike her; she had always been active, bustling about her home, tending to her garden, and checking in with Adamou and other neighbors. Now, even the simplest tasks felt like a mountain to climb. Her weight continued to drop noticeably. Clothes that had once fit snugly now hung loose, and her once vibrant complexion dulled.

Her appearance began to draw concern. Neighbors who came by commented on how tired she looked, how much weight she had lost. Family members who visited noticed the same changes. "Are you eating well?" they would ask. She would smile weakly and reply, "Oh, I'm fine. Just a little tired." But inside, she was beginning to feel that something wasn't right.

Despite multiple visits to the doctor, the answers didn't change. They repeated the same reassurances, prescribed the same medications, and sent her home with no real solution. She was the rock of the family, the one who had always been there for everyone else. To see her like this—frail, tired, and visibly unwell—was unsettling.

The woman we had always known as strong and determined was visibly struggling, and what was worse, we didn't know how to help.

Her son was preparing for his wedding in California at about this time, too. It was decided that she would travel to the wedding and use the opportunity to consult with doctors in the US as well.

Initially, when she began consulting with medical personnel in the US, very little information trickled back home. The whole process was shrouded in secrecy. There were bits and pieces that one could pick and put together, but overall, information was in very short supply. You could say the apple does not fall far from the tree, as my siblings were tight with information sharing. Right after the wedding, she saw a gastroenterologist who performed a colonoscopy and discovered a large tumor in her colon. She was diagnosed with stage III colon cancer, and the doctors recommended immediate surgery to remove the tumor.

She recovered well after the surgery, but had to carry a colostomy bag as part of her intestines had been removed. A colostomy bag, also known as an ostomy pouch, is a medical device that is attached to the abdomen of a person who has undergone colostomy surgery. This surgical procedure involves creating an opening in the abdominal wall, through which the end of the large intestine (the colon) is brought to the skin's surface, forming a stoma. The colostomy bag is then placed over the stoma to collect the feces and gas that would otherwise be eliminated through the rectum and anus.

It took a while for my mother to adjust to the idea of poop gathering outside of the body in a bag, but she learned quickly how to handle it. Soon, under the hot California sun, she was working outside in the garden at the back of the house, picking stones, raking grass, and helping my brother and his new wife settle down. This helped her exercise and made her feel needed again.

Even then, each time I called to discuss her health, she did not provide much detail. My siblings who lived in the US, Elizabeth, and Jubilant, were making most of the decisions relating to the treatment that my mother needed. Vivian was in the UK, and I was in Cameroon. We consulted very little because time was usually of the essence to make those decisions.

In the challenging journey of my mother's battle with colon cancer, it was my siblings who were primarily tasked with making critical decisions about her treatment. Elizabeth and Jubilant, residing in the United States, carried the weight of these choices, while Vivian was herself in the United Kingdom, and I, in distant Cameroon. The geographical distance separating us made it exceedingly difficult to have comprehensive discussions regarding the course of action required, and time, as we would soon realize, was a relentless adversary.

I had never heard of a colostomy bag, so it was not easy to comprehend. I soon learned that emptying a colostomy bag can be a challenging task, especially for those new to the experience. It is essential to empty the bag regularly to prevent leaks and discomfort.

One of the primary challenges associated with emptying a colostomy bag is managing the unpleasant odor. Fecal matter produces a strong and unpleasant smell, as we all know from pooping daily. Since she spent her time at home and was able to walk around, she managed it on her own. Later, when mobility issues arose, it became a bit trickier. Another challenge associated with emptying a colostomy bag is maintaining hygiene. Proper handwashing, both before and after handling the bag, is crucial to prevent the spread of germs and infections.

Emptying a colostomy bag may also be difficult due to the consistency of the fecal matter, which can spill or leak, or sometimes have a more solid consistency, making it challenging to release the waste from the bag. Removing the clamp was sometimes clumsy. While emptying, you had to apply just the right amount of pressure so the bag would not burst. She had been taught how to use it and, like the good student that she always was, there were rarely any mishaps.

When I visited my mother in Cucamonga, California, she showed me the whole process of how she dealt with her colostomy bag. She always had the necessary supplies within reach. These included gloves, a washcloth or paper towel, and a disposal bag. Having a toilet close by was a plus. She did not have to walk down any hallway to get to the restroom.

Colon cancer is a serious medical condition that can be difficult to diagnose early on. For my mother, her journey with this disease was made even more challenging by misdiagnosis. My mother was devastated by her Limbe misdiagnosis, but she would not let anyone know how much she was disturbed. It was evident that the doctors she saw in Limbe did not carefully consider her symptoms and medical history. They did not conduct proper testing and failed to consult with other specialists or even attempt to refer her to one. But since she had had medical issues before in far worse conditions and pulled through, she strongly believed she would get well again. But things only got worse.

She was put on radiation therapy. The radiation damages the DNA of cancer cells, which stops them from dividing and growing. However, the healthy cells in the area are also affected, but it is believed that these cells can repair themselves more easily than cancer cells. After the treatment, my sister thought the cancer had been cured. Little did we know that it started spreading like wildfire after the radiation treatment.

The doctors then decided that chemotherapy would be used as well. Chemotherapy uses drugs to kill cancer cells. Her sessions went on for some time, and she was able to do her own chemo at home. But this stage did not last either, and she deteriorated very fast after this and finally died on the 5th of November 2015.

One of the most common symptoms of colon cancer is pain, which can be excruciating. Every day, my mother had the same advice to tell anyone who could hear: "No one should ever suffer from pain like this." Sometimes she would have a sharp pain in her abdomen. As she described it, it was a stabbing pain.

As the days passed, the pain became even more intense, and the pain medication did not seem to help for long periods. There was also a fear of dependence. Then her condition began to interfere with her daily activities. She spent most of her time in bed. It was excruciating and debilitating, but she bore it with grace. In addition to the pain, her legs began to swell.

Lymphedema is a condition that occurs when lymphatic fluid accumulates in the tissues, causing swelling and discomfort. My siblings and I are unsure of what caused our mother's legs to start swelling. We concluded, however, that it must have come from the numerous procedures and treatments she had undergone, which had blocked her lymphatic vessels. At the hospital, the healthcare professionals advised us to seek non-medical therapies. Despite advances in medicine, science still has so many limitations. We started taking her to a trained professional twice a week who has experience in treating lymphedema through massage.

It was a one-hour car ride to see this new specialist, and often she could not sit up in the back of the car. So, she lay down on the back seat, uncomplaining, until we arrived, finished the process, and went back home. I spent my vacation time with her in Cucamonga, California, at my brother's house and took her to do the treatment three days a week. As I was leaving the US at the end of my stay, my sister came in from the UK to replace me. Together with my sister-in-law, they took her to wherever she needed to be.

The gentle, rhythmic movements of the skin in the direction of the lymphatic vessels were supposed to help reduce swelling and improve the overall function of the lymphatic system. After just a few days, the stark reality began to set in – the treatments received so far did not yield the expected results. The lymphatic massage we were trying to do certainly did not seem to be working. The human body, a marvelously intricate entity, seemed to confound our efforts. Each session of treatment appeared to merely shift the fluid from one part of her body to another. In a bid to alleviate this condition, a deep tissue massage was performed, a technique involving the application of pressure to the deeper layers of muscle tissue. Regrettably, the pain and discomfort it inflicted made it untenable as a long-term solution. It became increasingly evident that we were trapped in a seemingly futile cycle of time and resources.

In our collective quest to find a ray of hope amidst the darkness, we turned to our faith and the power of prayer, seeking solace from "Papa J," as my mum affectionately referred to Jesus Christ. Simultaneously, we delved into the depths of the internet, scouring for any semblance of guidance or insight that could potentially steer us toward a more promising path. We reached out to fellow Cameroonians grappling with cancer or their concerned relatives, desperate to uncover a hidden remedy or miracle.

In our hearts and minds, the conviction persisted that we could reverse this ominous descent into the abyss of death. We left no stone unturned, exploring alternative therapies and natural remedies such as soursop and boiled plant leaves for tea, driven by an unwavering determination to improve her condition. Yet, despite our best efforts, her health remained stagnant, and despair began to loom.

Debates ensued among us, laden with profound uncertainty. Should we transition her into hospice care at home or return her to the hospital? We even contemplated the feasibility of transporting her, frail and ailing, back to her cherished residence in

Mile 4, Limbe, Cameroon. However, her deteriorating condition left us with no choice but to focus on one unassailable goal – to alleviate her pain in her final days and bestow upon her the moments of happiness and comfort she so deserved.

During this trying period, some of her beloved grandchildren provided their unwavering companionship, seeking to uplift her spirits. And also, by her side stood her spiritual guide, a Nigerian Catholic priest. Each time she fell asleep, she told him it felt like she was taking her last breath, and she would wake up suddenly. He prayed with her, talked with her, and made light of death. She responded with her own prayer: "Papa Jee, may your will be done." The priest certainly offered her solace and serenity in the midst of the deadly storm that raged within her fragile human body.

In the final chapter of my mother's life, sadness permeated every moment as her health steadily declined. Her prolonged illness kept her in a constant cycle of hospital visits, her once vibrant spirit dimming with each passing day. I made the difficult decision to leave work for two weeks and journey to California, yearning to cherish whatever precious time remained with her.

As I arrived, her frail form greeted me, her legs swollen and her body weakened by the relentless battle against illness. That week we tried to make light of everything and found a bit of laughter. It was extremely difficult. We were racing against time and the inevitable. Alongside her hospital treatments, we also tried our own natural remedies. We tried soursop tea. We tried mango leaves. We had heard of cassava and tried it, even though she was eating only a very small amount. We researched various products online, and Juby would order them so we could try them out. It was a desperate attempt to hold on to our mother. I slept in the same room with her, waking up several times to help her to the restroom. With heavy hearts, my sister, Vivian and I traded places, my departure marking the beginning of Vivian's own vigil by our mother's side.

The weight of impending loss hung heavy in the air, a palpable tension that refused to dissipate. And then, as if the universe had conspired against us, the devastating news of her passing shattered our fragile hopes. I sat alone at my dining table, drowning in a sea of sorrow, when my brother's video call delivered the crushing blow.

With trembling hands and tear-stained faces, pretending to be strong, we bore witness to her final moments. As her breath grew fainter, my brother and my daughter shared a silent, heartbreaking farewell prayer, gently turning off the camera and shutting the doors. We let her go, and she slipped away from us, leaving behind a void too vast to fill. Reme had departed from this world, leaving us to navigate the depths of grief in her absence.

It was a challenging journey to bring my mother's remains back home for burial. She had been very specific about her final arrangements, reflecting her strong will and character. Despite the grim topic, she faced death with courage, showing her fearlessness.

Rather than formalizing her will through legal channels, she wrote it in her distinctive, scratchy handwriting, familiar to all of us. She outlined her wishes meticulously, from the way she wanted to be buried to the appearance of her corpse, which might seem morbid to some but was characteristic of her pragmatic approach to life and death.

In her will, my precious mom shared her property among us but emphasized the importance of caring for others. She urged us to ensure that nobody would endure the pain she faced during her battle with colon cancer, underscoring her selflessness and compassion.

Her final resting place outside her property in Mile Four, Limbe, under the plum tree she planted, symbolizes her connection to nature and her lasting legacy. It serves as a reminder of her values and the importance of honoring her wishes.

49

Legacy

In reflecting on my mother's life, I am reminded of the legacy she left—evidence of her resilience, strength, hope, sacrifice, and love. Her journey of impact and vision as a single mother was truly remarkable. From a young age, to know what she wanted as a mother was even more impressive.

Her life was far from easy, but her journey embodies these values at every turn. As a single parent raising five children on her own, she faced countless challenges and setbacks, yet she remained committed to ensuring that we all received the best education. Her own schooling ended with secondary education, but she never let that limit her dreams for us. She pushed us forward, showing us by example that hard work and persistence could overcome even the toughest obstacles.

Juggling the responsibilities of being both mother and father, she battled through health issues, daily financial struggles, and the pressures of colleagues and bosses at her government job. She ran small businesses on the side, stretching every franc to make sure we had what we needed. Even with all of this, she never compared herself to her old classmates who had gone on to prestigious careers as magistrates, prominent politicians, or government officials. Instead, she kept her focus on us, showing us her unwavering dedication through every sacrifice she made.

The values she instilled in us went beyond hard work and resilience; she also taught us the importance of humility and kindness. For her, the well-being of those under her care always came first, and she made sure we understood that our family, our education, and our community were worth every effort. She fostered a strong work ethic and instilled in us the drive to succeed, nurturing our dreams to become leaders and change-makers. She became a role model not only to us but also to others in the family and community, embodying the essence of a strong and independent woman.

One of my mother's greatest joys was singing, an activity that seemed to bring her a rare, quiet peace. When she burst into song, her voice would fill the house, often joined by her sisters or friends. Together, they created harmonies that felt almost magical, as if the music itself was an escape from life's burdens. These moments of song captured her spirit in a way words never could—a blending of strength, hope, and an almost palpable joy.

She made countless sacrifices, foregoing new clothes or jewelry, unlike other women who might have had husbands to buy these things for them. My mother, however, was alone, and her focus was always on providing for us. She rarely bought anything for herself and didn't begin buying clothes until we had all left home. Until then, her money went into raising us and giving us the best chance at success, often putting her own desires aside to make sure we had what we needed.

Her faith in God remained unwavering, becoming a source of strength for her. When life felt overwhelming, she would turn to prayer, often calling upon Mama Maria, the Mother of Jesus, when she felt she couldn't reach Jesus himself. She'd take up her rosary, praying with a quiet intensity until her worries lifted.

Her faith was her sanctuary, and she leaned on it through every hardship. Even now, the groups she belonged to still gather at her graveside each year, offering prayers in her honor, a testament to the lasting impact of her faith.

Perseverance defined my mother. She had incredible patience, yet she also knew when it was time to let go. "I've moved on," she would say if something became too heavy to bear—a gentle but clear indication that she had chosen peace over needless struggle. She had the wisdom to know when to stand firm and when to walk away, a skill she passed down to us.

Beyond her immediate family, she was a pillar of support for her extended family. She was always ready to lend a hand, offer advice, or simply be there for those who needed her. Her kindness and generosity were infectious, inspiring others to follow her example. Her legacy continues through her children, grandchildren, and great-grandchildren, who carry her values forward, giving back to their communities and impacting the lives of others.

Her daughter Vivian constructed "The Ark" in Mukundange, Limbe—a unique kind of orphanage designed not only to care for underprivileged children but also to support their families. Her daughter, Elizabeth, built the Grace House, having demolished the house that my mother bought in Church Street when we were children. Elizabeth has also written over 13 inspirational books, titles that reflect the very values my mother instilled in us, such as "Forty Days of Encouraging Words," "Love the Only Cure," and "Suffering with Grace." Many of Elizabeth's books are published in multiple languages, extending my mother's legacy of faith, perseverance, and hope across the world.

Perhaps the most inspiring part of my mother's story is how she turned every obstacle into a stepping stone. She saw education as the key to a better future and ensured that we all had access to it, urging us to strive for excellence. Growing up, we had no other life beyond school, the market, and church. She believed that with faith, hard work, and dedication, we could overcome any challenge, and her life was proof of this belief.

Even when faced with illness and the daunting task of raising five children alone, she never lost sight of her goals. Her story is both riveting and inspiring, a reminder that success is not determined by one's origins or limitations but by the willingness to persevere. Her teachings emphasized faith, resilience, and the transformative power of love and sacrifice.

Today, her legacy lives on through the lives she touched. Her son, a chemical engineer in California, his wife, and children, one of whom is named Suzie, epitomizes the success her sacrifices made possible. One of the children she nurtured has become a pastor, and another is a medical doctor in Nigeria. Through each of us, her enduring lessons and values continue to inspire. Her story teaches us all that no matter what life brings, with hard work, faith, and love, anything is possible.

Her achievements, as well as those of her children and extended family, testify to the power of resilience and the depth of her influence. Her legacy will continue to inspire and motivate future generations, reminding us that true strength lies in love, sacrifice, and the determination to turn life's challenges into a life well-lived.

Postscript

* * *

In the wake of my mother's passing, after a period of reflection, I felt compelled to share her story with the world. Susan Mbi Enoh was not just my mother; she was a beacon of love and strength in our family. Her life and success in raising her children serve as a testament to every single mother, no matter where they are, that determination and faith are all we need. That is what I wanted to capture—the very essence of this book.

This heartfelt memoir delves into her unwavering stamina, relentless optimism, boundless love, and unyielding strength, as well as the profound impact she had on those around her. As I penned each chapter, I found solace in reliving the moments we shared and the lessons she taught me. Through her example, I learned the true meaning of perseverance and resilience.

In *Against the Odds: A Single Mother's Battle for Love, Family, and Respect*, I poured my heart into recounting her journey. From her humble beginnings to her steadfast dedication to her family, every page is filled with memories of her forthrightness and courage. Despite facing countless challenges, she never lost faith or her ability to make things happen. Through poignant anecdotes and cherished memories, this book celebrates her indomitable spirit. It tells the story of a woman who knew no bounds, who knew no fear in every sense of the word.

Writing this book was my way of honoring her memory and ensuring that her legacy lives on. I wanted to share her story not just with those who knew her but with anyone who needs a reminder that single parents can succeed, overcome, and survive—even in the darkest of times.

In *Against the Odds: A Single Mother's Battle for Love, Family, and Respect*, her essence lives on—an affirmation of the profound impact of a life well-lived.

FINALE

As the sun dipped below the horizon, casting a warm, golden hue across the tranquil Limbe sea, I stood at the edge of a lush meadow, just by the entrance to the Botanical Gardens. Few people come to this stony place. I placed one foot in the water, feeling it rush over my skin, cool and calming. Behind me, a gentle breeze rustled through the tall grasses.

This was a spot I had visited many times before as a student at Government High School in Limbe, often after gathering fallen fruit from the "Banga school" trees. In that fleeting moment, nature's serenity enveloped me, and I felt an unshakable connection to the world around me. The symphony of chirping birds, the distant call of a solitary owl, and the rhythmic hum of crickets echoed the timeless rhythms of life. The flurry of bats and the occasional car racing past attempted—successfully—to break my concentration.

I hopped from stone to stone, sinking deeper into the idyllic landscape, allowing myself to leave behind the worries of the everyday. There is something essential about embracing the simple beauty of the natural world, where time seems to stand still and all that matters is the here and now.

Limbe on my mind.

Susan on my mind.

About the author

Tricia Oben is a journalist dedicated to capturing untold stories that inspire and empower. As the daughter of Susan Mbi Enoh, she brings a deeply personal perspective to her mother's biography, *Against the Odds*. Through her work, she honors her mother's legacy and celebrates the strength of single mothers everywhere.

About the Publisher

Spears Books is an independent publisher dedicated to providing innovative publication strategies with emphasis on Africana stories and perspectives. As a platform for alternative voices, we prioritize the accessibility and affordability of our titles to ensure that relevant and often marginal voices are represented in the global marketplace of ideas. Our titles – poetry, fiction, narrative nonfiction, memoirs, reference, travel writing, African languages, and young people's literature – aim to bring African worldviews closer to diverse readers. Our titles are distributed in paperback and electronic formats globally by African Books Collective.

Connect with Us: Go to www.spearsbooks.org to learn about exclusive previews and read excerpts of new books, find detailed information on our titles, authors, subject area books, and special discounts.

Subscribe to our Free Newsletter: Be amongst the first to hear about our newest publications, special discount offers, news about bestsellers, author interviews, coupons and more! Subscribe to our newsletter by visiting www.spearsbooks.org

Quantity Discounts: Spears Books are available at quantity discounts for orders of ten or more copies. Contact Spears Books at orders@spearsmedia.com.

Host a Reading Group: Learn more about how to host a reading group on our website at www.spearsbooks.org

www.ingramcontent.com/pod-product-compliance
Lightning Source LLC
Chambersburg PA
CBHW032034150426
43194CB00006B/274